BROWN BOYS AND RICE QUEENS

SEXUAL CULTURES

General Editors: José Esteban Muñoz and Ann Pellegrini

Eng-Beng Lim

BROWN BOYS AND RICE QUEENS

Spellbinding Performance in the Asias

NEW YORK UNIVERSITY PRESS
New York and London

NEW YORK UNIVERSITY PRESS
New York and London
www.nyupress.org

References to Internet websites (URLs) were accurate at the time of writing.
Neither the author nor New York University Press is responsible for URLs that
may have expired or changed since the manuscript was prepared.

Library of Congress Cataloging-in-Publication Data
Lim, Eng-Beng, 1973-
Brown boys and rice queens : spellbinding performance in the Asias / Eng-Beng Lim.
pages cm
Includes bibliographical references and index.
ISBN 978-0-8147-6089-5 (hardback) — ISBN 978-0-8147-5940-0 (pb)
1. Queer theory—Asia—Case studies. 2. Sex role—Asia—Case studies. 3. Asia—Race
relations—Case studies. 4. Orientalism—Case studies. 5. Postcolonialism—Asia—Case
studies. I. Title.
HQ76.3.A78L56 2013
305.3095—dc23
2013017728

New York University Press books are printed on acid-free paper,
and their binding materials are chosen for strength and durability.
We strive to use environmentally responsible suppliers and materials
to the greatest extent possible in publishing our books.

Manufactured in the United States of America
10 9 8 7 6 5 4 3 2 1

Book design by Marcelo Agudo

Also available as an ebook.

Dedicated to the ones
Who in the struggle for a more equal and just world
Face the unmitigated mutations of colonial and neoliberal discourses
Like infections that wear you out
The best among us
With the guise of care that protects the Self-same.
You watch in disgust, sickened
But know better
That nothing could wipe out your queer spirit
Or the labor of your kind
In the solidarity of our minds.

CONTENTS

PREFACE

The Queer Genesis of a Project

It is now twelve years since a queer sort of Asian encounter started it all. Shortly after I arrived in California from Singapore, my former adviser, in a moment of casual butch-camp ribaldry, asked for my thoughts on rice queens and a Balinese ritual purportedly choreographed by a German guy involving many Balinese men as monkeys. I was baffled and fascinated by her que(e)ry and affect as she tried to bring out the queer resonances of a colonial seduction scenario between the white man and the native boy survived by the trope of the Asian houseboy. It was a connection that could not be more far-fetched. The trope, though prevalent in the contemporary West, was not on my East Asian cultural radar. Even farther removed was the figure of the rice queen, a gay Asiaphile from Euro-America whose primary attraction is the nubile, innocent brown boy. The boy may be any (underage or adult) Asian male who fits the bill by virtue of his looks, affect, or infantilization. As for the gnarly tale of queer miscegenation in a traditional Southeast Asian ritual, I was simply flabbergasted for not knowing more. How could I have missed it? That burning sentiment, butch-camp ribaldry, and a set of queer question marks around the brown boy ignited this research project.

Growing up in Charlton Park, Singapore, I was raised on a steady diet of Chinese, Japanese, Cantonese, Taiwanese, and Korean popular culture that featured all-Asian pop stars, heroes, or protagonists. Hollywood films and an odd mix of mainstream British, Brazilian, and U.S. soap operas and sitcoms like *Mind Your Own Language, Isaura the Slave Girl*, and *The Cosby Show* supplemented my formative transcultural repertoire with glimpses of stereotypical racial performance and endless heterosexual storylines. My references did not include butch-camp, rice queen, and houseboy. I was more familiar with the transvestites on Bugis Street, an infamous red-light district area that was "cleaned up" by the Singapore government in the 1980s; its queer legacy was carried forth by a lone Indian drag queen, Kumar, at the now-defunct Boom Boom Room, where I spent many weekends as an adoring fan among beautiful boys. Lost in the cultural translation of our conversation was the fact that at twenty-five years of age, I was woefully ignorant of *any* gay racial fetish, let alone the campy seduction possibilities of white/ native, man/boy, daddy/son, master/houseboy that crossed Euro-Asian racial lines.

But I had, or so I thought, queer theory and postmodern sexuality under (alas, evidently *above*) my belt. My proudest academic achievement to date, an undergraduate thesis on Tony Kushner's *Angels in America* written at the National University of Singapore in 1998, had dutiful if also overachieving citations of queer, feminist, and performance theorists, from Michel Foucault to Judith Butler to Eve Kosofsky Sedgwick. Little did I know that the heady days of queer theory were about to wane, or so it was claimed, as I rode its last wave to graduate school. Despite how well it served me around the erotics and politics of angelic supersexuality, queer theory did not prepare me for this campy encounter or the irony of a butch bottom donning a Xena Warrior Princess T-shirt. "Now why would I be interested in queens working at the rice fields?" I asked with precious indignation as she flashed a wicked smile and with that insouciance cast the spell of the colonial dyad. It didn't take me long to catch up on what it all meant in the Castro District, and white man/native boy became my first major academic affair.

That tantalizing conversation with Sue-Ellen Case in her El Cerrito home planted the unnatural seed of this book. In retrospect, it also marked my lesbian feminist portal of entry to gay U.S.A. as well as the queer diasporic rims that connected Southeast Asia to California across the Pacific Ocean. The intersectionality of race, sexuality, and empire, which had heretofore been rendered invisible by my self-study of Euro-queer studies and by my "race" as part of Singapore's diasporic Chinese majority, became a fundamental analytic for all my critical inquiries. I turned to theorists who are committed to that intersection, or who see a connection between queer globalization and colonial afterlives. They included M. Jacqui Alexander, Gloria Anzaldúa, Rey Chow, Lisa Lowe, Joseph Roach, and Kobena Mercer. I was interested in how the circum-Pacific imaginary of Bali, Singapore, and Asian America encoded or enabled the queer erotics of colonial encounters in a transnational setting. The colonial dyad in question became a primary critical navigator as I examined a constellation of representative encounters in theater and performance that could be further described in ethnographic, intercultural, conceptual, or performative terms. I began by asking, What are the tropes and spells associated with the white man/native boy dyad in the wide spectrum of imaginaries and practices organized under the rubric of Asian performance or Asian encounters?

The book was written in the decade in which California, Washington, New York, Michigan, Rhode Island, and six universities—University of California, Davis; University of California, Los Angeles; University of Washington, Seattle; State University of New York, Purchase College; Michigan State University; and Brown University—became my home. Each move marked several transformations in disciplinary and institutional affiliations that reoriented how I read, produced, and thought of theater and performance as well as the dyad in question. While my primary appointment was always in either theater and performance studies or English, the permutation of my affiliations varied, from international studies, Southeast Asian studies, and drama (UW); to Asian studies, media, society and the arts, gender studies, and gay and lesbian studies (SUNY); to global studies, gender in a global context, Asian Pacific American studies, and advanced study of international development (MSU); to East Asian studies, American studies, race and ethnicity, and gender and sexuality (Brown). They demanded different, and sometimes difficult, adjustments in the way certain forms of knowledge about theater and performance are produced and privileged, or reproduced and re-entitled for the West as well as Asia and its diasporas.

Where the question of minority difference emerged, it was invariably embroiled in U.S. identity politics or the incorporative logics of university multiculturalism, and less often in the wider context of U.S./ Western imperialism or other forms of colonialisms such as Japanese or settler colonialism. Nowhere was the precariousness of global minority performance knowledge made clearer than in the resurgent pedagogic defense of Western practices under the guise of a neoliberal multiculturalism where considerations of the free market and the canon were strategically subtended so as to appear unquestionably supportive of "diversity"; or in the reiteration/recuperation of performance, particularly where it was thought to be discursively absent, through plays and other recognizable forms of theater production on the proscenium stage. In other words, performance is to be equated only with plays and theater productions of a more or less established repertory. The late Dwight Conquergood identifies this auto-recourse to the Euro-text and stage as "scriptocentrism," which for many in the theater department continues to be the foundational base of study even as it occludes dance-drama and other somatic, oral, or paralinguistic performance traditions. As I navigated through these critical terrains, performance studies and its crosscurrents with "queer" and "Asia" gave me a portal to imagine otherwise, sometimes by disorganizing the categories and chronologies upheld by Western theater studies and those among its followers who borrow the transdisciplinary cover of performance studies to do the same work, and other times by directly using the performance lexicon of theater histories as well as social and subcultural movements. These openings in productive critical infidelities enabled ways to think through performance cultures and histories less explored and less privileged.

Given the racial and sexual panics of neoliberal knowledge production, it came as both a surprise and a sobering realization that the dyad itself presented several challenges as an analytic because it seemed too close for comfort or too salacious as an actual or allegorical coupling. The dyad was, in other words, either overly personal or improper for academic study. To exceed the entrapments of identification (who's who in the dyad) or homophobia, I turned to a second question to clarify the stakes of this project: How might we reorient our understandings of Asian performance and/or encounter if we consider the dyad as its constitutive interface between evolving bodies and positionalities that sometimes preconditions meaning and sometimes prevaricates it for different outcomes or effects/affects? It turned out that this inherently unstable interface between body and positionality, or between queer and Asia in performance, is also a story of migration, memory, and misfits.

As one who has relocated extensively, I found the issues generated at this interface to be at once geographic, cultural, and personal; each move to and within the United States, from global city to midsize or midwestern city, from the West Coast to the East Coast, was also a migration to a different disciplinary setting, cultural surround, and time zone. Spatial and body memories both familiar and alienating permeated each site. Translocal temporalities were split asunder with old and new kinship structures. Being hailed as "G.A.M." (gay Asian male) took some getting used to. Still, I knew that the manner of my intellectual and queer "Americanization" was a variegated complex even within the United States. While this complex found an emotional analog in my dad's facetious name-calling—"Ah, my American son!"—it would never contain the epistemic and experiential cornucopias found therein. True, I learned gaysian fabulosity on Santa Monica Boulevard, but it didn't take me long to also learn what was pink in Singapore and Asia more broadly every "summer." Singapore, practically on the equator, appears to have the same summer-like weather all year round, but locals might be attuned to more nuanced characteristics. The Northeast Monsoon, Southwest Monsoon, and inter-monsoon periods, for instance, have their own subtle tropical expression around rainfall and humidity. Nonetheless, "Americanization" with its linear, developmental logic so cherished in colonial and capitalist narratives tends to valorize in discrete terms changes in identity and space or temporality and temperature as either a breakaway from or transition toward (the terms of) U.S.-American legibility, legitimacy, and landscape. The U.S.

measurement of temperature in Fahrenheit is a quick case in point. This familiar progress narrative, once owned by the colonials, is a hallmark of an exceptional U.S.-American modernity, and many have spoken to the human cost and violence of a singular "Americanization," including the mythology of the American Dream.

It bears note, even as it seems obvious, that the interface of migration and memory, and its concomitant effect in desire and identity, are a more complicated matter than simply a movement from point A to B. There are many more vectors involved, and also many more coordinates than merely two actual sites, affective relations, and states of mind. The configuration of Bali, Singapore, and Asian America as the Asias in this book is a way to consider the unexpected connectivities across locations that have traces of the dyad without necessarily using U.S.-America as the pivotal point. This is in view of an increasingly important but often overlooked fact: the United States is not, no longer is, or has never been the final destination but a nodal point of a larger diaspora for transmigrants whose relocations, either by choice or by circumstance, are often in flux over their lifetimes. Likewise, those who choose to remain at one site may have multiple affiliations, kinship arrangements, and identifications that exceed established categories. We might think in this regard with the theorists of Third World feminisms, queer and woman of color critiques, postcolonial studies, hemispheric performance theory, and minor transnational criticism. They have given us numerous stories, maps, and tools that speak to alternatives such as Sinophone, tri-national, or transcolonial identifications and other lateral diasporic grids. Conversely, from an Asianist point of view, the United States often drops out of the picture even as specialists trained in Cold War–era area studies bring an Americanist (or orientalist) agenda to the study of national traditions in Asia. As is well known, Said has spoken to an earlier iteration of this problem in the oriental studies of the European model. While it may be obvious that Eurocentrism and Asiacentrism have severe epistemic limits, their assumptions of proper objects, training, and temporality continue to organize much of disciplinary discourse and practice, such as in the mainstream theater arts and cognate fields that are regulated by the uncritical contours of normative study.

These assumptions and their auto-analytics saturate the planetary vulgate of disciplinary-speak and the cultural politics of everyday life. Hence, the performative logic of categorical naming, such as "my American son!," Asian theater, or gay Asia (which slurs suspiciously close to geisha), belies what is in fact incoherent or unknowable about the referent. More than that, their corollary conjunctures—East/West, First World/Third World, Western/non-Western—would also delimit the scope of inquiry as they tend to recede rapidly into parochial or monocultural nationalist outlooks. We might identify this practice as the auto-analytic of a predictable, comparative grid that ultimately upholds dominant perspectives. The reiterative logics of parochialism or nationalism based on existing or preconditioning notions of difference are then naturalized as "the way things are." This modality of knowledge production, at once a protection and a projection of modern categories of knowing, resonates with Foucault's postulations in *The Order of Things: An Archeology of the Human Sciences*, in which he uncovers the underlying conditions of truth that arranged what was acceptable as scientific discourse in the modern historical period, and by extension, the central episteme(s) organizing cognate fields of study. An old story with new guises, we might identify or experience these conditions of discourse in the canonical strike on what counts or does not count as knowledge, and how conditions of possibility or impossibility determine the core content and even the style of teaching or research in our respective disciplinary locations.

In tracing the genesis of the book's queer research and epistemic surround, I wanted to acknowledge the multiple portals of entry that have enabled my research for this book. They describe some beginnings that may account for the critical and personal impetus for this writing, and where or how I am located vis-à-vis the book's design and interventions. I hope it helps to consolidate the case I am making for a more expansive view of cultural difference and performance epistemology in the transnational era. Much has been said about the constraints of knowledge production in global studies around minority histories and figures without necessarily producing the conditions of possibility for more diverse pedagogy or research. We have to produce more than just critiques of limiting frameworks in theater and performance studies as well as in the broader humanities and the arts so as to resist the duplication of those frameworks in global contexts, particularly as U.S. universities set up academic outposts in Asia and the Middle East.

In a broader sense, this book is an effort to imagine what interpretive methodologies might be possible if we are not held hostage to disciplinary constraints and colonial hetero-binaries or their guises in the neoliberal superstructure of Western knowledge production. It is also a story of journeys taken by writers, performers, and artists with a colonial connection or who live with the legacy of that connection in the Asias, both as a geographic continent and a racialized phantasm. I hope that its intellectual vectors are a useful prophylactic against the unmitigated mutations of colonial and neoliberal discourses that, like infections, aim to wear out the best among us who are in the struggle for a more just and equal world, and against whom the odds are always already set. This insistent search for productive alternatives undergirds the formulation of questions and interventions throughout this book, and I have many to thank for giving me the critical access and aptitude to do this work.

ACKNOWLEDGMENTS

Sue-Ellen Case and Susan Foster recruited me to graduate school at the turn of the new millennium while Sue-Ellen was a visiting Fulbright scholar at the National University of Singapore. I learned from them the pleasure of epistemo-erotic senses attuned to the body, to writing, and to the world. Sue-Ellen in particular was instrumental in helping me forge my own set of connections while opening countless portals of entry for me.

Karen Shimakawa was a sharp reader of my work from the beginning, and presided over each phase of my career with the constancy of a devoted teacher, mentor, adviser, and friend.

In New York City, I found an alternative universe of progressive thinkers not known to follow the paths of inherited doxa. Electric and eclectic, they enabled and enhanced my work in myriad ways, and welcomed me into their transformative, often queer, and often overlapping circles. An example is the ad-hoc Ladies' Composition Society, led by the insuperable Lisa Duggan, where two chapters of my book manuscript were read with critical finesse and camaraderie. One couldn't ask for more than to be treated as one of the ladies among Gayatri Gopinath, Carolyn Dinshaw, José Muñoz, Tavia Nyong'o, Janet Jakobsen, Christina Crosby, Anna McCarthy, and Ann Pellegrini. I feed off their fabulosities and live to tell.

Being a part of the *Social Text* editorial collective energized my outlook on the possibilities of intellectual praxis, and gave me a venue to publish, edit, and think with acuity. Thanks especially to David Eng (for everything), Josie Saldaña, David Kazanjian, Brent Edwards, Neferti Tadiar, Jasbir Puar, Nikhil Singh, Randy Martin, David Sartorius, Roopali Murkherjee, Gustavus Stadler, Ioana Man-Cheong, Kandice Chuh (as well as Tavia, Ann, Anna, and José), and everyone on the collective for being all-around comrades.

At Brown University, I found a place to call home in an exciting interdisciplinary setting where several colleagues enabled or modeled ways for me to do my work successfully. My deep thanks to Rick Rambuss, Bob Lee, Evelyn Hu-deHart, Naoko Shibusawa, Corey Walker, Jacques Khalip, Susan Smulyan, Ralph Rodriguez, Tim Bewes, Lynne Joyrich, Elmo Terry-Morgan, Marcus Gardley, Kym Moore, Pierre Saint-Amand, and Susan Harvey. In the final stages of the revision, Matthew Guterl, Richard Rambuss, Ralph Rodriguez, Michael Steinberg, and my co-fellows at the Cogut Center for the Humanities took time to give me critical feedback. Colleagues from English, American Studies, Africana, East Asian Studies, Gender and Sexuality, the Center for the Study of Race and Ethnicity, Modern Culture and Media, Classics, and the Pembroke Center for Teaching and Research on Women also supported me in myriad ways by being readers, advisers, advocates, sponsors, collaborators, and friends. I would like to thank in this regard Karen Newman, Lina Fruzetti, Suzanne Stewart-Steinberg, Elizabeth Weed, Mary Ann Doane, Coppelia Kahn, Ellen Rooney, Philip Rosen, Kay Warren, Wendy Chun, Daniel Kim, Liza Cariaga-Lo, Debbie Weinstein, Gayle Cohee, Michael Kennedy, Shiva Balaghi, Tim Cavanaugh, Elsa Amanatidou, Jay Reed, Bersenia Rodriguez, Maitrayee Bhattacharyya, Chuck O'Boyle, Johanna Hanink, and Sam Perry. I will never forget that many of them affirmed the importance of my work when it mattered. Last but not least, thanks are due to everyone, particularly my senior colleagues in Theatre Arts and Performance Studies, who provided important feedback for my teaching, research, and service: Rebecca Schneider, Patricia Ybarra, Spencer Golub, Lowry Marshall, and Erik Ehn. I thank them for examining my work closely and pushing me to work at my highest level.

In the Michigan tundra, Karl Schoonover, Lloyd Pratt, Zarena Aslami, and I gathered in the now-defunct Morrill Hall to form our junior faculty Immorrill writing group, where a chapter of this book was hatched. Jen Fay, Jyotsna Singh, Scott Juengel, Salah Hassan, Ellen McCallum, Pat O'Donnell, Lisa Fine, and Justus Nieland offered warm, collegial support and invigorating conversations. At Purchase, thanks are due to Morris Kaplan, Michelle Stewart, Carolina Sanin, Jenny Uleman, Agustin Zarzosa, Michael Lobbel, Louise Yelin, Shaka McGlotten, Gari LaGuardia, Kay Robinson, and Geoffrey Field for helping me find my feet and keeping my sanity. At UW–Seattle, a convergence of exciting minds gave me a congenial place to think and work as a postdoctoral fellow at the Jackson School of International Studies, the Center for Southeast Asian Studies, and the School of Drama. Thanks to Rick Bonus, Laurie Sears, Chandan Reddy, Gillian Harkins, Alys Weinbaum, Celia Lowe, Caroline Simpson, Nikhil Singh, Tani Barlow, and Zahid Chaudhary for a special year. My heartfelt thanks also to the artists, activists, and writers who generously shared their work with me, and took time to talk to me at length, including Alvin Tan, Justin Chin, Alex Au, Việt Lê, Allen Kuharski, Alfian Sa'at, and Jeffrey Tan.

Writing a book is like climbing a volcano for a chance to see the crater and caldera lake. I have to thank many fellow risk-takers who climbed with me and showed me the value, ethics, and really the gift of mindful labor. With more than their brilliant minds, Roderick Ferguson and Chandan Reddy have been there with me every step of the way as my intellectual and survival guides in the academy. Together with Martin Manalansan and Lisa Lowe, they grasped the book's interventions better than I did and helped to reorient my theoretical gambit in exciting directions. Their collective wisdom and solidarity are matched by Nayan Shah, M. Jacqui Alexander, Grace Hong, Nadia Ellis, Hiram Perez, Sarita See, Andy Smith, Hiro Yoshikawa, Erika Lin, and

Jodi Melamed, who are always inspiring interlocutors. I can still hear their encouragement and call to finish the book. Always an emergency phone call away is Ramón Rivera-Servera, Joan Kee, and Todd Henry, and together with Patrick Anderson, Nguyễn Tân Hoàng, and Josh Letson-Chambers, they are my trusted conspirators and cheerleaders. Conversations with Sean Metzger, Sylvia Chong, Guo-Juin Hong, and Leo Ching were similarly influential in helping me reshape and rethink the contours of my work for the broader readership of Asian and Asian American studies.

I am embarrassed by how many more people I have asked to read or hear the book-in-progress, or subjected to my half-formed ideas. I owe so much to their attentive feedback and smart comments. Harry Elam and Jean Graham-Jones published my first article as editors of *Theatre Journal*, while David Savran read and commented on the introduction in its earlier forms. Shu-mei Shih and Francoise Lionnet were early supporters as directors of the UC Multi-Campus Research Group on Transnational and Transcolonial Studies. I also want to thank Carol Sorgenfrei, David Gere, Don Pease, Chua Beng Huat, Elin Diamond, Jill Lane, Ken Foster, Joe Roach, Kathryn Bond Stockton, Suk-Young Kim, Esther Kim, Janelle Reinelt, Diana Taylor, Richard Schechner, Charlotte Canning, Shannon Jackson, Harvey Young, Phil Auslander, Barbara Browning, Ara Wilson, Lara Nielsen, Tamara Underliner, Shannon Steen, Elaine Aston, Mike Sell, James Harding, Allen Kuharsky, Catherine Cole, Brandi Catanese, Ted Ziter, Jennifer Parker-Starbuck, Josh Abrams, E. Patrick Johnson, Shane Vogel, William Peterson, Craig Latrell, K. K. Seet, Dallas McCurley, Gay Cima, Katrin Sieg, Stacy Wolf, Jill Dolan, David Roman, Ken Elliott, Lois Weaver, Judith Hamera, John Treat, Janelle Reinelt, Anna Kuhn, Lynette Hunter, Henry Abelove, Douglas Crimp, Allen Isaac, Kiko Benitez, Wendy Ho, Kent Ono, Rosalinda Fregoso, Erica Stevens Abbitt, Una Chaudhari, Quah Sy Ren, James Harding, Lynette Hunter, Ong Keng Sen, Tracy Davis, Karen Tongson, Ron Grabov-Nardini, and Amy Villarejo. They have supported the project in more ways than they know.

I benefited during the writing of this book from the generous support of fellowships, grants, and awards: Humanities Research Funds, and Faculty Development Fund, Brown University, 2010, 2011; Research Fellowship, American Society for Theatre Research (ASTR), 2008;

Dissertation Research Fellowship and Thomas Marshall Grant, ASTR, 2003; Global Studies Grant, Michigan State University (MSU), 2010; Ellen Brown Award, MSU, 2010; Global Literary and Cultural Studies Research Grant, MSU, 2009; SUNY Junior Faculty Development Award, Purchase College, 2007; Provost's Faculty Research Award, Purchase College, 2005; United University Professional Development Fund, Purchase College, 2004, 2005; Greenword and Labadorf Fund, Purchase College, 2005, 2006; and University of California Pacific Rim Grant, 2003. I am also grateful for the research assistance of Ioana Jucan and Paul Tran, funded by Brown University.

I had the privilege of giving lectures at several venues where smart and engaging audiences deeply enriched my writing with their incisive critique and feedback. Thank you New York University, Harvard University, Cornell University, Columbia University, Barnard College, Dartmouth College, Yale University, Northwestern University, University of Washington–Seattle, UC San Diego, University of Birmingham, Warwick University, University of North Carolina–Chapel Hill, Brown University, Hofstra University, UC Davis, University of Minnesota, Texas A&M University, Stony Brook University, University of Virginia, Colby College, and Vassar College.

The librarians in the Netherlands, Singapore, and the United States have made this work possible. I would like to thank in particular the staff at Leiden University's library system for their tireless work in helping me locate Walter Spies's unpublished photograph collection. Special thanks go out to Dr. Marie-Odette Scalliet, Curator of South and Southeast Asian Manuscripts and Rare Books, who went out of her way to find the rare photographs and enabled me to have access to the archive in the Special Collections. J. A. N. Frankhuizen at the Special Collections helped reproduce the images. A quick shout-out to the librarians at UCLA's Special Collection, the Library of Congress in Washington, D.C., and the National University of Singapore's Central Library for their support.

My editor, Eric Zinner, has been a crucial and staunch supporter of this project from the start, and was the visionary force behind the eventual title of the book. I also cannot thank enough my series editors, José Muñoz and Ann Pellegrini, for their unwavering encouragement and steadfast belief in my work. Ciara McLaughlin and Alicia

Nadkarni were instrumental in steering the book manuscript through the production channels at New York University Press, and superb in their attention to details. Additional thanks are due to Rosalie Morales Kearns and Robert Swanson for copyediting and indexing my book, respectively. The two anonymous readers of this manuscript combined critical acumen and enthusiasm that propelled this project forward while helping to transform it for the better.

I am just so fortunate to have as my mentors, colleagues, and peers, thinkers and artists who have created the conditions of possibility for me to do this work. Everything I learned about the value of intellectual rigor and artistic integrity, I learned from them. I can only gesture at the monumental difference each one of them has made in my thinking and life. At the center of these transformative vortices are my mum and dad, for whom I will always be grateful for giving me the space, quite literally the world, to do my own thing. They are everything to me. My five siblings and the weasel club of nieces and nephews in Singapore, Australia, and Canada have given me more than I can ever repay. Thank you for everything.

* * *

A section of chapter 2 was published as "Glocalqueering in New Asia: The Politics of Performing Gay in Singapore," *Theatre Journal* Special Issue: "Theorizing Globalization through Theatre" 58 (October 2005): 383-405, and "The Mardi Gras Boys of Singapore's English-Language Theatre," *Asian Theater Journal* 22.2 (Fall 2005): 293-309. A section of chapter 4 was published as "The Epistemology of the Minor-Native in Transcolonial Borderzones," in *Performance in the Borderlands: A Critical Anthology,* ed. Harvey Young and Ramón Rivera-Servera (Basingstoke: Palgrave Macmillan, 2010).

INTRODUCTION

Tropic Spells, Performance, and the Native Boy

A Preamble to a Spell

The thunderous applause at Brooklyn Academy of Music's New Wave Festival opera *A House in Bali* (2010) reached an electric climax as the troupe of gamelan musicians and Balinese dancers filled the length of the stage. *A House in Bali* is based on a memoir of the same title published in 1947 by Colin McPhee, who is widely considered a progenitor of world music, particularly his transcription of Balinese ceremonial music for the piano.[1] Written by the MIT music professor Evan Ziporyn in honor of McPhee and their shared (but separate) pilgrimages to Bali in 1981 and 1931, respectively, the opera featured a lattice-like intermingling of Balinese gamelan with twenty-first-century composition and technology. It was a "multimedia phantasmagoria of Eastern and Western music" with a hyperkinetic mix of Western opera, fusion rock-n-roll-meets-contemporary-classical strings, piano, guitar, and percussion by a seven-member Bang on a Can All-Stars, a sixteen-member Balinese gamelan, and Balinese singers.[2] Onstage, the mise-en-scène included a roving videographer feeding images in real time to two large screens atop the action juxtaposed with archival photography, while four principal dancers in the traditional mode were accompanied by live music. The excitement of this clangorous sonic and visual experimentation may be compared to the exclamation by McPhee's character in the opera on first hearing the gamelan: "Listen to it! The confusion of sounds, jangled dissonance, merging to form constantly surprising harmonies in this absolute music."[3]

While music played a big role in the show, the most fascinating discovery that evening for the audience was the character of Sampih, an eight-year-old Balinese dancing boy who was the love object of the thirty-one-year-old Canadian musician Colin McPhee. In fact, there was so much enthusiasm for him that the actor playing the part joined the curtain call to a literal gasp in the auditorium.

With the boy on center stage, the audience shot to their feet to affirm the Balinese collectively as the stars of the show rather than the three European opera leads—the actors playing Colin McPhee, the anthropologist Margaret Mead, and the painter Walter Spies—who had disappeared backstage. This was an uncanny moment: the boy had become a star, as he had in McPhee's memoir when the Balinese dancers toured the United States and appeared on the *Ed Sullivan Show* in New York City in 1952. The Balinese, indistinguishable as historic characters and actors onstage, seemed like a living flash/flesh from the past.

As the clapping turned manic, I joined the standing ovation with an apoplectic ambivalence that first seemed customary of middle-class theater etiquette, unsure if standing up was in fact a voluntary or compulsory act. My friend Tavia, whom I had convinced to see the show, clapped politely but would complain later that the New Wave Festival was increasingly pandering to the cosmopolitan multiculturalism of the Brooklyn art set. "I see what you mean now with the boy," he said with his eyes widening. There was something palpably seductive and "wrong" about the spectacle to be clapping so hard, though I could not say what it was just yet; for the record, it has nothing to do with being a theater curmudgeon. I had rather enjoyed the show. So there we were

standing before the altar of the Western proscenium stage like adoring
fans reliving the silvery rhythms of pure gamelan magic with the final
treat of this intoxicating native tableau vivant. I couldn't help clapping
harder, maybe even tearing up a little, perhaps out of guilty pleasure or
the sheer conceit that my book had just been given yet another staging.
More than middle-class decorum or postcolonial sentiment, my ambivalence was taken over by a swirly mix of contradictory feelings. I was in
fact fighting a possession: the ethno-visual splendor of brown bodies,
male torsos, and costumes shimmering en masse under the floodlight
with gamelan music in my head. I was spellbound and sick, euphoric
and catatonic.

I have taught and written about the nativized spectacle and its sen-
sory history for years, so I was surprised that its performatic logic and
rapture were tangling before my eyes and in my body that evening over
a Balinese dancing boy. If the audience saw the Balinese as the scopic,
sonic, and sensual centerpiece of an opera that is ostensibly a multimedia phantasmagoria of Eastern and Western music, video, dance, and
performance art, were they also applauding the love story between Sampih and Colin McPhee, the queer pedo-phantasmagoria at the heart of
the opera? Could it be that the rush of "Bali high" from the 1930s channeled through Sampih was displaced on a spell so magical and addic-
tive that its queer content was taken for granted and even celebrated at
this 2010 cosmo-multicultural festival? Or was the queer content simply disavowed and evacuated for a mesmerizing Balinese experience, an
experiential magic that we might also call the native burden of Asian
theater traditions on the world stage? These questions engage and yet
also exceed the matter of valorizing colonial exotica or the primitivist
grid of contemporary performance in the West as echoed in such brilliant and now familiar indictments as "going primitive" (Marianna Tor-
govnick), "orientalist melancholia" (Rey Chow), and "imperialist nostalgia" (Renaldo Rosaldo). They point to and pivot on the open secret
of the native boy, so feared and beloved in the opera and by the audience, as a minor figure dancing his way onto the world cultural stage.
He is the disciplinary love object of colonialism and those who live by
its shadows, identities, and myriad afterlives.

The Sampih-Colin pedo–love story is not exceptional, though rare
in its extensive coverage of a single native boy's identity. One need only

survey the life and work of André Gide, Paul Bowles, William Bur-
roughs, Lawrence Durrell, Gustave Flaubert, T. E. Lawrence, Edmund
Backhouse, John Moray Stuart-Young, and E. M. Forster to find myriad
examples of this coupling in the Western literary world. My main interest in foregrounding this well-known and yet unspeakable love story
is the way that it serves as an allegory for the white man/native dyad
that organizes the production and reception of Asian performance writ
large. In this regard, the space for debate is how "Asia," to the extent that
it is cast as an actual or conceptual native boy, is part of a pedophiliac
Western modernity bearing the homoerotics of orientalism. Moreover,
how does Asian performance encode this colonial legacy or wrestle
with the pedophiliac tendencies of Western paternalism?

To be clear, this is neither an abolitionist project that seeks to free the
boys from servitude or predation, nor a corrective to right the wrong
done to subaltern boys by giving them a voice or future.[4] Nor am I interested in the business of identifying colonial pedophiles in the style of the
NBC series *To Catch a Predator*, or engaging the moral anxieties of the
"good colonial versus bad colonial" dilemma that accompany defensive
debates about the virtues of exceptional Europeans and Americans.[5] The
latter's broader manifestation as an apologia for the U.S. nation-state,
what many have rightly identified as American exceptionalism, is strikingly etched in the redemption narrative of Hollywood films like *The
Green Berets* (1968). As is well known, the film ends with the American
hero Colonel Kirby, played by John Wayne, comforting a helpless Vietnamese boy ("What happen to me now?") crowned with a green beret as
they walk holding hands along the beach in the sunset, with the promise
of the colonel's fatherly care and patronage ("You let me worry about
that, Green Beret. You are what this is all about!").[6] I am clarifying what
the book is not doing partly in response to the common charges raised
by respondents at my lectures and partly to highlight how the disparities
haunting the dyad also give credence to a West that has all the power vis-
à-vis the helpless, nubile, innocent native boy. Moreover, in spite of the
liberal, Western concern for the boy, the focus is invariably redirected
back on the white man as the subject or main character, whether he is
the complex genius and hero or whether he is even proximate to "the
colonial condition." Remarkably, the critical discourse would always
eschew any significant study of homoeroticism as it pertains to the boys.

For instance, Joseph Boone's important essay "Vacation Cruises; or, The Homoerotics of Orientalism," as well as others, addresses the strictly European tourist who sexualized and romanticized boys in North Africa.[7] This foundational essay offers a nuanced reading of T. E. Lawrence and other white male travelers in the "Sotadic zone" and is centered on the predicament of the white male "going native" over there in North Africa and the Arabian Peninsula.[8] Boone also interprets how these "spells" were conjured in major European novels. Historically speaking, the silent native boys are represented either as a curiosity, mystery, or source of fascination, their discursive absence or silence marked by their anonymous faces etched on paintings and photographs; their performance ephemera irrecoverable or sustained only in memory and oral transmissions. Even in leading gay novels, such as *The Swimming Pool Library* (1988), the depiction of African boys is deployed merely to enable the grace and virtuosity of the novelist. Studies such as Boone's take a curatorial, literary approach to cultural artifacts that examines the role of the colonial writer but continues to ignore a study of the boy himself. I am interested in how "the homoerotics of orientalism" may be deployed to understand the representation of the boy.

In the case of Colin McPhee, the late musicologist Philip Brett notes that he is enjoying "a small revival as a result of art music's unreflected admiration of Orientalism."[9] Hence, like the work of the (straight) minimalist composers Steve Reich and Philip Glass, the composer's reflection is focused on the "degree of originality of the Occidental composer," or his genius cross-cultural aesthetic. Unlike the politics of exploiting "a so-called primitive music," McPhee is said to have incorporated in his most ambitious work, *Tabuh-Tabuhan* (1936), widely received as a transcription of the gamelan, "cross rhythms, irregular ostinatos, sectional structures, and layered textures" that had preexisted in his own work in the 1920s.[10] The genius of McPhee is that he "did not simply tack on exotic effects," and "met the East on its own terms."[11] The musicologist Carol Oja went as far as to say that *Tabuh-Tabuhan* "occupies a singular—even a leading—position within works of ethnic inspiration as well as the whole of twentieth century American music."[12] But, for McPhee, meeting the "East on its own terms" or finding with Balinese music and its people "an empathy that was extraordinary"[13] was not merely a musical affair. It also involved Sampih as muse, son, adoptee, houseboy, trophy dancer, and lover, a matter that Oja hints at ever so coyly. Consider the differing accounts of the original encounter between Sampih and McPhee by Oja and McPhee, respectively:

> Sampih was a child of about eight when McPhee first met him in 1932 while the house was being built. As McPhee tells the story, one day he walked down to the river below his house and was suddenly caught in a flash flood. Sampih saw him struggling, leaped in, and led him to safety. The two struck up a tentative friendship, and soon Sampih was stopping frequently at the McPhee house. Eventually he came there to live. McPhee probably never adopted Sampih officially. In *A House in Bali* he does not use the term "adoption," although he talks of custody negotiations with the child's parents. Katherine Mershon also took in a boy; hers was named Murda. She has claimed she paid Murda's family about a dollar a month so she could keep the child.[14]

> One afternoon I had gone down the hillside to the river and waded to the other side to walk along the edge of the rice fields . . . a few yards above the level of the water. A crowd of small boys splashed in midstream, leaping from rock to rock. Their wet brown skins shone in the sun as they danced up and down in the ecstasy of nakedness. They were completely wild, agile, and delirious as a treeful of monkeys. . . . while I was walking along the river's edge . . . one of these floods occurred . . . I soon found myself in deep water where the current was far too strong. The children shouted excited directions from the shore, but I could not hear what they were saying. It was then that one of the more boisterous, one whom I had already noticed as the leading spirit, threw himself in to the water, swam to a boulder and jumped over to where I was struggling. He knew every shallow and hollow in the river bed, for he quickly led me ashore. . . . When we reached land this naked, dripping youngster and I stood facing one another. He was perhaps eight, underfed and skimpy, with eyes too large for his face, daring and slightly mocking. I offered him a cigarette, but he suddenly took fright and was off into the water before I could say a word.[15]

The metaphor of the phallic cigarette that frightened poor Sampih is a subtle sexual reference in McPhee's alternately pornographic and loving gaze about his first encounter with him. Details of the Balinese boys as a "treeful of monkeys" dancing in "the ecstasy of nakedness" articulate a queer vision that is rampant in the era's colonial postcards and photography.[16] Like it or not, the eloquence of his desire for Sampih and the boys is part of the memoir's appeal that has also made it a must-read for those purportedly interested in the structure and sound of Balinese gamelan music. In this regard, Oja's dry codification or denial of the encounter's homoerotics, calling the Sampih-Colin relationship a "tentative friendship," seems rather disingenuous. She has in fact read McPhee's memoir but chooses to highlight the common practice of recruiting houseboys instead, noting that his heterosexual dancer friend Katherine Mershon also "took in a Balinese boy." While we may speculate on Oja's disinterest in bringing out the queer erotics of the encounter, we might also point out what is obvious: the colonial dyad is at once identified and disavowed for a narrative focus on Colin McPhee as the subject, and Sampih as the object. Similarly, the opera skirts the issue by vaguely acknowledging the centrality of Sampih's role in McPhee's story of personal and artistic transformation in Bali. It went as far as to suggest that his fixation on this beautiful dancing boy was more than a matter of discovering and nurturing local talent, but does not ever develop its queer subtext. As a disgruntled review notes, "it's like a coming-out story in which nobody ever really comes out."[17]

The historical narrative dictates that Sampih's fame and even existence as a dancer hinge on McPhee's patronage and life story, neatly cataloged in the archives at UCLA's ethnomusicology collection. Though Sampih's story meets with the requisite tragic end for the native boy (he was brutally murdered at age twenty-eight in 1954)—he is at the very least known by his first name. This is in contradistinction to countless other boys who remain nameless and anonymous even as they are photographed, written about, or endlessly reproduced as a trope. The term "native boy" refers both to minors like Sampih and to nativized men who are treated as less than adults. This rampant form of racialization resonates with various official discourses that infantilize gay men as no more than boys even as "boys" remains a popular term of endearment in gay circles. These blurring lines of the term index the problematic that attends each inquiry and encounter about the queer dyad that is the white man/native boy.

INTRODUCTION

[handwritten annotation: one stop at a time... (and relationships of pedophilia can be problematic — discuss)]

Paradigm

Brown Boys and Rice Queens proposes that while orientalist dyadic formations are chronic and persistent in twentieth- and twenty-first-century intercultural encounters, queer couplings such as the white man/ native boy remain under the critical radar in spite of their prevalence. This queer dyad is, to put it facetiously, everywhere and nowhere at the same time. The book begins by asking why this has been the case, and then performs a comparative study of this queer coupling as a primary object of performance history and analysis. Three sites configure a mapping of circum-Pacific performance in the Asias: Bali, Singapore, and the United States. This study will argue that an understanding of Asian encounters in a colonial-transnational frame is not merely incomplete but lacking in its central substance if it does not take account of queer couplings exemplified by the white man/native boy's conceptual, historical, and sexual couplings.[18] It will assume that this dyad and its cognate formations must be rendered a commensurate visibility in critical studies of performance, theater, and culture, whether as a queer episteme or a colonial one, or both, intertwined throughout the encounter. Such a wager considers queerness and a perverse love for the Asian boy as central to traditional and transnational epistemologies of "Asian performance."

[handwritten annotation in left margin: stakes]

The historical dimension of this gambit is based on a set of dichotomies. In the classic colonial/native encounter of post-Enlightenment modernity, the purchase of Western power is accepted as a matter of intelligibility. The perception and interpretation of that encounter is organized through the Western perspective. It is a dyadic structure that organizes an uneven distribution of power through paradigms that are both colonial and gendered, focused on both labor and seduction. The colonial man inscribes, reasons, and directs the encounter with singular finesse, while the nativized objects appear as dancing, laboring, grumbling, and seducing. While the colonial subject is imbued with gravitas and mobility, the nativized object is made to seem infantile, tricky, and bound by tradition. The subject inspires a biography, while the object disappears into a mob; the subject is rational and distinguished, the object remains erratic and mysterious. These performative iterations and their requisite affects are regulated by an age-old orientalist logic

native woman's relationship gets discussed, but not native boy's

whose most familiar dyadic formation is also a gendered one: the colonial is a white man and the "native" is a brown woman. In the Western canon, the familiar image of the lovelorn female Asiatic woman has been immortalized in Puccini's *Madame Butterfly*, or she appears as a hypersexual prostitute, as in *Miss Saigon*. In the social imaginary, she is the tragic Indian *sati* widow, and the oppressed Afghan woman in burka. All of these images are set in narratives in which the iconic native woman is to be loved or saved by the white man. They compose the colonial deployment of East-West relations as heteronormative in structure. The uneven distribution of power is mobilized by codes of masculinity and femininity.

The critical focus on the native boy is crucial since he, unlike the brown woman, is often cast as a superfluous character, a neglected critical trope, or simply missing from the archives. In this work, the focus brings the erratic sightings of the nativized boy from the backdrop, or the wings, to the foreground, using as its material the incandescent realms of theater and social production, narrativized fictions, filmic recordings, and the queer "porno-tropics" of the global arena.[19] The variability of these sightings constitutes a broad spectrum of types and sites. He is, for instance, the possessed Balinese dancing boy in colonial photography; the faceless victim of child sex tourism in Southeast Asia; one in a mob of cannibalistic brown boys in Tennessee Williams's *Suddenly Last Summer* or in the non-cannibalistic mob in the film *Slumdog Millionaire*. But beyond identifying these images, the study seeks to interpret their significance and connection. The book reads the native boy as a figurative consignment of colonial modernity, at once the love child of predatory capitalism, queer orientalism, and the white male artist-tourist on the casual prowl for inspiration and sex. In one regard, the native boy is a sign of conquest, the trope of an Asian male or nation infantilized as a boy, a savage domesticated as a child, and a racially alienating body in need of tutelage and discipline.

Paired with a white man, the allegorical figure of colonialism, the dyad enters the discourse of colonial piety and subjugation with various anxieties, chief of which is racial and (homo)sexual panic. The boy's homologous manifestations, located in the three chosen sites (Bali, Singapore, Asian America), signify a transnational formation across the colonial time-space of the last century where his body is passed from the hands of the colonial empire to the postcolonial nation-state to neo-liberal globalization. Read through such semiotic figurations, the traffic in native boys between white men and their different care packages is also an allegory of Asia infantilized and emasculated as a nubile boy/child in the face of colonial whiteness and modernity. The persistence of the trope of the white man/nativized boy informs the global system of representation that positions the racialized embodiments of the Asian male in transnational queer performance and everyday life, hailing the queer underside of what Michel Foucault calls a "history of the present," an open, productive space to "detect those things which have not yet been talked about, those things that, at the present time, introduce, show, give some more or less vague indications of the fragility of thought, in our way of reflecting, in our practices."[20]

Assemblies of Interpretation

By way of introduction to the full study of the paradigm I have developed above, I want to briefly address the critical paradox of the colonial dyad and the native boy (both as a part of and apart from the dyad) that resides within queer inquiries by formulating a number of axioms, conceptual rearrangements, and critical interventions around "Asian performance." The sections in this introduction propose a consortium of tools, texts, terms, and maps to think through the site and surround of Asian encounters in a transnational complex. They consolidate the book's critical hedges in theater and performance studies as its primary cross-fields while engaging queer and global studies, postcolonial and ethnic studies, and Asian, Asian American, and American studies (what I shall henceforth refer to as Asian/American studies) to elucidate every encounter. They serve as a signpost of ideas rather than an end point, and a way to navigate the transnational and sometimes unruly itinerary throughout the book, including "queer f(r)ictions," "bringing out tropic spells," "glocalqueering native boys," "butterflies gone berserk," "trans-colonial borderzones," "epistemology of minor-native," "dyadic performativity," "G.A.P. (Gay Asian Princess) drama," "performance in the Asias," and "ethnic camp." The plurality is meant to trouble the ascribed unidirectionality of critical and complicit energies and logics that often accompany the provenance of "Asia" as a stable and static category in twentieth-century area and theater studies.

Bali, Singapore, and Asian America organize a configuration of the queer Asias predicated on the material and historical particularities of their performance cultures, and each is treated in separate chapters. Anchoring this study is the Balinese *kecak*, Singaporean gay theater in English, and Asian American performance art. The legacy of colonialism hovers over the broader argument describing all the chapters together, haunting the contemporary postcolonial queer Asian (both queer and female examples included) in ways best analyzed through performance. While each chapter may be read as dealing with what is prototypically colonial (Bali circa 1900-1942), postcolonial (Singapore, 1990-2010), and diasporic (Asian America, 1990-2010), the theater and performance forms I examine both address and exceed each designation when read through the consortium of critical formulations that relate Asian encounters to transnational queer performance. The three sites are explicitly connected in a transnational and transcolonial complex where colonialism and its legacies manifest in ways that exceed or deform conventional hierarchies of national and colonial time-space with queer couplings, turns, and feelings. That is, they involve a turn from the enforcement of top-down/bottom-up to the artifice of same-sex top/bottom, or the facetious substitution of "East gone rogue, gone missing" for the West-to-East or East-to-West model of exchange. Theater and performance are ideal for staging this complex while being a part of its very constitution. Its sensate acuity for people rubbing against each other (in all manner of speaking), speculations of actor agency, and critical (de-/re-)composition of reality are all crucial for shoring up the conditions of possibility for the native boy. A centerpiece of this complex fiction is thus the boy himself, including his movement, action, and affect vis-à-vis the desiring white male gaze in different locations, bodies, and guises.

Whether he is performing for the postcolonial father-state, the United States, the white daddy, the impresario of ethnic drag, or the Western theater director, the boy brings to bear the historical valences of an originary colonial encounter as well as the queer and racial legibilities and deformities that attend to his role-play, erotic identification, and figurative power.[21] The book conjures the dyad as constituted by the complex and multidirectional desires and resistances that are deployed to fuel the colonial and postcolonial encounters between the West and the Asias. It makes provisions for a spectrum of feelings and histories that may or may not be commensurate with official or unofficial accounts about the boy or the dyad. Understanding the native boy in multiple contexts is therefore crucial to the erotohistoriography of performance traditions in the Asias, and each given site demands a particular assembly of critical tools and reference points.

Read together, these performances, situated within their individuated sites, animate the stakes of queer Asian/colonial encounters across spaces and temporalities gauged by transnational processes. My hope is that different contingencies and combinations of Asian encounters and queerness could be activated around the shifting set of concerns, outlooks, and issues that these performances prompt. Let's turn to one assembly of these modes of interpretation.

Queer F(r)ictions — *explanation of terminology*

The transnational vectors I have in mind in this section proceed from two major points of departure whose critical trajectories have for the most part and until recently run on parallel tracks. The first point of departure is derived primarily from U.S. queer of color critiques and Australian AsiaPacifiQueer studies, what we might call as a shorthand, Asian/Pacific/American (A/P/A) performance epistemologies.[22] The other major vector proceeds from notions of postcolonial queerness that link directly to multinational identifications and the comparative histories of Asian performance in American understandings of race and sexuality. The implicit backdrop for this vector is the rise of global Asia and the return or transmigration of Asian American artist-scholars to China, India, and Southeast Asia. Thus, the first point of departure organizes an Asian identification within national and regional boundaries, such as American, or Australian, or Pacific Island, and the second point of departure takes the global Asia as its starting point. The fact that these critiques run on parallel rather than shared tracks creates something like a bipolar condition, with varying effects, including a methodological impasse or critical blind spot.

1) Asian identified in other non-Asian spaces
2) Looking at Asia as a whole (and how it's viewed globally)

12

Rather than privileging one of these approaches over the other, I want to regard their convergences and collisions as transnational f(r)ictions. By "f(r)ictions," I have in mind the anthropologist Anna Tsing's notion of "friction," which brings out the "awkward, unequal, unstable, and creative qualities of interconnection across difference" through the "sticky materiality of practical encounters" around the world.[23] This is a way of refusing dominant myths such as the singular discourse on— or what Tsing calls the lie of—"global power as a well-oiled machine."[24] Rather, it provides critical traction for minor scales in the grip of worldly encounters, or frictions produced by people (including those other than the usual suspects) with varying agendas and desires rubbing up against each other. The rhetoric and methodology of Tsing's friction reconfigure how universal terms are often only seen as being rearticulated in the local idiom from a top-down direction when both (universal/local, dominant/other) are always mutually constitutive in "zones of awkward engagement"; one changes over place and time through contact, and the other stakes out claims beyond its locality.[25]

I want to bring this idea together with the collective theorizations of scholars whose queer and women of color critiques uncover the "fictions" within "the ruptural components of culture" such as "the restrictions of universality, the exploitations of capital, and the deceptions of national culture."[26] In this regard, we might follow the leads of its theorists to say that queer f(r)ictions are a way to track the unpredictable connectivity of the queer dyad, or the "heat" of its tropes, across the multiple scales and interfaces of the postcolonial/diaspora, native/ethnic, Asia/America animating all Asian encounters in performance. These disarticulations of entrenched coherencies are a move to see opposing fictions and fabrications in action, or the inherently dramatic force driving the performance of queer f(r)ictions. They have several implications for reading the native boy as the *other* half of the dyad whose "new" visibility is based on uncovering different histories and conditioned agencies in performance that would also mark the disunity and instability of the dyad's dominant fictions.

For one, they carry stories of hope and dissension that "rub" against each other with complex transformations in the subjectivity and politics of those who care about the potential of queer acts to imagine otherwise. Trouble or pleasure, queer f(r)ictions are crucial for interrogating all the explosive issues accompanying the native boy's presence, whether as a queer episteme, critical affect, performance conundrum, or historical trace. These involve various queer couplings, romances, and disputes wherever the two (colonial/native, white/ethnic, poco-daddy/cosmo-homo, patriarch/boy, rice queen/Asian houseboy) may meet. While the focus at each geographic location is on different versions of the native boy, the objective is not to present a homology or taxonomy of boys tied neatly to colonial, national, and diasporic predicaments. Rather, queer f(r)ictions facilitate a comparative spatial study, what I call a transcolonial borderzone, of different Asian encounters with an eye toward a different outcome than simple negation or negativity. It engages the hope in José Muñoz's conception of queerness as "essentially about the rejection of a here and now and an insistence or concrete possibility for another world."[27] Such cruisings, to intermix Muñoz's and Tsing's critical heed, involve a staggering range of people, places, and performances that are brought into the fray of frictive and fictional contact onstage, in everyday life, and in imagined futures.

Additionally, the question of scale around each encounter with the native boy calibrates a different set of Asian encounters based on the queer congeries of local/global, local/regional interactions. These are attuned to native self-invention vis-à-vis colonial spells of difference in Bali, postcolonial state policies around pink capitalism in Singapore, and U.S. imperial histories in Asian America and the Asian diaspora. Hence, he is simultaneously the one to be tutored and disciplined by the white daddy, a trope for the racial minority in colonial and postcolonial Asia and the United States, and the one to be saved in the global proliferation of rights-based Western lesbian, gay, bisexual, and transgender identity movements in Third World countries. Each of these salvific and disciplinary encounters with the Asian boy in theater and performance as well as their surround is an opportunity for understanding the liberal (and false) apology for U.S. colonial management and neoliberal triumphalism in or on Asia, and the effects of that history on Asian/America. A way to make sense of all these variable Asian encounters, that is, the boy as a trope of Asian performance or a native of the Euro-American tropics, is through a critical formulation that I am calling the "tropic spell."

Bringing Out the Tropic Spell

[handwritten: more terminology explained]

From a lexical perspective, a spell originally meant a "narration," which gives a discursive structure to its current popular meaning as "a form of words used as a magical charm or incantation."[28] A spell is also an exemplary performative as words that not only do things but perform the act of doing things: it can quite literally conjure things into being with the right organization of words and conditions. In spite of these structures, much like theater or dance-drama, its effects are not always predictable with bodies in motion. In fact, a spell is never able to fully determine how subjects think, produce, consume, feel, or act. Besides, there are all kinds of unplanned effects during such an encounter, contingent upon the spell's duration, histories of the space in which the encounter occurs, the actors' bodies, loose affects, secretions, the labor of production teams, and how others see or interpret what is taking place.

Brown Boys and Rice Queens asks why performances produced from or read through Asian encounters and dyadic couplings have such allure or magic; why global queer theater and racial performance are or seem to be easily given to their spellbinding scenarios. Such an approach opens up a space for an explicit play with the requisite affect, speech, and identifications of the dyad as well as the design, casting, and history of each Asian encounter. These are all basic inquiries of performance analysis but also fundamental components of a tropic spell. There is nothing "natural" about a white man/native boy pairing. Its legitimacy or legibility is contingent on the naturalization of the other's performative attributes. Hence, the point of my staging the Asian encounter is not to look at a spell as simply that which is cast by one over the other, or on us as readers and spectators. Rather, it is to understand how the spells are mutually constitutive in performance as a technology of representation and sustainable across a web of relationalities, including other dyads, triads, communities, and so forth. This is a gambit for configuring a range of critical reading practices about performance in the queer Asias. I am not interested in a nomothetic and singular notion of Asia or naturalized connections of bodies to space, time, and bodily regimes of action. Bringing out the tropic spell of the colonial imaginary begins

[handwritten margin note: Why does the native boy/white man dyad and Asian culture in general have special performative allure?]

15

to denaturalize the dyad as well as Asian performance as a queer design with many faces.

Performance is crucial for understanding the spell of the dyad as that which gives Asian encounters and other hegemonic cultural conventions their appeal and durability. By performance, I mean to invoke its variegated and contested meanings as an embodied practice, critical trope, and interpretive methodology with an eye toward bridging "segregated and differently valued knowledges, drawing together legitimated as well as subjugated modes of inquiry."[29] As Dwight Conquergood argues, such an approach models a radical research agenda that attends to the "epistemic violence" of scriptocentric Western regimes of knowing by procuring minor performance knowledges that are "tacit, intoned, gestured, improvised, coexperienced, covert."[30] The burgeoning field of transnational theater studies, a cognate of performance studies in an ever-changing cross-field, is also crucial in this critical venture. Together, they turn a critical eye on the blind spots of dominant epistemologies stuck in colonial (straight white male) ocular-centrism, print-based literacy, and self-legitimating productions. In this regard, both theater and performance are particularly suited to examining the dyad's queerness as a mode of subjugated, covert, and "illegitimate" form of living.

The queer intelligibility of a colonial scenario is both performative and allegorical. The performativity of the dyad's queer coupling requires that the native boy corporealize the elements of the fantasmic power relationship. His performance is an embodiment of the flexible genders (more often feminine) and exotic magic assigned to Asia. Unlike the native girl, he is perceived as either male or female, a double-faced agent who performs modern feelings but acts in familiar traditions. The boy is nativized by virtue of precisely his "boyish" aspect, his seeming underdevelopment of secondary sexual characteristics, his smaller size, and his propensity for graceful, "primitive" ways. Toward this curious object, the white man feels lovesick, possessed, and paternalistic. He has fallen for the spells cast by the West, even as the magic appears to emanate naturally from the boy's nativized and flexibly gendered body.

The hyperbolic emotional and sexual affect of this Asian encounter is registered in the scenario, to use Diana Taylor's term, of colonial-orientalist encounters, and sets up a queer account of the racialized subjectivities they produce. At stake in such a scenario of global encounters is the way that the corporeal imaginary and its performance can theatricalize the queer and nativized affect enforced or naturalized as a matter of the uneven distribution of power. Describing the dyad's differential manifestations in/as performance not only serves to display the ways power is imagined as corporeal and seductive, but also serves to create an interface with performance traditions along the global crossings in the Asias with resonant particularities at each site. It attunes us to the "other" traditions of corporeality, theater, and performance that play alongside, against, and with the colonial scenario. Together, and apart, these performances stage this open secret of queer couplings at once dirty and tender, patronizing and enabling, real and fantastic, which continues to condition transnational queer performance across time and space.

In the first chapter of the book, I take a close look at the Balinese *kecak* as a prime example of the tropic spell. *Kecak* is often performed with traditions of ritual possession (Sanghyang) from which it is derived in nightly tourist shows at Ubud, Bali, to conjure an "ancient tribal hypnosis." More strikingly, its adapted, current choreography may be understood through the classic white man/native boy dyad put in place by the German expatriate artist Walter Spies. Spies was instrumental in this adaptation based on his love for the Balinese brown boys, who portray the *Ramayana* monkeys within the spectacle. Although the monkey is a god in the story, the agile, playful, and yet also threatening portraits the boys enact are at once youthful, seductive, and threateningly elusive. In his daily life, Spies employed a host of nameless boys who served as his houseboys, models, lovers, and inspiration during the interwar years of the twentieth century, when Spies and a queer enclave of Western transplants made Bali their home. The seduction of the brown boy theatricalized in the ritual's polyrhythmic gyrations and cacophonous chants is an explosive, open secret whenever Spies is invoked as a cocreator in its history of development. Its intractable and "invisible" queerness sounds off the problematics of authenticity in traditional Asian ritual forms whose preservation and evolution in the past century are tied to a violent colonial history. Not only is this history of the development of *kecak* elided, its subsequent academic and historiographic representation by both Western and Balinese scholars have actively sought to marginalize or invalidate the troubling queerness at the origin of the form's "revival." But the queer encounter of Spies and the boys is part of the Balinese paradisal idyll, a discursive invention of the Dutch colonials who also made Spies a famous "victim" of their raids against buggers and sodomites. The aesthetic success of such a queer dyad suggests that the man/boy coupling is constitutive rather than deformative of the colonial scenario.

Contemporary criticism of Balinese dance forms attributes a rather patriarchal neutrality and authority to Spies, who is said to have saved Balinese "native" performance, in adapting it for consumption by tourists. Yet Spies actually knew very little about the originary status of the performers and the performance. Spies may have been the creator of the conceit of performing possession, of playing possession for the Western anthropological gaze—what some scholars have provocatively called ethnopornography. Likewise, Spies's "ethnophotography" stages the languid gaze, entranced posture, and wry smile of both Spies and "the boys," who appear to be in on the joke about their queer masquerade. But the scholarship is nearly silent on this Asian encounter due to either structural conditions of the archive or a lack of desire, casting a pall over the historical texture of the Balinese performers or the material conditions for their reengagement of *kecak*.

I bring up the example of Spies (which I examine more extensively in chapter 1) to illustrate the practical workings of the tropic spell. Spies represented this spell in his life filled with Balinese "boy" lovers, in his re-creation of them in the choreography of the *kecak*, and in his ethnophotography. I am interested in how his biography and work suggest a shifting range of mutually constitutive queer fantasies that motivate conflicting claims and disavowals around its cultural ownership or co-optation, and how we might use the tropic spells found therein to theorize transnational queer performance. I do not mean to suggest that the Balinese men who were involved with Spies, as lovers and as performers, were simply objects of his gaze and his affections. The seduction of the tropic spell is not simply the invention of a colonial individual, but a condition within which the queer coupling found a seductive scenario to play. As Spies illustrates, tropic spells are both identitarian or social positions and theatrical, aestheticized conceits.

Tropic spells are at once colonial and postcolonial in their effects and tricks, and they demand a range of queer reading practices attuned to the dyad's critical and complicit orientalist formations. In my analyses, I will use contrapuntal (in Said's sense) interplay between sometimes discrepant and sometimes mutually constitutive visions, worldviews, or experiences of *both* the (former) colonizer and (formerly) colonized. The point is to not singularize one or the other subject position—white man or native boy, colonizer or colonized—but to approach it as a dyadic formation that takes into account "both the metropolitan history that is narrated and . . . those other histories against which (and together with which) the dominating discourse acts."[31] The dyad is, in other words, mutually constitutive, and the spells are cast in both directions.

Bringing out tropic spells as theatrical conceits or performance in(ter)ventions is a way to make legible, audible, and palpable the shifting temporal and spatial positioning of the "Asian" subject in various performative genres. When the queer exigencies of various Asian subjects, performances, and discourses are carefully limned, the stereotypical rendering of the white man/native boy dyad is also being actively decomposed. This is in contrast to the way some have written about the disciplinary technology of colonial "tender violence" where the assumptions are primarily based on an ocular fetishization of the native as at once sexual, primitive, and modernizable.[32] Little has been said about how the panic of otherness is sublimated in professions of love that vacillate between romance and patronage, care and surveillance, through queer, dyadic formations. These affective polarizations attract and repel one from the other endlessly in a tricky relationship. It is a relationship that takes on multiple guises around the world, pointing to a confluence of queer connections and unspeakable possessions from the colonial past to the transnational present. Such giddy guises and codependencies open a new set of questions about the role of queerness in colonial (re)formations and orientalist legacies in Asian performance, and how Asian encounters inflect transnational queer performance (or vice versa). As a flexible allegory, the dyad is not confined to the colonial scenario per se but key to understanding various ethnic and queer (de) formations in transnational worlds wherever the East and West have intermingled, including postcolonial and postwar contexts.

The mutuality of the queer dyad of man/boy may be within, but is clearly different from, the dominant reception of the East as infantilized.

A comparison of Spies's aesthetic with the familiar image of General Douglas MacArthur screwing up a Japanese boy toy could help illustrate what I mean. Allegorizing U.S.-Japan relations after the war, MacArthur's characterization of postwar Japan as "a boy of 12" relative to the Anglo-Saxon, who was, "say 45 years of age in development in the sciences, the arts, divinity, culture" is an unvarnished reference to the unqueer, nonconsensual white man/boy dyad.[33] Defeated, the Japanese were represented as children, made pliable and teachable, justifying the Occupation. Occupation is more brutal, more authoritarian, and more nationalist than the tropic spell. It also moves the boy toward the eventual payoff of occupation: the Japanese "boy" will mature into the Westernized man, and take on "the responsibilities and privileges of an advanced society."[34]

As is clear, this particular iteration of the native boy as "impressionable, vulnerable Japanese 'children'" is an assertion by Americans and Europeans who saw "something immature and undeveloped about the 'small' Japanese and their 'toylike' nation."[35] The MacArthur-Japanese boy doll encounter is thus ensconced in the subject-object designation of white man/native boy with no escape for the joyless Japanese "kid" in a hetero-orientalist framework, an update of the Pinkerton-Japanese bastard child. While we may queer the conventional sexual metaphors of this conquest scenario, it is not queerness but a violent homoeroticism that is at the heart of the image's racist paternalism. This accounts for the structure of legibility predicated on the "truth" of Japan as a machinic doll and the West as a manly officer in charge. I want to stress that this operates differently than the "magic" of tropic spells I have in mind, where racial fascination and queer affection are mixed with bewitching scenes of seduction from both sides even where cross-cultural understanding ultimately fails. But these performative positions, the interplay between exploitation and patronage, subterfuge and romance, suggest that the dyad is constantly negotiating the effects of its own spells. Yet such queer distillations of orientalism in the Asias are rendered with a set of affects that must feel like orientalist déjà vu, from the joyful nativization or racialized sufferings of the boy to the loving patronage and knowing paternalism of the colonial. These affective registers are generated in tandem with the dyad's binaries—white/brown, man/boy, rational/exotic, clean/dirty, First World/Third World—accompanying contemporary spells of difference.

reversing the binary to focus on boy?

Placing the Asian boy at the center of the colonial/native imaginary means that the dyad's encounters also become key to understanding performance in the queer Asias. The dyad's spells are ultimately uncontainable because it has perennial tropic heat, in the sense that its tropes and body logics continue to be pervasive and naturalized in the pornotropics of the Asias. But performance is well situated to play with its magic. It would require that the native boy come out as a critical subject on the transnational stage with his white male other (in hand or absently) in a dyadic but not necessarily committal relationship.

Dyadic Performativity, or Butterflies Gone Berserk

As I have illustrated in the Spies example, the history of such encounters is crucial in transnational configurations that push against the contours of accepted cultural logics and histories about Southeast Asia. That is, they interrogate how "Asian performance," both as a theatrical genre and as an encounter, is also a queer transcultural amalgam. "Tradition," in this regard, has to be viewed as an evolving form that exceeds discrete national history and identity. Just as there is not one unchanging tradition, there is not one native boy. He has to be understood within the logics and structure of specific colonial, national, and diasporic projects and their relational affinities. The multiple histories, memories, and desires of these intersecting projects bind his coherency and incoherency to a politics of recognition—Who is the native boy? How is he recognizable? What is his story? Why should we care?

In *American Tropics: Articulating Filipino America* (2006), Allan Punzalan Isaac argues that the "enigmatic unrecognizability" of the gay biracial Filipino American killer Andrew Cunanan, best remembered for the 1997 murder of Gianni Versace, is part of his figuration as a native boy. Isaac argues that his unrecognizability is part of a U.S. "imperial grammar" with "blind limits of the U.S. racial imaginary and its misreading and incomprehension of its imperial history."[36] Hence, the suicide gunshot that completely disfigured Cunanan's face indexes how he was figuratively and literally unintelligible to the U.S. public as an American citizen of Filipino descent. This violent forgetting or cultural amnesia is also tied to an "American dis-ease with homosexuality," which manifested through the media's salacious obsession with the frenzied "gay underground."[37] This paradox, of forgetting and obsessing, of disavowal and knowledge, is symptomatic of a central anxiety around the white man/native boy dyad—the danger of homosexuality and racialized depravity—that conflates sexual and racial otherness.

For the U.S. public, the lasting image of this story is Cunanan's mangled body in a pool of blood on a gleaming white houseboat. This violent clash of colors, one in which the "glaring, if not blinding, whiteness" obscures all else, adds to a long list of poetic fatal endings for the native boy.[38] The "grammatical structure" of recognizability in this sensational case is also a theatrical one, staging Cunanan as the "shape-shifting Filipino rent boy" of the national media, and the "altar boy" of U.S.-Filipino immigration and Catholic mythos. These different media viewing points incite more questions graphing the historic and psychic links in the Asias: Is Cunanan's case an American story? Is it a Filipino story? Is it a Filipino American story? Is it a tragic "gay" story? Or is it all of the above, marked with traces of America's empire?

The dyad is embedded in these questions through a set of tropic scenarios in which Cunanan as Filipino "rent boy" and "altar boy" is vividly set against the white American star (Versace) and the pope or father figure. The story of this Filipino boy is, in other words, part of a historically specific instantiation of the dyad tied to U.S. imperialism, proselytization, and the colonial management of Filipino American masculinity. He is thus framed around a particular set of racial and heterosexual panics involving the "secret" histories of an unrecognizable gay Filipino other within the borders of the United States. Cunanan represents a terrifying racial allegory of gay Asians in the diaspora who fail to assimilate into Western society. But rather than using Cunanan to naturalize the narrative of the native boy's "pathology," we might consider the case in relation to dramatic representations of gay Asians in Asian/America. David H. Hwang's *M. Butterfly* (which I will read in chapter 3) and Chay Yew's *Porcelain* (1992) are key examples that bring out what I am calling the drama of butterflies gone berserk.

Yew's play concerns the psyche of a nineteen-year-old Anglo-Chinese student, John Lee, who commits a crime of passion after discovering his older male lover, Will Hope, "cottaging" with other men.[39] Written as a chamber play and framed around a set of interweaving interviews with a court-appointed criminal psychologist, a priest, a reporter, and others, the play presents Lee as a lone character onstage responding to four disembodied voices that represent each of the aforesaid roles. The voices also produce other soundscapes such as the streets of London. Based on salacious tabloid headlines around the entrapment of gay men who have public sex in the toilets of East London, *Porcelain* is at once fictional and ethnographic, invoking the blurry and risky boundaries of gay desire/internalized homophobia and obsession/love. It plays with the orientalist premise of queer encounters organized by the dyad by inverting the expectations one may have about each position. Within the dyadic structure, John Lee is the native boy from Hong Kong whose immigrant parents speak little English. But he is the protagonist who has a multifaceted psyche, a racially ambiguous name that could pass as British, and a future as a Cambridge-bound scholar. In contrast, Will Hope is, as the auxiliary verb in his name suggests, only disposed to something like the feeling that what is wanted can be had. He is working-class and married, and has stereotypical taste (his favorite opera is *Madame Butterfly*). In spite of the reversal of fortune, the spell of orientalist intoxication is indexed by the pathology or predilection of both characters, though Lee bears the burden as the murderer hearing all kinds of voices in his head. This is an interesting comparison to *M. Butterfly*, where the central character, the French diplomat René Gallimard, is also in an incarceral space, both physical and psychic, as he tells his enchanted story through flashbacks. Both Lee and Gallimard are differentially possessed and pathologized but undeniably taken by the dyad's spells.

Similarly, the "Balinese light youth," the Thai go-go boy dancer, and the Chinese Mardi Gras boy in Singapore have their own sets of spells. To confront each tropic spell, rather than to be taken by it, one has to consider how the native boy's theatricality is contingent upon the seamless reiteration of various truth-effects, tropes, enactments, and embodiments organizing "the way things are" in the empire. I have in mind the Dutch, British, and U.S.-American empires in the twentieth and twenty-first centuries. The "set pattern of behavior or action" of native boys in the empire or after-empire is in this regard the effect of a regulatory order naturalizing particular racial and erotic expectations.[40] It reiterates what has been taken for granted in terms of how queer and racialized subjects (should, might, or ought to) act, desire, and speak in the face of whiteness; and how colonial figures assume particular entitlements or privileges around how they act, desire, and speak with the nativized. Those who are infantilized as Asian boys, for instance, are part of the lineage of the perverse, primitive other successfully tamed by and displayed for Western modernity. This is the classic underpinning of racial performativity in the West.

It bears note, then, that the colonial dyad, let alone the boy, continues to be explicitly disavowed or disallowed as a queer formation with significant histories and stakes in performance across the Asias. This has sometimes enforced their absence, erasure, or unreadability in the institutional archive as well as in artistic practice. Buggery with male natives, for instance, is considered such a threat that colonial penal codes against sodomy were introduced in all the British colonies. Notably, lesbian sex or the white female/native female coupling has no such provisions in the statutes. Such a female queer coupling is deemed either impossible or simply insignificant in the colonial Victorian mindset. However, the specificity of directives against the male-male dyad suggests the undue potency of queer couplings involving the native boy who as a boy is potentially disruptive of the dominant colonial imaginary of Asia as a woman, and yet also crucial for consolidating the same imaginary as the perverse other—a boy who is or acts like a girl.

The anthropological dimensions of this colonial history mean that Eurocentric notions of Asianness often overdetermine actual encounters with Asians, including many contemporary Asian encounters.[41] As James Moy notes, "the notion of Chineseness under the sign of exotic became familiar to the American spectator long before sightings of the actual Chinese."[42] The ambiguity around who might be "the actual Chinese" is tied to a racialized curiosity around who is a real "native" in the West. Hence, the "freakish" spectacle of a "Chinese lady," Afong Moy, at the American museum in New York City in 1834 resonates with how Goldie Cheung, a forty-eight-year-old Hong Kong immigrant in the United Kingdom, was sensationalized as a hypersexual Chinese contestant on the British television show X Factor in 2011. Their common "foreignness" was deemed sufficient novelty for visual entertainment, but Cheung had to be more than just a passive Chinese body on display. Auditioning for a spot on the popular series, she was singled out for her outlandish racial burlesque, singing and dancing as if she were a new

Suzie Wong on the loose one week, and a female Chinese minstrel show in Tina Turner drag another week.

Her native boy counterpart is William Hung, the Chinese American student (also from Hong Kong originally) whose off-key and off-rhythm audition on the 2004 *American Idol* went instantly viral on the Internet. Hung was widely embraced as a racial joke with his nerdiness, buckteeth, and Chinese accent, and had a media blitz lasting a few years playing "himself" in this stereotypical Asian role in films and television shows. Both Cheung and Hung gained short-lived notoriety and public attention as the legible and laughable other, or as the native Asian woman and native Asian boy respectively in the United Kingdom and the United States, and were "adored" for their aberrations. But they are hardly exceptional, since representations of Asians as unassimilable aliens or celestial beings have a long visual and narrative logic in the Western media. This marketable logic with the dyad as its silent imprint continues to regulate portrayals of Asians in the West, though the rise of China as an economic power, and Asia more broadly as a consumer market, appears to be slowly changing the terms of representation.[43]

By dyadic performativity, then, I do not mean to unfix or "correct" these scripted racial identities but to place them within a relational matrix of power in performance that has a colonial history. Hence, while the colonial hand wavers between a strong arm and a tender touch, the nativized occupies a range of positions and affects that are sometimes docile and sometimes resistant. But rather than once again putting the boy to the use of the colonial, one might examine the complex senses of magic, affection, and fascination, bewilderment and disgust, as differentially shared by both parties rather than simply as the experience of one over the other. This "two-way street," as it were, necessitates a discussion that includes but also exceeds clear indictments of colonial hegemony and native complicity. I have in mind questions of pleasure, prohibition, and romance mixed in with exigencies of queer survival (on both sides) that are sometimes expressed through self-preserving and exploitative acts, and sometimes through self-reflexive and ironic play. (This exceeds questions of authorial intentions where biography or cultural background is often used to account for doing certain acts.) The alternating critical foci between the two positions in the dyad allow for a level of flexibility in addressing a spectrum of queer issues wherever and whenever the two meet under the thrall of an Asian encounter or Asian performance. Importantly, these alternating foci afford a space for considering the Asian boy explicitly as a queer episteme and dilemma of theater and performance studies in a transnational frame.

Native Boys in Context

While each native boy has a unique story with different connections to colonialism and performance, his story is often wrapped up in joyless questions of agency and volition as if these were the only ways to understand his predicament. The mutually constitutive queerness of the white male desiring gaze and the nativized innocent nubile boy is also lost in the alluring logics by which each becomes recognizable in broader contexts, from the technics of ethnic self-display in the West, the programming of the mass media, and the curatorial dictates of mainstream theater circuits to the masculinist ethos of postcolonial nationalism. In chapters 2 and 3, I will address the recoverability of the dyad's presence primarily through the visibility or invisibility of the native boy as the Asian boy, and propose to read these performative iterations as "glocalqueer" in Singapore or New Asia, and as "G.A.P. (Gay Asian Princess) drama" in Asian/America.

These formulations assume the permeability and porosity of Asian encounters across time and space, and are an analytic for understanding tropic spells. In "The Global Asian Queer Boys of Singapore," I explore the state's tendentious investment in pink-dollar capitalism and the blind spots of global queering as a discourse for the country's recent, English-language gay theater. My major case study is the theatrical trilogy *Asian Boys, Vols. 1, 2, and 3,* by the Malay playwright Alfian Sa'at, whose work alongside that of other local artists raises important questions about the boy's autoexotic display and gay agency in the region. I suggest that the theatricality of the Asian boys has to be read as a glocalqueer production that serves a number of critical functions, including the way it can undo the binaries (West/East, First World/Third World, legitimate/fake, advanced/backward) often internalized in studies about queer and postcolonial productions.

The dyad's postcolonial transformations enact a crucial spatio-epistemic shift from the interpretive paradigm of global queering, which has focused narrowly on how so-called local queer subjects are adopting Western-style gay, lesbian, and transgender identity for their own agencies. The coordinates of such a global/local, West/East binary tend to reinscribe a problematic ontological premise for international queer subjects by making the assumption that a queer, sexual Being exists on stable, identitarian grounds across time and space cohesively structured. The stability of this identitarian base is consolidated by the prominence and permeability of Western queer culture and identity. This means that the politics of queer representation and encounter in trans/national contexts often uncritically privilege the prominence of Western modalities and mobilities of queerness. Consequently, queer cross-cultural exchanges are invariably reduced to a quandary around ahistorical identity claims, and focused on the iconicity of the white gay male. There is thus a sense of epistemic narcissism in which global queering is all about or only happening in relation to Anglo-American men or the Western gay male gaze. For instance, classic liberal questions using this approach include "how gay identities will change as 'Asians' recuperate Western images and bend them to their own purposes";[44] and the perennial curiosity—"Are Chinese, Indian and Malay gay men (closeted) like American gay men?" This internal logic undergirds the problematic bifurcation between Western or Euro-American LGBT and the ethnic/world gay, without seeing how shows like *Asian Boys* paradoxically constitute and confound tradition, queerness, and the diaspora in the Asias.

The transmogrification of native boys as "Asian boys" bears some elaboration in the context of Singapore. Asian boys represent one of several types of "queer boys" circulating in the global gay market, and is itself a contested term. In the Western context, the white, urban, gay male youth is a generic icon of queer boys, while Asian boy is a subcultural category referencing the racialized fetishes of an older white male for the diminutive and effeminized Asian male. The emergence of Asian boys in Singapore and their theatricalization in local plays like *Asian Boys* both reiterate and transform the Asian houseboy trope. For instance, the play's critique points to the Singapore state as a substitute for the white male in the classic colonial/nativized boy coupling: Are global Asian queer boys the state's unspeakable fetish as it turns to queer capital to sex up its insipid image as a draconian father-state? One might note that the Asian boy is already imbricated in the state's use of Asia as cultural capital for touristic, economic, and political ends. The Singapore Tourism Board has been quick to exploit such an imaginary in its autoexoticizing construction of this multicultural "Lion City" as "New Asia." In an interesting turn, the queer dimensions of this imaginary are brought out by critics who argue that the imaginary of "New Asia" has also been constructed in part by the idea of a "queer Asia."[45] Based on a queer and exotic interculturalism, Singapore's claim as the nexus of New Asia—the "heart of Asia" fusing "Occidental and Oriental influences"—is inscribed on the bodies of its transcultural Asian boys. Importantly, however, the focus on global Asian queer boys does not mean in any way that queerness in Singapore, inflected by differentials in class, race, and gender, is reducible to this trope or intelligible only through the performativity of the white daddy/Asian boy binary.

The prominence of Chinese males as Asian boys, for instance, is tied to the rise of East Asian economies. Having frenetically advanced to First World status within three decades of independence, Singapore's rapid economic development is a singular achievement in the relatively impoverished ten-member Association of Southeast Asian Nations (ASEAN) of which it is a member. The combined nominal GDP per capita of ASEAN was US$1,154 in 2001, which was less than 6 percent of Singapore's national GDP per capita of US$20,659, a figure that rose to US$59,900 in 2011.[46] Hence, Singapore is often imagined outside this geopolitical grouping of Southeast Asia as an "Asian tiger" with South Korea, Taiwan, and Hong Kong.

Singapore's imagined transportability across Asia feeds into the racialized construction of "Asian boys" in the tourist porno-tropics. The boys, in other words, help to configure the island nation within the miracle spell of an East Asian economic imaginary waiting to be consumed. According to the "brand development" manager of the Singapore Tourism Board,

"New Asia—Singapore" is the tourism brand that Singapore Tourism Board launched in 1996. It aims at positioning Singapore as a unique city-state at the heart of Asia, by expounding on the curious blend of Occidental and Oriental influences, of things old and new that have made Singapore unlike any other in the world. It also spoke of Singapore as being a vibrant, dynamic Asian country celebrating the best of her diverse cultures and traditions, and preserving and nurturing her Asian heritage, even as the country embraced the economic marvels of high technology.[47]

In this touristic master narrative, Singapore's cultural identity as an Asian state takes on a continental proportion as "New Asia" while amalgamating the wonders of an intercultural space fusing "Occidental and Oriental influences" in the "heart of Asia."[48] It is an Asia waiting to be "discovered." The didactic memo, reminiscent of colonial makeover projects in the Asia Pacific, is the postcolony's reverse exotic narrative sanctioned by its own Asian patriarch.

Singapore's global Asian queer boys are figures caught on the cusp of epistemic, ontological, and political im/possibilities in the face of this postcolonial daddy. Are they a resistant figure or do they merely laminate the "liberative" possibilities of a queer globalism over racialized sexual tropes like the Balinese brown boys? Is the colonized native boy reprised in Singapore, where the male citizen who does not participate in the country's heteronormative national production is identified or prefigured as no more than a "boy" with dreamy escapades? These questions point to the complications and multiple meanings generated and forestalled by glocalqueer Asian boys who stand in for contemporary embodiments of the native boy.

Enabling and yet complicit in neoliberal and nationalist agendas, Singapore's global Asian queer boys and their troubled visibility foreground the difficulties in understanding the contingencies of, or what counts as politically efficacious, queer representation in a multicultural, multiracial metropolis. They are a crucial case study that demands close readings of native boys in context: Where do local gay male bodies fit within the state's nationalistic mantra, "One People, One Nation, One Singapore," in the geopolitical imaginary of New Asia, and in other such official cultural blueprints as "Renaissance City" and "Global City for the Arts"? How are such representations, voices, and performances of the native boy to be read and understood in a glocalqueer world?

Transcolonial Traditions

It bears note that the queer politics of Asian performance traditions tend to be contentious when a "tradition" is tied to one ethnic heritage, often with a vested interest in preserving its native "authenticity" as a matter of national pride. This directed investment in authenticity or in one pristine tradition is often under the influence of a colonial spell with heteronormative assumptions. The Asian boy hovers over such a traditionalist turn as the tropic influence that dare not speak its name. Tellingly, the "community's" unspoken fear of the boy's deracinated masculinity is expressed obliquely through postures of ethnic muscle, such as the early cultural nationalism of Asian America. Traditionalism is often couched as a heteronormative and patriarchal institution, whether it is espoused by the postcolonial father-state such as Singapore's "Asian values" campaign from 1976 to the early 1990s or by the Big Asian American "Aiiieeeee," led by the authors Frank Chin, Paul Chan, and others in the early 1970s.[49] Both projects are in search of or in sync with an Asian paternal figure on top, and are keen to obliterate the native boy's innocence or infantilization. As is well known, Singapore's deployment of Asian values is a cultural nationalist campaign against the hegemony of Western liberal democracy based on a regional solidarity model (with Malaysia, China, Vietnam, Cambodia, and Myanmar) that is self-legitimating. Instead of internalizing Western exceptionalism, it willfully depicts the West as morally decadent, inept, and arrogant. The move is not, however, only a rhetorical posture or a cultural war about clashing civilizations. Rather, it is used, as some have argued, to consolidate the postcolonial state's authoritarianism under the cover of "Asian democracy" and "Asian capitalism."[50]

The substitution of the Asian communitarian father for the colonial white daddy sets the path for the heteronormative Singaporean to come out as a good Asian who sees, if paradoxically, the value of privatization over welfarism, consensus over conflict, collective over self, and national interest over individualism. This is a postcolonial rebuke of the bad Western. The crude and hyperbolic bifurcations are a play on and reversal of the dyad's power relations based on ludicrous orientalist tropes (colonial daddy/Asian son) in the first place. Their successful reiterations, however, are contingent on a careful staging and valorization of particular cultural assumptions that are often also bureaucratic inventions. The Asianizing of the Singaporean citizen, for instance, involved a massive Confucian ethics education at schools, designed by eight foreign Confucian scholars. Apparently, no one in Singapore was familiar with the field even as it was purportedly part of the country's cultural constitution. Notwithstanding its Sinic cultural heritage, Confucianism was deemed "universalistic" and "humanistic" as an Asian cultural form in multiracial (Chinese, Malay, Indian, Caucasian) Singapore.[51] As a Confucianist ethos was literally imported to authenticate Singapore's Asian identity, its founding prime minister, Lee Kuan Yew, was consecrated "a modern Confucius." This performative consecration marked the rise of the Asian father vis-à-vis Western demagoguery. Lee's old sage act as Confucius is also a theatrical counterpoint to Singapore's nebulous identity as the region's youngest and most Westernized country, or a native boy gone rogue, quickly wise, and more Asian than Asians. As Slavoj Žižek sees it, this inventive Asian encounter is between (Chinese) Singaporean capitalism with Asian values and Anglo-Saxon neoliberalism.[52] To put it differently, it is a battle between the efficiencies of two closely related regimes, one authoritarian and one neoliberal, that also marks the end of the marriage between capitalism and democracy.

In Asian America, Frank Chin and his compadres sought to disrupt the logic of racial domination and emasculating stereotypes produced in part by the historic 1882 exclusion laws (and their subsequent restrictions) against primarily Chinese and later all East Asian immigrants. This discursive pushback was chiefly concentrated against the racist debasement of Asian men relegated to doing soft or "feminized" labor, such as laundry, cooking, and grocery shopping service on the one hand, and being no more than asexual sociopaths and moral degenerates like Fu Manchu and Charlie Chan on the other hand.[53] The deviancy of Asian gender and sexuality has to do, in other words, with its "estrangement" from white norms or as a form of reaction formation against racialized oppression. In each case, the figure of the Asian boy haunts the discourse, collapsing emasculation with feminization. In other words, being less than a man (or a boy) is like being a woman. As several critics note, colonial gender logics are internalized in Chin's cultural nationalist project, which promotes a unitary Asian American identity using Chinese and Japanese American testosterone, male muscle, and male worldviews as a corrective.[54]

In Chin's 1972 play *The Chickencoop Chinaman,* Tam Lum, one of the central Chinese American characters, remembers his boyhood hero, the Lone Ranger, as a Chinese male in disguise about to bring "Chinaman vengeance on the West." The hyperbole of racial substitution in this white man/Asian boy encounter appears to be a casual reference to a childhood memory for Lum, but it also underpins what Chin calls the "embodiment of Asian-American manhood."[55] In other words, the man/boy dyad is formative of Asian American cultural nationalism, and an alternative manhood can be generated only by substituting cross-racial identifications and solidarities between black, Japanese, and Chinese American adult males for the Lone Ranger. But this manly call against institutionalized racism and white dominance is seemingly unaware of its sexism or Eurocentric gender ideology. Lisa Lowe, among other critics in the field, points out that their insistence on a fixed masculinist identity "can be itself a colonial figure used to displace the challenges of heterogeneity, or subalternity, by casting them as assimilationist or anti-ethnic."[56]

Crucially, such a colonial figure is also a queer problematic since it invokes the historical exclusion of the Asian male from "normative" masculinity. The Asian boy haunts this discourse of gendered exclusion in the United States, and his exclusion is obtained wherever and whenever the universalizing subjectivity of whiteness is assumed as the given standard or pivotal point. This racialized predicament is necessarily queer (or has to be queered) insofar as it aligns "manly" identifications with whiteness and heteronormative legitimacies. As is clear, the realness of a white man having gravitas or the Asian male being a native boy is a myth of white supremacist patriarchal capitalism. As a theatrical conceit, the purchase of such tropes and its continuing reiterations in the signifying economy are obtained by what one is not, or whom one is defined against. Hence, one's a man and the other's a boy, one is American whereas the other's forever foreigner. Where these are or thought to be conditions of his survival, they also produce a nativized body with symptoms of racial grief, rage, and hysteria. In this regard, the native boy is a paradox incarnate: he carries the residue of colonial or imperial history, and is ineluctably (for he cannot but be) a player in scenarios of fantasy and conquest; yet he is also a theatrical iteration who plays out the fantasy and conquest as incoherent, and even ruined. Between scenarios of colonial interpellation and queer intervention, he is caught in a range of charged debates about agency, exoticism, exploitation, and eroticized subjecthood.

The comparative, transcolonial context I outlined above between Singapore and Asian America lends itself to a number of queer scenarios that can potentially relieve the critical impasse of representation around the Asian boy using ethnic camp. In chapter 3, "G.A.P. Drama, or The Gay Asian Princess Goes to the United States," the scenario of conquest is parodied through the figure of the rice queen who is desperately in love with the diasporic gay Asian male in the United States standing in for the native boy. I examine this scenario as a dramatic predicament by revisiting David H. Hwang's *M. Butterfly* using the native boy as a central figure, and subsequently with a queer solo performance by Justin Chin based on an adaptation of the novel and film *The World of Suzie Wong*. The unlivable scenario under the regime of the rice queen is a mock protest performance in ethnic camp, a queer commentary on the racialized conditions targeted by Frank Chin and his compadres with their war cry against a racist Euro-America. But G.A.P. is also queering, or at least endeavoring to queer, the lives of all nativized Asians in the world! The native-ethnic transmogrification here is at once real and parodic, and points to the racial legacies of the queer dyad in the postcolonial and diasporic borderzones of Singapore, China, Thailand, and Asian America. Such a campy reading opens up a new set of questions about the bewitching politics of transcultural magic, and the mutually constitutive spells that the dyad casts in the production of art in the Asias.

In the final chapter of the book, which serves as a conclusion, "Toward a Minor-Native Epistemology in Transcolonial Borderzones," I expand on the native-ethnic intersection by formulating a reading practice that brings together Native American studies with performance in the Asias. It imagines a different return to the conventional hetero-orientalist scenario where the brown woman is the scopic center by considering the productive outcomes of the boy "rubbing up" against this scenario. The queer f(r)ictons of this simple "rub" wrest the brown woman out of the seemingly entrenched hetero-orientalist setting and into an-Other comparative framework with Native America. Using Chin Woon Ping's *Details Cannot Body Wants*, a Peranakan (Straits Chinese) Asian/American solo woman show, as an exemplary case of transcolonial performance, I set the brown woman next to other minor scenarios in native and ethnic studies, and postcolonial and queer studies. This is suggestive of future critical directions in which studies about the native (woman) is informed by dyadic queerness or comparative racialization in the Asias rather than the standard orientalist configurations in the West. In other words, a transcolonial paradigm of tradition can potentially bring out an alternative set of analytics for the Asian boy and Asian woman. Between Asian/America, Native America, and Southeast Asia, their "jumps" in the Asias can potentially exceed even the dyads examined in this study by triangulating them in nondiscrete geographies.

Performance in the Asias

Facing the vast reconfigurative scope of these inquiries, one might ask, why even assume that the Asian boys' spellbinding allure continues in the transnational Asias, from the Anglophone postcolony to the Asian diaspora in the West? How is performance in the Asias situated vis-à-vis Asian theater? Where is Asia in all this? In using "the Asias," I mean to invoke the contesting imaginaries, aesthetics, and interregional and diasporic formations that make up Asia, itself a term of no easy definition. Yet Asia is generally settled (in official parlance and some academic fields) as a stable geographic referent, or the originator of various, apparently self-evident ethnicities. The historian and literary critic Naoki Sakai postulates that Asia is neither a "cartographic index" nor a sensible identificatory label. Rather, it emerged in the late nineteenth century as a heteronomous term when "a few intellectuals began to advocate the plausibility of constituting the transnational and regional subjectivity of Asia."[57] If "the word *Asia* originated outside of Asia," formulated ostensibly by "Europeans to distinguish Europe from its eastern others," its genealogical gridlock with the West would also produce a conceptual dyad whose legibilities are contingent upon that history:

> Only through the acknowledgment of its lost autonomy, of its dependence to the West, or only in the mirror of the West, so to say, could Asia

reflectively acquire its civilizational, cultural, ethnic, or national con- *Asian is not*
sciousness. The defeat is registered in the genealogy of the name itself.[58] *comprised of its own culture—its simply been histed*

Asia can therefore be spoken of only as the "negative of the West," and
to "talk about Asia is invariably to talk about the West."[59] This history,
refracted through the institutionalization of Cold War–era area studies programs, has a number of implications for Asian theater studies as
a nationalist and culturalist formation. Significantly, the notion of an
Asian theater from a "distinct" geographic area with a knowable history coincides with the rise of the United States (following Europe) as
an imperialist power with military bases in Japan, Korea, Taiwan, the
Philippines, and Vietnam. As the historian Vicente L. Rafael notes, the
"systematic instrumentalization of foreign languages to serve nationalist ends runs far and deep in American thinking," most evident
in the production of "area studies experts whose knowledge of other
cultures would help shore up 'our way of life.'"[60] Translation is in this
sense a national security issue that "protect[s] ourselves from them
and . . . ensure[s] that they remain safely within our reach whether
inside or outside our borders."[61] The geographically deterministic study
of theater traditions in Asia follows the logics of this organization.
Asian theater is thus either presented as the (radical) other of Western
forms or nativized as local traditions with ancient, timeless aesthetics.
Imperialism is not relevant in such studies, just as there is little interest
in transcolonial approaches focusing on shared orientalized histories or
regional performance vocabularies facilitated by trade routes, religion,
or migration. Rather, the West is the point of departure and return. *—all Asian cultures are computed together*

The role that "Asian theater" plays in recent world theater textbooks
may be helpful in illuminating this point. I am referring to the newer
textbooks that aim to globalize theater studies, and are generally speaking a welcome departure from their Eurocentric predecessors. In the
Longman Anthology of Drama and Theatre: A Global Perspective, for
example, the editors condensed the myriad theater traditions of India,
China, and Japan into one chapter that stood out for its geographic
demarcation rather than the rich periodization reserved for Europe.[62]
The Middle Ages, the Renaissance, and the late seventeenth and eighteenth centuries, for instance, continue to be the exclusive temporal
domains of Europe. Making space rather than time for this excursion

to the non-Western world, the move indicates the timeliness of Asian traditions for a global perspective that is nonetheless predicated on their timelessness. The editors claim nine generalizable characteristics that are common to Asian theater, a designation for over twenty-five thousand theater troupes covering over two billion people.[63] In predictable fashion, the pointers include Asian theater's spiritual or mystical origins, lack of realism, and the use of dance, mime, masks, painted faces, and gesture as its main theatrical language. Their schematic fabulation bifurcating "Balinese (Asian) Theater" from "Western Theater" is offered this way:

BALINESE (ASIAN) THEATER	WESTERN THEATER
Mystical	Realistic
Gesture and Signs	Dialogue and Words
Ritual and Transcendence	Ethics and Morality
Metaphysical State	"The Here and Now"
Does Not Rely on Rational Continuity	Causality
Transcends Reality on Stage	Creates Reality on Stage
Abandons Illusion	Creates Realistic Illusions
Uses Platforms and Spaces	Uses Scenery and Setting
Sounds and Rhythms	Speech[64]

As is clear, this chart by the editors neatly summarizes the main characteristics already offered, but this time by way of its otherness to Western theater. Hence, while Balinese (Asian) theater is "mystical" and "does not rely on rational continuity," Western theater (which one?) is realistic, logocentric, and driven by "causality" and "ethics and morality." The editors claim Antonin Artaud's manifesto *The Theatre and Its Double* as their inspiration. For Artaud, however, the performative setup of otherness or otherworldliness renders a portal to transcend the "mausoleum of the (Western) mind" with "the alchemical theater" that seizes upon "what is communicative and magnetic in the principles of all the arts," and thereby combine the two.[65] Such a visionary alchemy is partly conjured by the "theatrical operation of making gold" from nothing, alluding to the centrality of performance as both a method and metaphor of integration and disintegration—the stuff of magic.[66] While Artaud's thought experiment is more cosmological than geographic, spectral rather than monolithic, the editors' approach is precisely the reverse in their singular and geographically determined study of theater in China, Japan, and India. Their irreconcilable binary polarizes Bali and the West, and fixates on an alterity that is binding rather than doubling. Their reductionism distills Artaud's "magic," an oft-cited charge of his orientalism, with their own spell of difference about the Asian exotic.

Yet this is evidently not a spell that the editors are aware of in their sensible illumination and standardized pedagogy about Asian theater. Instead, they make a veiled charge of orientalist visuality against a dead white man less known for his rationality: "Artaud compares the theaters of the West and of the East, though his comments reflect a Western bias."[67] An insouciant declaration validates their version of theatrical inquiry on Asia using facts, an enlightened optic, and an inclusive global curriculum. This cover updates the salvational ethos by orientalists without whose knowledge and dissemination the theatrical traditions of Asia would perish. Rey Chow posits this kind of work by specialists in a cognate field, East Asian studies, as sharing an episteme with primatology, calling out the "self-interestedness" of those who refuse to engage the colonial-orientalist nexus of Asian cultural formations.[68]

What I have been intimating is that in each of these encounters—Asia and the West, U.S. area studies, and Asian theater within a global perspective—various spells of difference organize an entrenched position, a nationalist epistemology, and a culturalist pedagogy. Artaud's magical ruminations about Balinese performance are therefore not exclusive or an eccentric exception but a different manifestation of the same logics. On the question of magic in colonial encounters, the anthropologist Michael Taussig posits that mutually constitutive spells are cast between the colonizer and colonized in an "epistemic murk," where figurations of the "Wild Man" engender all kinds of imaginary infections, nativized nightmares, and erratic terrors on the one hand, and healing properties on the other hand.[69] His specific case study involves a regime of terror and genocide in the Putumayo River area of Colombia in the late nineteenth and twentieth centuries, where a cabal of British rubber barons sought to impose a capitalist mode of production by eliminating any indigenous resistance to its agenda. Their demented obsessions about the native male are symptoms of among other things *mal aire*, which means "evil wind," a complicated, polysemic index of *infideles* (pagans, heathens, infidels) from the preconquest era capable of causing illness or even death. Yet this may also be a manifestation of Indians killed in the colonial conquest returning to haunt the colonizers.

Such an affective complex forms an "implicit social knowledge," which some have characterized as a brew of "rotting, sickening mess" where the "stinking by-products" of official history—"the senselessness and amorality, the cruelty, the maddening fear, the losses, the tragedies, the suffering, the misery"—are amassed and forgotten.[70] This is a "non-discursive knowing of social relationality and history," different from conscious ideology and empirical fact-finding missions in its "inarticulable and imageric" constitution.[71] Rather, it "moves people without their knowing quite why and how, with what makes the real real and the normal normal, and above all with what makes ethical distinctions politically powerful."[72] Since man is never cruel without impunity, the colonizer's violence of subjugation has also produced a spell of perception from the winds of pulverized corpses in his interaction with the living native as the slave/shaman: "The master maltreated his slave, but feared his hatred. He treated him like a beast of burden but dreaded the magical powers imputed to him."[73] In other words, fear has also produced an (over)investment in the terrific magical powers of the shamans. And such a scenario is consummately restaged by the natives in an autoexotic display of demonism:

> So it has been through the sweep of colonial history where the colonizers provided the colonized with the left-handed gift of the image of the wild man—a gift whose powers the colonizers would be blind to, were it not for the reciprocation of the colonized, bringing together in the dialogical imagination of colonization an image that wrests from civilization its demonic power.[74]

Notably, the "Wild Man" possession is a consumptive experience involving healing rituals in which the white colonizers partook as an antidote to various sorceries. The colonizers believed that the wilder the Indian, the more powerful his healing power. In Taussig's ethnographic account of a séance during which he himself took yagé, a hallucinogenic and purgatory drug, this ossified colonial view of the shaman as the half-devil, half-god wild man gives way to the shaman as "a strategic zone of vacuity, a palette of imageric possibilities."[75] Importantly, performance organizes this encounter with no truth beneath the surface enacted by actors bearing its requisite spells of wonder.

But where Taussig, Sakai, and Rafael stop in their implicit formulations of a conceptual dyad with a queer sexuality, one must proceed with its queer scenarios in full view. Throughout this introduction, I have argued that historiographic and theatrical (re)enactments help to frame the dyad's speech acts, desires, and bodies as representations with historical meanings rather than "the way things are." This staging is important insofar as the colonial extraction of the dyad's scenarios is sublimated as cultural transactions in fields of study such as Asian American and Asian theater studies. This is in contrast to the recent performance scholarship in the Americas where the politics of such scenarios are more explicitly foregrounded. This has rendered the assumption of Western equanimity, prestige, and patronage as benign or even wondrous. Some of this has to do with the fact that the point of view of the incumbent hegemon, invariably the colonial specialist, or those who are or may be so identified is still dominant. These enduring functions of orientalist hegemony and their queer derivatives have real effects in the reconfiguration of performance practices with both mythic and cultural specificity.

Performance in the Asias, like Asian theater and Asian diasporic performance, is embroiled in overlapping claims of national authenticity, self-identity, and the collective survival of Asian art and artists in its most pragmatic sense. But this struggle is only one part of the story regarding the native boy. Like Taussig's "Wild Man" or Sakai's "Asian," his bodily manifestation is contingent upon a set of performance conditions with identity formations that are potentially deformative rather than fixed, transformable rather than preordained. He is thus a dissipating European invention and a diasporic re-creation, a desperate houseboy and a pink-dollar poster boy, and an Asian nation that is at once economically advanced but also infantilized as a boy with "developmental" issues. The paradox of his queer transmogrifications will always be an orientalist riddle involving the requisite fantasies and fears of the West vis-à-vis the Orient and his autoexotic display as a pageant child in need of discipline and adoration. His symptomatic manifestations in the theater, performance, and media have to be examined as a matter of ethnic and cultural critique, and postcolonial and transcolonial study.

Last but not least, the dyad's queerness saturates the drama and fictions inherent in the myriad scenarios outlined above by introducing native (as well as ethnic and diasporic) camp to colonial performativity. It reiterates with mock austerity a compulsory love for the white man and his institutions amid the native boy's transmogrifications across time and space. Using this facetious perversion as a basic premise, the book explores performance in the queer Asias as a way to disrupt the naturalized repetition of various acts constituting the regulatory ideals, legibilities, and identifications of a colonial order and its global guises. To put it differently, it drags the "originary" colonial scenario, already eminently stageable, to its limits by uncovering its scattered queer histories and corrosive effects across the Asias. This orbit of Asian encounters with different dyadic configurations is a way to consider critical solidarities in transcolonial configurations of the Asias. But more than that, the tropic spell organizing how queer "Asia" is experienced and executed in performance is a necessary analytic for understanding cultural production in today's and tomorrow's transnational complex. I hope the set of reading practices proposed here can foreground the magic of tropic spells as a historical trace as well as a function of performance in the queer Asias, and thereby open our eyes to the ways race, sexuality, and empire are embroiled in a set of interconnecting issues on the global stage.

As I said this morning to Charlie
There is far too much music in Bali
And although as a place it's entrancing,
There is also a thought too much dancing.
It appears that each Balinese native,
From the womb to the tomb is creative,
And although the results are quite clever,
There is too much artistic endeavour.
—Noel Coward to Charlie Chaplin

A COLONIAL DYAD IN BALINESE PERFORMANCE

[handwritten marginalia: Tropic spell is magnified by the nativity, primitivity and mystery of Bali]

By the 1930s, when Noel Coward turned to Charlie Chaplin with this
ditty about the surfeit of "artistic endeavour" in Bali,[1] reports had been
filtering out to Europe and America that the island, "not Fiji or Samoa
or Hawaii, was the genuine, unspoiled tropical paradise, known as yet,
even by reputation, only by the cognoscenti, a category with which all
of the more affluent world travelers sought to identify themselves, as
did a certain few more or less learned scholars."[2] Coward's wry ascrip-
tion of magic to the Balinese native, at once a kind of Asian encounter
and a colonial spell, is also a queer repartee between two men undoubtedly among the cognoscenti on vacation in Bali. While one can only
guess whether the generic or gender-ambiguous "Balinese native" so
central to the island's magic is a brown woman, brown boy, or both,

it is clear that a colonial dyad is involved in the making of the native's creative queerness from "the womb to the tomb."

The poem's opening couplet, with lines ending in "Charlie" and "Bali," sets up the dyad as an informal relationship and suspends it across the remaining rhyming couplets, "entrancing/dancing," "native/ creative," "clever/endeavour," for a seductive and incantatory effect. Like a spell that is contingent upon the arrangement of words, the tightly woven metrical verse brings out the magic of Coward's performatives while indexing Charlie's amused if not entranced posture in Bali. Tellingly, Coward hints at the native choreography as a design that is in fact unnatural, parodying the prevalent discourse about how "everyone in Bali is an artist" with the bio-claim that the Balinese "womb" incubates creativity.[3] One can thus interpret his ironic quibble about the surfeit of creative production—"*far* too much music" and "a *thought* too much dancing"—as a queer moratorium on colonial artistic production even if "the results are quite clever." In other words, Coward's version of the queer dyad is set apart from, even as it is imbricated in, the colonial invention of the Balinese native and the island paradise of Bali.

Bali's makeover from "feudal" and "vestigial Dark Age"[4] to "unspoiled tropical paradise" is a remarkable testament to Dutch colonial "ethical," "protectionist," and "conservationist" policies implemented in the 1910s.[5] These policies sought to preserve selected traditions, customs, and performing art forms that the Dutch deemed essential to native Balinese culture while also appealing to tourists. Within two decades of Bali's annexation by the Dutch in 1908, Bali's nativized performing arts became a magical trope for the island's idyllic character and gained a seemingly indissoluble cultural currency thereafter.

One of the nativized rituals that became iconic of the island's cultural traditions is *kecak*, the Balinese performance at the heart of this chapter.[6] Widely known to tourists as the "monkey dance," *kecak* features a large Balinese male chorus performing a polyrhythmic chant with synchronized gestures and throbbing bodies in a multilayered circular structure. Much of its appeal centers on the transmogrification of the men into entranced monkeys from the *Ramayana* epic. *Kecak* and its possessive embodiments is a key analytic of the tropic spell cast by or cast upon the queer dyad. It enables a reading of the ritual's choreography as the interplay of colonial, indigenous, and queer crossings.

Such crossings of the dyad inflect colonial power with a queer cognate fraught with paradoxes, and have several implications for studies of race and sexuality as they pertain to performance in the Asias. The spell is thus a different kind of magic than the one generated by the colonial mandate or its cognate anthropological gaze, which together resulted in the rabid exoticization of the island's cultural traditions.

Even as *kecak* is performed as a secular dance, spectators are charmed by the tantalizing assumption that it is a trance ritual that serves as a magical portal to the island's religious and cultural essence, a "primitive" Balinese experience, as it were. Tapping into such a popular imaginary, *kecak* is often used to reify Bali's spiritualized exoticism as tourist spectacle. Pictures of *kecak* are iconic of this tropical paradise and can be found in myriad books, postcards, and films on Bali. In *kecak*'s most vivid image, the density of "possessed" Balinese male bodies huddled closely together bare chest to bare chest invokes a queer memory from the 1930s, when its choreography was formalized as part of an island-wide paradisal transformation that started more than two decades prior to its invention.

Following tourist brochures produced as early as 1914 that hailed the island as the "Garden of Eden" and an "enchanted isle," Bali appears seamlessly interpellated as the exemplar of "paradise" throughout the twentieth century and in contemporary discourse,[7] from travel literature (*The Last Paradise*, 1930),[8] musical theater and film ("Bali Hai" in Rodgers and Hammerstein's *South Pacific*, 1940s and 1950s),[9] and scholarly publications (*Bali: A Paradise Created*, 1989; and *The Dark Side of Paradise: Political Violence in Bali*, 1995),[10] to newspaper headlines ("Paradise Lost," 2002, 2012).[11] These paradisal representations tell the story of colonial fantasy, possessive vision, and transnational love. It is a love story that is mostly understood through the figure of the brown woman since the gender of Bali, as produced by the dominant discourse, is female; and "Bali as a woman" is subject to the Western male gaze or patronage and penetration. The iconic female Legong dancer, for instance, is representative of this gendered imaginary or romance. Meanwhile, the queer erotics of the colonial encounter, particularly the figure of the brown boy imbricated in Bali's cultural transformation as paradise, are obfuscated in the mix of hetero-fantasy, possession, and love.

But among the glittering circle of visitors attracted to this "tropical Shangri-la" in the 1920–1930s is a queer cast not known for their fidelity to orthodox practice, including Coward and Chaplin as well as Colin McPhee, Margaret Mead, and many others. They form an influential group of stars and scholars, writers and artists whose time in Bali created a cultural legacy that reverberates across the world of performance from Broadway musical to Hollywood film as well as ethnomusicology, anthropology, modern art, and photography. At the center of this "charmed circle" is the German expatriate artist Walter Spies, whose café salon is the epicenter of their Balinese encounters.

As the charismatic host, Spies led his visitors to what he deemed the most authentic parts of Balinese life, such as cockfights and trance rituals. Those spellbinding encounters then became the basis of their creative or scholarly—and often very personal—output. Their letters, photographs, films, and ethnographies helped to concretize the grand colonial narrative of the island as a beautiful but politically bankrupt dreamland sustained by such spiritual and romanticized precepts as "balance," "harmony," "order," and "happiness."[12] Spies's queer vision or (per)version of Bali is in that sense constitutive of the Western imaginary of the paradise island, since many were spellbound by Bali's traditions as seen through his eyes as a quasi-colonial cultural attaché.

Accordingly, the first images about Bali were all focused on the most spectacular ritual, trance, and mystical aspects of its dance-drama. As part of a colonial visual technology, films like *Sang Hyang and Kecak Dance* (1926), *Calon Arang* (1927), *Island of Demons* (1931), *Goona-goona* (1932), and *Trance and Dance in Bali* (filmed in 1939 but released in 1951) helped to promote Bali's dance-drama as the cornerstone of its exoticism. These films typify the colonial study and consumption of the native through visual and aural representations while pointing to a way in which theatricality, cinematography, and ritual embodiment are central to the spell of the Balinese exotic. The groundbreaking short film *Trance and Dance in Bali,* for instance, is famous for documenting Balinese dancers in violent trance seizures as they turn their krisses (sharp daggers) against their breasts without injury. It inaugurated the genre of visual anthropology, which rendered a form of native verisimilitude (or "the way things are") in a simultaneously cinematic and scientific gaze. The shift from written field notes to recorded field images or documentary films was a major methodological move in the twentieth century. Photography and film footage became an important archive as well as a portal to Balinese culture. The idea is that one can infer as much if not more about a culture through careful photography and meticulous filming rather than through written notes.

makes — sense — Seeing is believing

Though Margaret Mead is widely known as the writer, narrator, coproducer, and codirector of *Trance and Dance in Bali*, the film was a team effort involving Gregory Bateson (producer/photography), Jane Belo (photography), Katherine Mershon (notes), and Colin McPhee (music), all members of the aforementioned café salon with Spies at the helm. In the film, the viewer is directed by Mead's narration to focus on the most spectacular trance occurrences from the Calonarang dance-drama. Consider her description of Rangda (the "witch") and the possessed devotees of Barong (the "dragon") in a segment known as "Kris Dance":

> These are the dragon's followers falling to the ground at the glance of the witch, up again when she turns her back, down again when she looks at them. . . . She trips through their ranks, runs away, and as her back is turned, up they get again, rush to the attack, but as she turns, her glance forces them back, back, back, back, and she stands, back, back, and then turns away, indifferent, this is slow motion, the followers of the dragon with their krisses in the air, ready for the attack, but falling down again before her glance (normal speed), the witch dances again and then two by two, they run up and attack her. She doesn't resist, she submits as a rag doll, but overcome by her power, they fall and lie in deep trance. Two more come up, fall also. Members of the club come and arrange them on the ground while another pair attacks the witch. They lie arranged in two rows in deep trance, compulsively twitching. And the dragon comes back to revive them, . . . comes back in a somnambulistic state, comes back in. The witch meanwhile has fallen into a deep trance, and being carried away . . . (the dance in slow motion).[13]

As the transcript suggests, Mead is staging a theatrical encounter with Rangda, an archetypal figure in Balinese ritual whom she calls "the witch" and a figure of immense fascination to Westerners, using slow-motion editing and a highly animated commentary. Rangda's bewitching spells are rendered through her glance, and her attackers are possessed into a deep trance. Even as Mead sought to give an objective and scientific account, the controlled modulations of her voice, the exotic cinematography of the film, and the emphatic repetition of words—"her glance forces them back, back, back, back, and she stands, back, back"—like stage directions to intensify the dramatic account of the trance possession, give her away. The text could well be describing a scene from an occult or horror film. In fact, Mead's disembodied presence was often more captivating as a vocal performance than the actual ritual spectacle. It also bears note that the trance focus of the documentary was part of a research project funded by the Committee for Research in Dementia Praecox, and a series in "Character Formation in Different Cultures."

Mead's "objective" visual approach to advance an intercultural study about the prevalence of possession (or schizophrenia) among the Balinese is in stark contrast to Walter Spies's relationship with the "Balinese male youth." Unlike Mead's approach, Spies's visualization of Bali is much less interested in the purchase of a scientific façade. Rather, it veered toward art. At the archives of Leiden University in the Netherlands, his unpublished photography includes a large number of solo portrait shots of Balinese men and boys in a variety of languid or martial poses as well as those that capture the ritual possession of *kecak* dancers with an unmistakable spell of kinetic wonder. The collection blurs the lines between photography and painting, and the way that art is archive and vice versa. As I sat contemplating the images at Leiden, they began casting a different kind of spell, a spell of the onlooker rather than of the subject of the gaze. The spell was on an entranced Spies looking on the boys as they speak back with expressive eyes and wonder not only to him but to me through him in a triadic encounter. This homosexual encounter, like D. A. Miller's cruising of Barthes's texts, restages the colonial encounter by queering the Euro-ethnographic hetero-gaze on the native boy, and creates a witty visual repartee or dialogue with "the natives." For instance, a Balinese man peering out of his mask with a wry smile appears to be playing with Spies, the camera or onlooker. He smiles as if he were well aware of the queer encounter; the peering poses a premonition of a tropic spell that has heretofore been without a name or history.

Figure 1.1
Balinese man peering out from mask.
Leiden University Library, Collection
Marianne van Wessem, shelfmark Or.
25.188-II-46.

Figure 1.2
Balinese man in sampan.
Leiden University Library, Collection
Marianne van Wessem, shelfmark Or.
25.188-II-66.

Figure 1.3
Balinese men in martial pose.
Leiden University Library, Collection
Institute Kern, shelfmark Walter Spies
80-1315.

Figure 1.4
Balinese man in languid pose.
Leiden University Library, Collection
Institute Kern, shelfmark Walter Spies
80-1490.

How to Do a History of the Dyad

To trace the history of the colonial dyad in *kecak*, one has to reach beyond the conventional parameters of research based on the mnemonic archive such as books, letters, maps, and texts or a mode of reading that is uncritically phallogo- or scriptocentric. The alternative, to use Susan Foster's method, is "to grant that history is made by bodies, and then to acknowledge that all those bodies, in moving and in documenting their movements, in learning about past movement, continually conspire together and are conspired against."[14] This is a form of proprioceptive affiliation by the historian that attends to a "kinesthetic empathy between living and dead but imagined bodies."[15] This way of history writing is aligned with the formulations of several performance theorists, including Diana Taylor's notion of the repertoire, or enactments of "embodied memory: performances, gestures, orality, movement, dance, singing . . . [or] ephemeral, nonreproducible knowledge,"[16] and Joseph Roach's "surrogacy," the mediation of radical social loss through enactments of cultural memory by substitution.[17]

In literary criticism, it resonates with what D. A. Miller calls the epistemo-erotics of a gay writing position that burrows deep into the text for evidence of "illicit" knowledge privy only to the writer and the reader as "homosexual encounters."[18] These "albums of moments" model methodologies of historical study necessitated by the inadequacies of Western worldviews or archives that continue to be masculinist, patriarchal, heteronormative, and logocentric. They present an alternative way to understand the performance vocabulary of *kecak* around the dyad's absent presence, queer somatic transmissions, and shifting contact zones. Put simply, there is no conventional method for documenting queer erotics, particularly in a colonial context of prohibition, and there is certainly no dedicated archive for the dyad's myriad encounters. The question then is not just whether there is a different, non-logocentric way to record alternative histories and memories, but *how* the production and transmission of knowledge as they pertain to queerness can be accessed or activated in both the archive and repertoire of *kecak*.

These methodological quandaries are directly related to the issue of queer intelligibility and access as well as the affects surrounding the dyad and the native boy. These will be duly explored in later sections.

Spies's protected legacy and the "traditional" status of the ritual have meant that the role of the colonial dyad in *kecak*'s aesthetic formation is either wholly rejected or trivialized as a gay issue irrelevant to its performance history. This has to do with, on the one hand, the denial of homosexuality—Spies's estate, for instance, has stipulated that homosexuality be excised from his biography—and, on the other hand, the taboo of besmirching the history of a "sacred" Balinese ritual with a cross-racial, same-sex encounter. More than that, a lack of desire to understand the ritual through the native boy has also rendered him an unintelligible historic presence. The dyad thus persists as an epistemic curiosity in the closet of the ritual's history even as its queer deeds are an open secret, both a doing and a thing done. This paradox of unspeakable knowing and unknowable apathy means that a mere mention of this history elicits either knowing smiles or vociferous denials from the Balinese as well as Western Baliophiles.

This internalized homophobia is symptomatic of a larger problematic in intercultural studies where the white man/native boy dynamic is the structure (more often unmarked than explicit) of artistic exchange or collaboration between the West and the East. This dynamic is still rampant at theater festival circuits featuring distinguished star directors or choreographers from the West and their young, ethnic protégés or native others from the East. The queer politics, intimacies, or affects of the dyad are therefore an unspoken descriptor of the patronage or exchange system of intercultural, aesthetic study. In the case of *kecak*, the queer and orientalist history of Bali's colonization as prefigured by the dyad could serve as a model for thinking about the homoerotic strands of interculturalism that have yet to find their place in theater and performance analysis.

To bring out the dyad in *kecak*, we have to first locate it within the context of Dutch colonialism and Spies's oeuvre, which includes his writing, photography, and film, before examining the dyadic affects, memories, and intimacies driving its tropic spell. The performance or prohibition of sexual travesty and loving so delicately lived by Spies and the Balinese boys is part of the dyad's epistemic tension and possibility. Encoded in the choreography of *kecak*, it points to a way in which art, colonial fantasy, and queer nativization conjoined to perform a foundational version of Bali's exoticism. Put another way, *kecak* has a material and performative value in accounting for the history of Balinese exoticism and for how queer erotics may serve very different ends in a colonial context. To unravel this queer story, it is necessary to first recount the history of Bali's conquest by the Dutch and then situate the dyad in the wildly successful makeover of Bali into a nativized art paradise, using *kecak,* Walter Spies, and the Balinese boys as our primary guides. We will then consider the legacies of this queer dyad in subsequent colonial, theatrical, and novelistic stagings of paradisal Bali.

Disciplining Bali with the Arts

Situated a few degrees south of the equator, Bali is an island on the vast Indonesian archipelago covering more than seventeen thousand islands. For about three hundred years until 1945, when Indonesia became an independent republic, much of the archipelago was under Dutch rule. For an island of its size relative to the rest of the country (Bali's population of over 4 million is a small fraction of the country's 237 million), Bali enjoys a disproportionate amount of international attention that resonates in the academic, literary, filmic, and theatrical worlds. Distinguished in the Islamic archipelago as a stronghold of Hinduism, Bali's economy is highly dependent on cultural tourism, one in which dance, drama, and music are generative of myriad forms of exotic consumption, pleasures, fictions, and spectacles.

This thriving Balinese cultural industry is a colonial legacy. Tourism gained momentum in the 1920s after Dutch colonials successfully engineered an elaborate makeover of Bali as a "harmonious, exotic and apolitical" tropical island.[19] As part of a carefully planned colonial program that conflated "tradition" with forms of primitive nativism, a traditional Bali was imaged reiteratively through its indigenous art forms and spiritual practices. The familiar picture of a smiling Balinese native preoccupied with spiritual practices and artwork was thus embedded deeply in the cultural imaginary of Bali. While such a traditionalized Bali served as a postcard for the commercial tourism that the Dutch actively promoted, it also pointed to a colonial policy of cultural transformation and containment. And bizarre as it sounds, it was also an act of colonial atonement for the massacres at Badung in 1906 and Klungkung in 1908. As the political historian Geoffrey Robinson suggests, using the bifurcatory logic of Dutch colonialism, a traditionalized Bali immersed in the arts would be politically castrated: a "cultural" people could not at the same time be "political"; so long as "Balinese 'culture' remained strong, 'political' influence would be weak."[20]

The dramatic change of Bali from "savage, perfidious, bellicose"[21] to a place where "everyone is an artist"[22] has thus to be understood in the context of colonial conquest and disciplining. Bali was one of the last islands to be subjugated by the Dutch as part of its aggressive and punitive territorial expansion in the region. The Dutch had first attempted to conquer the island in 1846 with an unsuccessful military offensive. Two years later, the Dutch forces were again repulsed by the Balinese, who unified their resistance among the small kingdoms. With military reinforcements, a third attempt in 1849 by the Dutch proved more successful due to feuds among local lordships. The Dutch would exploit such feuds in the subsequent decades by pitting one small kingdom against another or use the feuds as excuses to invade the rest of Bali. Some rajas were also offered degrees of autonomy in exchange for terms of submission. In such prevalent "soft" conquests, the Dutch ruled by proxy using local aristocrats as figureheads, and systematically replaced commercial administrators with colonial officialdom. The gradual but violent annexations of Bali culminated in two bloody incidents that colonial officials termed the *puputans* of Badung in 1906 and Klungkung in 1908. The Badung and Klungkung incidents were pivotal for marking the threshold of Dutch colonial rule over the entire island. Subsequent dominant discourses have adopted *puputan* as standard lexicon for the massacres following this colonialized terminology.

Before 1906, *puputan* was merely a way to describe certain Balinese combat practices, but Dutch colonials had deliberately orientalized them as a "kind of amok" in which Balinese men dressed in white and "armed with lances and krisses" threw themselves on the enemy, "seeking death."[23] Colonial narratives of *puputan* revolved around the fatal "ritual" or "mass suicide" of Balinese aristocrats in the last moments of their "heroic" defense against the invading Dutch forces. Margaret Wiener argues that by romanticizing the bloody end of Balinese resistance forces with a term like *puputan* (the morpheme *puput* means "finished"), the Dutch were able to refigure practices for local agents and reified "particular instances of Balinese agency into a fixed cultural form."[24] The complete evisceration of Balinese martial tactics in the

Dutch versions of *puputan* ("great Amok" and death wish) marked a way in which local practices were both inflected and reified by colonial design for ideological purposes.

Wiener's account of Bali's colonialized history puts in perspective narratives of *puputan* in which the Balinese rulers, dressed in white, were believed to have stabbed themselves to death with krisses in a terminal act of nonsurrender before "horrified" Dutch soldiers. Such colonial folklores of *puputan* invoke orientalist notions of the Balinese "natives" as uncontrolled, senseless, impotent, and ultimately "tragic" figures as they go into a trance state wielding their krisses before a colonial firing squad. In this vivid spectacle, the dominant image is a vision of indistinguishable Balinese men in white gathering en masse to die a grisly death, with their families, also dying, in the background. Consider an account of this "ghastly scene" as recounted by a Dutch witness: "the corpse of the king, his head smashed open and brains oozing out, was surrounded by those of his wives and family in a bloody tangle of half-severed limbs, corpses of mothers with babies still at their breasts, and wounded children given merciful release by the daggers of their own compatriots."[25] Inspiring pity and fear, such representations of conquest helped establish, if ironically, the Enlightened and European "aesthetic" of rational, colonial rule.

In contrast, Balinese responses to the event, expressed in poems like "Bhuwana Winasa" (A World Destroyed), cited the *puputans* as disturbing events in a genealogy of omens and wars with the Dutch.[26] The Dutch authorities quickly isolated the resistance as episodes of "futile and feudal pride" that had no bearing on the ordinary people of Bali.[27] Clearly the portrayal of an arrogant, wasted, and despotic Balinese ruling class set up a politically efficacious transition to the progressive rule of the Dutch colonials. It is important to note that the colonial depiction of *puputan* as a mythologized and distant episode devoid of political meaning for its contemporary Balinese peasants was reinforced by many Western writers and artists, whose uncritical and romantic versions of the massacres only seemed to confirm the culture/politics divide endorsed by the Dutch. For instance, in Vicki Baum's 1937 novel *A Tale of Bali*, the two *puputans* were evacuated of any political content and depicted as little-known "tragic episodes" of no consequence and social relevance.[28] They were similarly obliterated of any vigor as forms of Balinese combat practice and martial tactic in Clifford Geertz's famed anthropological study of Bali as a "theater-state."[29] As Wiener glibly notes of Geertz's study, *puputan* was characterized as all "ritualized sound and fury, ultimately signifying nothing."[30]

I have discussed at some length the politics of *puputan* to uncover the punitive violence from which Balinese exoticism germinated and to foreground this history in the colonial production of "traditions" as pleasing aesthetics. By exploiting the romance of the rehabilitated native in an ageless paradise, the Dutch colonials were able to diffuse the political heat over the violence of *puputan*.[31] In its actual execution, the artful and guilt-induced "ethical policy sought to protect selective traditional Balinese culture from changing under Western influences." These so-called preservation policies were in actuality extensive transformations of Balinese practices based on peculiar and idiosyncratic Dutch notions of what constituted authentic "native" culture. Here the nativizing effects of constructing Bali as an island filled with "traditions" were remarkably pronounced in the visual and performance arenas. For instance, there was an overt and sudden change in the colonial outlook of Bali in pre- and post-conquest images: "intense, challenging stares are replaced by the mild and friendly expressions now familiar from countless guidebooks and postcards."[32] Just as the "look" of Bali changed, the bogus constructions of tradition went on to gain wide acceptance.[33] These traditions were evidently invented as a way to know Bali, serving a mystification of the island that also reified a nativized paradise.

There are two dimensions to this seamless cultural transformation into "paradise island," both of which indicated a covert politicization of cultural and knowledge production about Bali. The first dimension was a colonial academic field known as "Baliology," which generated dominant epistemologies of Bali through ethnographic, philological, and legal studies, particularly during its peak from the late nineteenth century to the 1920s. The second dimension was the work of cultural producers under the auspices of late Dutch colonialism. In this regard, Walter Spies emerged as a leading figure after becoming a permanent expatriate on the island in 1927. A fabled German artist and musician, Spies hosted an influential enclave of Euro-Americans from the scholarly and art worlds who stayed at his "salon" in Ubud, Bali, in the 1930s. Together, their publications, films, music, and paintings reified colonial visions of Bali as the island of smiling natives, temples, demons, and gods. Like the colonials, Spies and his friends sought to preserve what they deemed to be the native Balinese way of life, and even wanted legislation to make this happen:

> Having leisure, my friend Spies and I started a scheme which would tend to slow down the invading forces from the West and keep the Balinese in their happy, contented ways for a few decades longer. . . . We want to make of Bali a national or international park, with special laws to maintain it as such.[34]

This "scheme" would materialize in a version of the "park" concept when Spies configured Bali as a "living museum,"[35] and provided precise contexts for visitors to see the "real" Bali, including the field-defining anthropological work of Margaret Mead, Gregory Bateson, and Jane Belo. Spies's notions of what constituted authentic Bali widely influenced the production of film, painting, dance, drama, anthropology, ethnomusicology, and literature about the island. In his varied roles as director, musician, artist, tour guide, and cultural attaché, Spies concretized his vision of Bali as an "international park" to a glittering circle of visitors from Europe and North America.[36] The traffic of stars, scholars, millionaires, and diplomats that embraced Spies included the sexologist Magnus Hirschfeld, the dancer Katherine Mershon, British aristocrats like Lady Delamere (Lord Mountbatten's sister-in-law), the ethnomusicologist Colin McPhee, the dancer-writer Beryl de Zoete, the writers Miguel Covarrubias and Vicki Baum, the Baliologist Roelof Goris, the academic Claire Holt, the Woolworth millionairess and Cary Grant's ex-wife Barbara Hutton, and stars like Noel Coward, Cole Porter, and Charlie Chaplin. Under Spies's watch and lore, Bali became a legendary destination in the 1930s and thereafter. Throughout the interwar decade, an eclectic group of people visited the island with him, saw much of Bali through his eyes, and then communicated their "discoveries" to the Euro-American world.

With varying degrees of separation from the colonial administration, Spies and his cohort of cultural producers helped to materialize every claim that the Dutch colonials made about the people of Bali, including how they were "more interested by nature in art, culture, religion—dance, music, painting, carving, ceremonies, festivals, and so on."[37] Miguel Covarrubias's exclamation in his 1937 best-selling novel *Island of Bali* imprints such a typical sentiment: "[e]verybody in Bali seems to be an artist. Coolies and princes, priests and peasants alike, can dance, play musical instruments, paint, or carve in wood and stone."[38] By the 1930s, the Dutch authorities were said to have described "with a tedious uniformity" the construction of a cultural Bali through copious "bureaucratic memoranda."[39] The dry, bureaucratic language would be recast into the beautiful photography, dance, and prose of writers and artists. Together, the colonials and their unwitting creative affiliates celebrated Bali as a politically bankrupt dreamland saturated with art, music, and ritual.

Two decades after the bloody scene of the last *puputan* in Klungkung, Bali was to be systematically disciplined both by colonial design, using the arts intrinsic to Balinese culture, and by the anthropological and artistic imagination of Western writers and visitors. For much of the twentieth century onwards, this performative spell and its attendant tropes would script Bali as a mysterious and alluring locale through such lasting manifestations as Bali-Hai in Rodgers and Hammerstein's *South Pacific*; as oriental hieroglyph in Artaud's influential manifesto *Theatre and Its Double*; as proto-paradise in travel writing, music television videos, ethnography, and journalism; and in intercultural performance projects where Balinese dance-drama is routinely relegated as the native marker. The early formulations of this cultural magic that Spies helped to notate would congeal with his adoration for Balinese males in his choreography of *kecak*. Spies's role in the colonial project of *kecak* is at once curatorial and choreographic, and *kecak* would quickly come to iconize the island's living spells as a leading spectacle of spiritual traditions put on ritual display for tourists.

Choreographing the Queer Eye

In "traditional" *kecak* as it is practiced in Bali today, a chorus of men (anywhere from seventy to two hundred) sits closely huddled in concentric circles that are configured like penumbrous loops. The setting could be a temple or palace in Ubud, a village square in Bedulu, the beach in Kuta, a traditional pavilion, or just an open space up Mount Agung. The men, who are bare-chested in the manner of quotidian ritual practice, face inwards to the core of the performance circle, which then extends outward, forming a multilayered circular structure with the outermost circle encompassing the smaller ones inside. Using *cak* as a syllabic beat, the men vocalize a polyrhythmic chant before a centralized light source such as a bonfire or oil lamp placed in the heart of the circle. As entranced monkeys from the *Ramayana*, the Indian epic poem, the chorus enacts famous episodes with the help of a few external dancers taking on key roles like Rama, Sita, and Ravana. To signify its ritual contours, three equidistant white dots are painted across the temple on the men's faces with the middle dot between the eyes to signify the Hindu trinity of Shiva, Vishnu, and Brahma. Two flowers, typically a plumeria and a hibiscus, are placed on the man's left and right ear respectively. The consistency of the spectacle achieved by the men's synchronous chants and movements is further emphasized by their highly coordinated costumes. Everyone is clad in a black *babuletan* (loincloth), *saput* or *podong* (black and white checkered sarong), and *umpal* (sash).[40]

Given its attention to prototypical Balinese looks and ritual practices, it may come as a surprise that *kecak* is performed only to tourists, and has no actual function as a spiritual practice. This is unlike other dance-dramas such as Legong, Calonarang, and Sanghyang Dedari, which have a separate ritual function outside tourist cultural shows. Under the friendly banner of the island's cultural immersion program, the largely foreign audience enjoys the trance and native elements of *kecak* as part of its intrinsic appeal from a distance. Few if any would perceive the combination of different dance movements and costumes of the *Ramayana* dancers within *kecak* apart from their sheer, visual impact as incomprehensible tribality. But *kecak* is in fact a kind of intracultural display as it features a mix of classical Balinese dances such as *Wayang Wong* or *Kebyar*, the costumes of *Gambuh*, *Wayang Wong*, and the modern Balinese *Ramayana* ballet or *Sendratari Ramayana*. By mixing the design and choreography of these dances, the staging promotes an authentic, traditional feel that transcends any specific ritual function. Its guise as a native ritual is also reiterated in dubious but tantalizing claims about its origins. On the cover of a popular tourist DVD of the show, for instance, *kecak* is sold as "an ancient ritual to listen to god's voice under mass hypnosis."[41]

Kecak's "100 naked men" and "beautiful women in their tribal costumes," tag lines of Bali's cultural tourism, sell a popular version of native exotica first perpetuated by the West.[42] The dance theorist Marta Savigliano in her study of tango calls this form of self-expressive exoticism in a postcolonial context an autoexotic display.[43] Both the colonial and contemporary tourist versions of *kecak* rely on the myth of the primitive to generate or intensify touristic voyeurism and excitement. The heterosexual assumptions of *kecak*'s aesthetic composition, however, belie the queer encounter at the heart of its traditional masquerade. If the pleasure of an appealing exotic gaze is contingent upon the sublimation of its queer history, then this sublimation brings with it the fraught issue of queer evidence, which quickly raises the stakes of using the dyad as an analytic. What is queer about *kecak* and what constitutes the queer evidence of a tropic spell in a traditional ritual form suddenly become incendiary questions.

A group of historians, writers, and pundits of Bali have, for instance, reacted very strongly against the study of Spies's homosexual relations with Balinese males in relation to *kecak*.[44] From their point of view, uncovering Spies's sexual relations with Balinese boys in the homoerotic milieu of 1930s Bali is tantamount to having a wrongful "agenda."[45] Such an "agenda" proves, if anything at all, my own "fantasy" and "obsession with his [Spies's] sex life."[46] Besides, one might "truly" know *kecak* only through an objective, linear study of its chronological development. In this regard, the homoerotic issue is charged with an "undue fascination" with Spies's "sexual proclivities."[47] It is "improper," "outdated," and "irrelevant."[48] Conversely, dominant readings of *kecak* have tended to obfuscate or suppress the question of colonial homoerotics while demonstrating a strange ethic of adulation for Spies. In other words, a proper discourse on a traditional Balinese ritual dictates certain terms of "decency" and excludes Spies and the boys altogether.

Spies's sexuality and the multiple valences of sexual conduct in Bali in the 1930s are a lightning rod for controversy, particularly among the Baliophile defenders of his legacy. They object to a project that in their opinion willfully characterizes Spies as a sexual predator, and fails to account for how a more benign Dutch colonialism substituted for a Balinese feudal system in which male servants were brutally treated; how the Balinese practiced their own experimental gender and sexual fluidity (in contradistinction to rigid Western sexual mores) that made

[handwritten margin note: Native Balinese culture is ... more ... accepting & homosexuality]

homosexuality more acceptable; and how the boys' parents had come forward on their own to say it was their privilege that their sons played with Spies. "Do you know the ages of the boys?" one queried. "Can you say you have not enjoyed the thrill of watching half naked Balinese men wielding krisses yourself?" These provocations, curiously defensive of colonial honor and pleasure, are raised in the name of Balinese "agency." They are a way to speak for the Balinese subaltern who has been ignored in my study, the one who is "saved" from the local despot by the white man, and complicit in his own oppression.

If the brown boy is the salve of colonial hurt feelings, Spies's esteemed status is protected by the dominant view that "Balinese and foreign scholars tend to view his time (and contributions) in Bali positively."[49] At an early stage in my research, I posted a leading question on the transnational Balinese Arts and Culture News (BACN)[50] listserv:

> I am a graduate student at UCLA working on Walter Spies's involvement in the creation and development of kecak. If you have information about Spies's involvement as well as his ties (cultural, sexual, social) with Balinese men/boys between the late 20s and early 40s when he was in Bali, can you please be in touch with me. I look forward to your thoughts and information.[51]

The reactions from Western Balinese scholars and writers were not what I expected, especially respondents who immediately accused me of "playing up a sordid angle."[52] Many were aghast by my inquiry about Spies's sexual relations with Balinese males and considered such an approach to the study of *kecak* improper and culturally disrespectful. They objected to the (homo)sexual angle of my inquiry even though the question I posed was broadly couched. The colonial dyad threatened to entangle Spies's life and Balinese "tradition" in some unspeakable personal and cultural dishonor; a lot was at stake.

There was apparently so much to guard against this less than respect- *[handwritten margin note: it's easy to judge from the hegemony perspective]* ful attitude that many joined in the chorus against my work or what they conceived of my work on the listserv. They were nearly all white male writers, scholars or Baliophiles who seemed personally aggrieved by the way I had besmirched Spies's legacy as a pioneer artist on the island. A white male journalist living in Bali posted, "[this author] seems more interested in the sex life of Walter Spies than the origins of Kecak and this is sad. Maybe it had a role to play in what he achieved but let's not trivialise the accomplishments of an outstanding character (Walter Spies) who has been dead for 60 years."[53] Taking aim at the homoerotic angle of my inquiry, a German professor observed that "[c]reating art is too complex to be mystified in such a limited direction," and advocated "religion or belief in a more overall sense of spirituality" as alternative ways to study the composition of this fusion performance ritual.[54] He claimed that if (homo)sex were such a "primary motor of inspiration," he would "stop to compose and become a peasant."[55] A U.S. ethnomusicologist noted that the "intercultural and physical contact between Spies and Balinese men" is not "relevant" and suggested that one should study Balinese arts as they developed from an exchange of "ideas."[56] Another Dutch man who wrote his MA thesis on Walter Spies acknowledged that Spies had "relations with young men," but insisted that kecak represented a "creative collaboration of Spies with modern Balinese artists—who were equally interested in creative interpretation of dance."[57] He added that insofar as "dance is a celebration of the beauty of the body, male dance might be homoerotic by definition," but denied any vestige of homoeroticism in kecak per se.[58]

In the midst of the exchange, a journalist living in Bali confirmed that the official German biography on Spies supported by Spies's family was written with the "avowed stipulation that his homosexuality not be mentioned."[59] An art historian who claimed to be "close to several people who were acquaintances of Spies" also informed the list that "Spies's sister permitted him [Hans Rhodius] to use Spies's private letters for his book under the condition he expurgate all overt homosexual references."[60] There was apparently no Balinese point of view in this exchange. An Australian academic who had written about Bali reported that "there may still be one or 2 old men around Ubud who worked with/for him" but they have since passed away.[61] But apart from these exceptional revelations, all the other men were in a state of denial about Spies's homosexuality and fondness for brown boys. Though there is little documentation of what transpired between Spies and his boys, court records show that Spies was twice incarcerated for having sex with a minor under Dutch colonial law. At one of his court hearings, Margaret Mead defended him for not knowing the age of the boys because all Balinese males looked so young. While this was an attempt to vindicate him of any wrongdoing toward the "Balinese light youth" (Mead's phrase), it also signaled a way local males including adults were routinely infantilized as boys by Westerners.

While I was slightly taken aback by some of these responses, it was the vehement refusal to consider the politics of queer relationality in the context of Balinese arts that seemed puzzling. The myth of cultural purity, along with the objections converging around the "good name" of Spies as a "hero for the culture conscious," has become "a kind of lit-any"[62] for both the Balinese and foreigners alike. The name of the "late, lamented Spies" would not suffer, as one might gather from the panic reaction and disavowal, the indignities of a (homo)sexual inquiry. On the Balinese side, the sole voice of I Wayan Dibia, a master artist of *kecak*, advocated seeing the form as a Balinese performing art form and a vital, evolving tradition; queerness is again irrelevant.[63] In his seminal *Kecak: The Vocal Chant of Bali*, I Wayan Dibia accounts for the history and mechanics of this ritual as a prototypically Balinese art form while eschewing any mention of Walter Spies, as if to protect the cultural identity of *kecak* as a pure Balinese creation. Almost all who responded to my various inquiries used old school intercultural theater theory to obliterate queerness or homoerotics from consideration in *kecak*'s aesthetics or history. They all pointed to more "proper" ways of studying *kecak*—artistic collaboration, religion, tourism, and the cultural evolution of traditions. Questions of race and sexuality in a colonial context appear to have no place in such a study.

The heated exchanges on the listserv and at my lectures index the problematic of studying queerness and performance in a cross-cultural frame. They demonstrate the enduring controversies of the dyad and the way issues of evidence and discourse conspire to uphold colonial epistemology and affect. Contemporary Western and Balinese scholars who zealously guard what is a proper inquiry of *kecak* only reiterate colonial structures that control the flow of information on what Bali and Balinese *kecak* "really" are. It seems fair to ask, given this history, how a queer encounter in the Asias is circumscribed by the colonial dyad. Consider the famous overwrought scene of the lone Balinese brown boy singing outside Spies's jail window while he is incarcer-ated for pedophilia. It depicts the scenario of the young brown boy displaying his sincere and selfless love to the old white man, a familiar hetero-orientalist scenario restaged with a homosexual cast. Importantly, it points to the performativity of colonial love with its requisite drama—the singing native boy, the jailed white lover, the inseparability of the two—and attests to the power of tropic spells as a force field in the queer and/or Asian encounter. Such an uninterrogated notion of love is said to triumph over all power dimensions at work, but colonial affect and emotional binds are often part of its loving formations, rendering certain intimacies possible and others untenable.[64] Imagine the reverse scenario in which a young white boy is singing a love song to an old Balinese man jailed in Germany or the United States for "playing" with him. Is this conceivably romantic?

Today *kecak* is performed to global cultural tourists and used in intercultural theater projects in which it often serves as a native marker. In none of these venues is *kecak* ever a signifier of that queer contact between Walter Spies and his beloved Balinese "boys." Spies's biography and records, however, point to his inextricable involvement in the ritual's formation. Throughout his permanent stay in Bali from 1927 to 1942, he enjoyed intimate contact with Balinese males who served his social, artistic, and sexual needs. Even as he was "a friend of the Balinese," his status as a white male expatriate meant that he was able to live with a sense of entitlement. The issue in hand is therefore not so much locating proof of his homosexuality or sexual predilection as it is his queer position in the colonial matrix. Such a position is complicated by his love for the brown boy, which expressed a "repudiation of the kind of dominance and submission, authority and dependence, which he associated with European culture."[65]

Yet, as Joseph Boone has noted, "where the occidental traveler by virtue of his homosexuality is already the other, the presumed *equivalence* of Eastern homosexuality and occidental personal liberation may disguise the specter of colonial privilege and exploitation encoded in the hierarchy white man/brown boy."[66] In other words, the disparities built into such a dyad may be obscured by the commonality of erotic interest, sexual emancipation, or romance, but there is no mistaking its "colonial privilege and exploitation." One might speculate, following Boone's critique, that Spies's quest for a lateral *equivalence* between his Balinese same-sex encounters and escape from Western sexual oppression found expression in the fetishization of native boys and the production of a new ritual form tied to orientalist art. This conclusion may be precisely what the Baliophile dissenters feared or objected to, but given what we already know about the orientalist legacy in Western art, such an observation is not wholly remarkable.

Rather, the more difficult que(e)ries have to do with how the colonial past can be rewritten (in an Asian performance touched by the dyad's tropic spell) without reinscribing Eurocentric hetero-biases. Can it be successfully reimagined by postcolonial and queer contestations of "truths" and "facts" that will not be marginalized as "irrelevant" or "improper"? With discursive, heteronormative strongholds guarding a "proper" point of view, a performance historian interested in the colonialization and homoerotics of *kecak* is faced with a seemingly insurmountable task. But the recuperation of "irrelevant" or "improper" histories is fundamental in formulating a critical optic attuned to the queer eye of a choreographer. Queer legacies imbricated in (neo)colonial or collaborative productions of art are not a more or less legitimate line of inquiry; they are critical intersections that have to be addressed as a cognate of power. The queer historiography of *kecak* is, in this regard, a crucial link to Bali's past, present, and future. With this in mind, let us now turn headlong to the queer erotics of *kecak* as we continue to unravel the tropic spell cast by the dyad.

Queer(ing) *Kecak*

One of the most striking images of *kecak* is the proximity of numerous male bodies jolting incessantly together within fixed and seemingly inescapable circles. The proxemics of these homosocial circles produces a sensual, collective male union with a homoerotic charge. This charge is sustained even in the more static states of the chorus as the performers are clustered very closely together with an expectant, latent energy. Within the communal, concentric circles, bare-chested young men enact variations of sensuous bodily movements, from subtle, rhythmic throbs to sudden, jostling strokes. The sheer spectacle is erotic by virtue of its irresistible physicality and fascinating rhythm. There is palpable vigor as heated, tactile male bodies pulsating without end channel the vibrations of each other's kinetic emissions. Each man sits cross-legged and reproduces with precision a vocabulary of synchronized movements that involve close contact of shoulders as well as back, torso, pelvis, and leg. These strokes of bodily contact happen most dramatically when the chorus collapses backwards, surges forward, sways sideways or rises to their feet. Every man moves in sync with each other without missing a beat. The metronomic *cak* beats are sustained throughout the performance, powering the incessant throbbing of naked chests, heads, arms, and shoulders. Every so often, the men will jolt to their feet with their hands upraised, digits wholly spread out and flickering to complete a section of the chant before huddling back in quick retractions to close the circle. A homoerotic, sexual energy peaks at several points in the ritual with the insatiable spectacle of countless, pulsating male bodies penetrating en masse into the inner circle with full force.

These palpably erotic effects of *kecak* can be traced back to the 1930s in colonial Bali, when Spies choreographed its originary form with his local conspirators. In *Dance and Drama in Bali* (1938), a book Walter Spies coauthored with Beryl de Zoete, the homoerotic appeal of *kecak*'s progenitor form, the *cak* chorus in Sanghyang or "god-inspired trance-dance," was tellingly noted: the "exorcistic circles of sitting men" were "naked except for a small loin-cloth, and wearing fantastic freshly woven hats, adorned with flower garlands of every hue."[67] The attraction of the men was evidently found in their presentational allure, a *nativized* spectacle of men decorated with flowers and "fantastic hats," and arranged in "exorcistic circles." This all-male Sanghyang *cak* chorus to which Spies referred as the "voice-*gamelan*" was the trance-accompaniment that he would subsequently develop into *kecak*. There were a couple dozen Sanghyang dances in Bali featuring a mixture of female and male choirs, and boys and girls.[68] Spies's choice to develop an all-male *cak* chorus affirmed the aesthetic appeal of Balinese male bodies.

In an even more telling affirmation of this aesthetic, Spies expanded the Sanghyang *cak* chorus to over a hundred men and was said to have implanted a gas lamp in the center of the circle to dramatically cast light on the male torsos and faces. He eliminated the Sanghyang girls in trance possession as well as the female *kidung* chorus, secularized the form, and added the *Ramayana* narrative to serve as a dramatic backdrop. These crucial structural changes attributed to Spies as he innovated the Sanghyang *cak* chorus into *kecak*, pointed to many homoerotic elements. It was clear that his choreographic eye to "increase the dramatic impact" of *kecak* was driven entirely by a male aesthetic.[69] Without the nymphs and female chorus, Spies's "visually exciting"[70] *kecak* was now wholly male, and focused on the spectacle of bare-chested men wearing nothing but "a small loin-cloth."[71] As the Asian theater scholar Craig Latrell noted in his study of the form, the homoerotic markers of Spies's "new" performance ritual were much too pronounced in his visual and choreographic composition of *kecak* for the development to pass as incidental or "as if the dance had naturally evolved from the earlier sanghyang."[72]

Part of this transformation was documented in the 1931 film *Island of Demons*, where the male chorus was clearly the visual centerpiece during the ritual segment representing the climax in the film.[73] The chorus used their incessant *cak* chants to build suspense around the Rangda/ Barong confrontation and provided the possessive beats to the crucial and most dramatic moments of expurgation during the exorcism. Conceivably, Spies directed this visual, aural, and sensual emphasis on *kecak* as the film's "ethnographic consultant." In comparison, the female *kidung* chorus in the same film was more frequently heard than seen. They also had barely any physical action or gestures and were often out of frame. The Sanghyang nymphs also did not share the kind of close-ups and camera focus as the male chorus. In corollary, the erotic appeal of the Balinese males was accentuated by their dominance in the filmic spectacle and the attractive kinetics of their varying movements. Male bodies gyrated en masse in very concentrated frames amid light and shadow cast by a gas lamp on the men's bare torsos and faces.

The spellbinding quality of this spectacle has to be appreciated in tandem with Spies's "texts" on the form. Going back to his seminal book *Dance and Drama in Bali*, we learn that *kecak* had an "ecstatic ritual character" and was embodied by "naked, swaying bodies." It was a "terrific" dance featuring "monkey jabberings, squeakings, angry squawks" as "some invisible monkey sports with another."[74] Continuing with the queer vision, the "monkeys twine and wrestle, biting, teasing, ceaselessly jabbering. Now the opposing half swells furiously up against the monkeys. Alternately they rise against each other in two fierce hosts, each in turn leaning like a great cloud above the prostrate group."[75] The dynamic and mystical physicality of these entwined monkeys was clearly layered with sexual meanings. As one group of Balinese males "swelled" and "leaned" on the other "prostrate group" in fierce action, another was "jabbering," "wrestling," and "entwining."

These graphic textual descriptions supplemented Spies's palpably ecstatic photographs about the ritual. In one representative photograph titled *Transformation of Ketjaks into Monkeys*, Spies captured the trance-like moment when the male chorus stretched their arms upwards with their digits spread fully apart before the gas lamp. The men with their gaping jaws were mimicking monkeys in a dark and magical atmosphere. It is clear that the photograph aimed to convey the visual thrill of *kecak* through the recognizable tropes of the "native" featuring, in this case, erect male bodies in some kind of possession. As the book would also tell us, the crisp and rhythmic movements in *kecak* were complemented by such "native"-like affectations as "reiterated bird-like cries."[76] Without question, these enthralling movements and sounds about the ritual were *nativized* by the text. More than that, the text also eroticized the male performers with fairly explicit sexual metaphors and innuendos: "erect but rising, rising, rising"; "hoarse ejaculations"; "broods like some monstrous toad with wide-spread legs and arms, then rises again to his utmost stretch."[77] In this regard, the circles of *kecak* were also a palpably homoerotic fantasy about Bali and materialized a site in which to channel Walter Spies's desire "for the boys."

The semiotics of other photographs depicting his life on the island reveal even more "monkey business." Smiling wryly, Spies poses with his pet monkey next to images of Balinese men performing *as* "monkeys" in *kecak* or crouching around him as innumerable crowds of "native" male youth in the village. There is an uncanny and striking resemblance between the encircling mobs of village crowds and the agglomeration of "monkeys" in *kecak*. In the photographs with the Balinese youth, Spies is nestled among them in the center of these neatly arranged semicircular "group" shots staging his exceptional immersion with the Balinese males. Then in photographs with his pet monkey, the animal is lovingly cradled in his arm like a baby or perched on his shoulder while he dips in a pool. In the switch between these photographs, a campy, semiotic slippage seems to occur between *kecak* "monkey," Balinese boys, and pet monkey. This slippage was part of Spies's affectionate and humorously anthropomorphic fantasies about Bali's mythic and "primitive" landscapes, with him in the foreground and the boy in the background, as in the picture.

Figure 1.5
Balinese men performing as *kecak*
monkeys.
Leiden University Library, Collection
Institute Kern, shelfmark Walter Spies
80-1149.

Figure 1.6
Balinese men in early choreography
of *kecak*.
Leiden University Library, Collection
Institute Kern, shelfmark Walter Spies
80-1355.

Figure 1.7
Walter Spies with pet monkey, parrot,
and Balinese houseboy.
Leiden University Library, Collection
Daisy Spies, shelfmark Or. 25.773-D-3.

Spies's appreciation for the Balinese, Javanese, and Sundanese was starkly focused on their bodily appeal: "The people . . . are so incredibly beautiful, so delicately built, brown and aristocratic, that everyone who is not one of them should be ashamed."[78] Unlike the prevalent focus on Balinese women by Euro-American painters and photographers, Spies's artistic oeuvre focused on young Javanese and Balinese men bearing erect poses. These would invariably focus on the male head and naked torso, including the individual's boyish face, parched lips, bare skin, and innocent allure, which gave the paintings a soft, phallic appeal. The expressionistic agrarian landscapes of his paintings call attention to the natural cosmology of Bali, and male figures infuse them with a dreamy sacredness and enchanting harmony. With Spies codifying his romanticized, homoerotic fantasy of Bali in so many different "readable" ways, one is struck by the omission of a more explicit address of colonial homosexuality and homoerotics in the discourse and choreography of *kecak*.

Compulsory Love for the White Man: Reading "Walter Spies"

Since the queer twist in the story of *kecak* congeals around Walter Spies, one might ask, Just who is this man? To give an idea of Spies's legacy on Bali, here are some of the ways he has been described: "artist," "painter," "composer," "hotelier," "curator," "hedonist," "musicologist," "self-appointed host," "tour guide," "inspiring mentor," "father of modern Balinese art," "impresario," "choreographer," "director," "theater documentation [expert] and historian," "photographer," "teacher," "Bali's adopted son," "participant in the traditional arts," "conductor," "cognoscente," "interventionist participant observer," "prisoner," "homosexual," and "lover of young Balinese boys."[79] These descriptors, gathered from a wide variety of sources, illustrate the ubiquity of Spies, particularly in Balinese studies, and illustrate an overwhelming discursive disparity of the dyad. As is obvious, information on Spies is readily available in numerous publications, which begs the question, Why is his life so singular and romanticized? I raise this rhetorical question to expound on what I call a compulsory love for the white man in contrast to the oblivion of native boys. To read "Walter Spies" as biographical performance is one way to denaturalize the triumphant life story of another intrepid European traveler in the East. Importantly also, this is not a biographical cause-and-effect analysis around sexual identity: I am not arguing, for example, that Spies, a proven homosexual, choreographed a gay ritual orgy with natives, or that *kecak* is a gay ritual because one of its choreographers is a gay man. I have been surprised by how often such a fallacy is deduced by readers of my study. Rather, I am interested in the convergence of queer and biographic fictions of "Walter Spies" and *kecak* in discourses of compulsory love.

The social anthropologist Graeme MacRae points out that the narratives on Spies have become "a kind of a litany taking a hegemonic hold over the history of Ubud (the cultural nerve-center of Bali)."[80] The hegemony of Spies, evident in his "great name" in the performance and cultural imaginary of Bali, indexes an expressive universality of the white man. By focusing on Spies in this section, I am not interested in reproducing another storied narrative about a "handsome," "blonde," and "blue-eyed" artist from a quasi-aristocratic background who died a "tragic death." Yet playing a version (or aversion) of this dominant biography is necessary to convey the privilege and romance associated with the white man. In contrast to the countless, nameless native boys who are rendered invisible in the annals of colonial history and memory, Spies has an estate, an archive, and a following. He has a foundation to his name, and a special collection of his photography is currently housed at Leiden University in the Netherlands. In the contemporary art circle, one of his paintings recently sold for half a million dollars at The Hague. His eminence is in deep contrast to the Balinese men and boys, including his *kecak* collaborators, who enjoy no such interest. Hence, even in abbreviated form, his biographical content would prove to be extensive and overwhelming relative to the anonymous brown boys with apparently no recordable life story. Instead, they invoke an incomprehensible native mob (reprised as the multitudes of the Third World) in a classic scenario of exotic otherness. In contrast, the white man arrives in the foreign land with a star identity, life story, and complex individuality. In such a setup, he is always the centerpiece, the one who commands attention by eliciting desire and curiosity from onlookers. Like a dramatic character, he is the one who drives the plot with a grand objective, such as the "making of modern Ubud." The combination of omniscience and assumed gravitas helps to elevate the colonial figure. A self-justifying act, his ubiquity and importance demand the public's compulsory love while making the anonymity and privation of brown boys acceptable.

The critical disparity of the dyad cannot be emphasized enough: In opposition to the singular, privileged white man endowed with a colorful past, the erasure and anonymity of the native males foreground the methodological problematic of recovering or remembering history in a colonial context. The discourse is always inherently unequal. Besides, the way that Spies is lionized next to the scores of nameless, indistinguishable, and forgotten Balinese men has to do with how his life is remembered within an exclusive expatriate club setting: "Spies was seen as an extraordinarily creative, altruistic and well-loved individual amongst the white friends who shared his cultural values and his lifestyle. . . . It is less clear how he was seen by the Balinese themselves and also what range of opinions existed about him amongst those with a lesser voice in terms of the documentary record."[81]

Reading this disparity through Edward Said's *Orientalism*, one might say that love for the white man is much ado about self-love, or a white-on-white romance framed in an exotic location. On a discursive level, the magical Western "self" in love with himself is remarkably pronounced in Spies's biographies, which are all written by "Westerners who tend to reflect the cultural and ideological position of those Westerners."[82] Moreover, such a self-same love is perpetuated through the white man's access to Western cultural institutions. The biographical romance of Spies is another Western myth for the West and the world. Often, his life was portrayed like a cinematic story with intrigue, glamour, and a lot of drama. The narrative would invariably start with him growing up as the son of the German consul general in prewar czarist Russia before noting how high art, ballet, opera, meeting Rachmaninoff, and conversing in French, English, and Russian were all in a day's work for the young Spies. Around the First World War, Spies was interned in the Siberian Urals, but was supposedly spared from typical prisoner hardship owing to his luck as a "strange child of fortune."[83] A typical passage written by his friend about Spies's internment in war-stricken Russia sums up a poetic and charmed life that is part of his magic:

> Sometimes he tells of those days. Springtime on the steppes, broad miles of cobalt flowers; a week later, and the plains all garbed in yellow.

Butterflies. Days with pallet and easel. Days with the piano. Rocks upon the heights, with rich luminous crystals and sea-born fossils. Flat plains that changed their levels in sudden precipices; winter snows that leveled everything; and houses beside the cliffs, snow that leveled everything. . . . Tongues to be learned, Russian, Tartar, Persian. Books. Long winter nights with the lore of lands beyond the Himalayas. Such were the war and the Red Terror to Walter Spies.[84]

The dreamy prose that is used to describe the internment years as a carefree adventure in the beautiful countryside belies the violence and upheaval of the Russian revolution. But its ostensible effect is to strip the account of any political content and to accentuate Spies's sweetness as the happy-go-lucky, bohemian artist. We also learn of his early cross-cultural experiences, how he learned foreign traditions, languages, and dances in the mountains, and how he committed to a lifelong spiritual connection with nature and its cosmology. As we've come to expect of the genre, these experiences are linked to Spies's love for agrarian and mystical Bali in his later years. After the war, Spies threw himself into the world of arts, gave piano recitals, exhibited his paintings, and mingled in a glittering circle of European stars, filmmakers, and artists. He was already well known in Europe as a painter and a rising star in 1923, well before his voyage to the Dutch East Indies. These networks undoubtedly boosted the appeal and success of his well-known travel "salon" in Ubud, Bali.

In "Margaret Mead's Balinese: The Fitting Symbols of the American Dream," Tessel Pollmann reported that Spies was a "charming, cosmopolitan, and intelligent host" who was widely loved for being a "friend of the natives."[85] Pollmann's breezy characterization of Spies in an otherwise critical article is consistent with several accounts portraying the paradisal environs of Bali as the backdrop of his perfectly beautiful life. The myth of Spies and his goodness continues to be reiterated at the expense of any productive inquiry about his colonial status as a white man, obfuscating the ways he helped to install a "well-organized, money-oriented modernizing [Balinese] society" that had "all the comforts of the West and all the charms of exoticism."[86]

Spies's love for Bali is part of a larger Western discourse about the romance of the East. He is said to have dived headlong into the

[handwritten marginalia: — how history is told — omitted to glorify Spies ↓ becomes the face for loving the East]

75

unencumbered freedom "over there" because Europe was draining his life: "You don't understand at all how unhappy I feel living among those impassive and emotionless people in Germany! They don't have anything natural! Everything is false and artificial."[87] Spies's sudden and permanent departure for Bali was supposed to reflect the popular romantic thinking of his generation about shedding the restrictive mantle of civilization that governed rational Europe for a more natural existence with natives. In a recent study, however, Geoffrey Green speculated that Spies might also have been running away from prosecution for "having sex with a minor," foreshadowing similar charges in Bali for which he was multiply jailed.[88] Yet another speculation posited that he was trying to flee from Friedrich Murnau, his "possessive" lover or "special friend."[89] As is well known, Friedrich Murnau was a director from Weimar Germany famous for films like *Nosferatu* (1922), *Faust* (1926), and *Tabu* (1931).[90] Spies lived with Murnau as his lover for several years and actually worked on several of his films, including *Nosferatu*.[91]

Murnau bequeathed much of his estate to Spies, and their liaison was to have an aesthetic influence on Spies's artistic work. Many have read Murnau's expressionistic style in Spies's photographic technique and art and suggested how the use of its emotive charge enhanced Bali's exoticism: "Walter planned his camera angles with great care, and this low-angle photograph makes the Rangda loom menacingly. They emerge from the mist brandishing their talons. The effect is reminiscent of Murnau's *Nosferatu*."[92] Apart from Murnau, Spies had other white male lovers, including the German composer and academic Jürgen von der Wense. The strand tying all these details is a starry fascination with Spies's life and art. Much of the writing is tinged with magic, fantasy, and tantalizing conjectures that compel a love for the white man, a tropic spell in itself. Such a complex and fictionalizing fascination is not about to fade. The cinematic dimensions of these narratives are being considered for an actual feature-length film on his life, *Walter Spies and Bali*.

What's Love Got to Do with This?

In *Reminiscences of a Balinese Prince*, Tjokorda Gde Agung Sukawati (the prince himself) notes matter-of-factly that Spies's art depicting

Bali's exotic charms produced at his very comfortable abode "commanded such a high price that one painting gave him 3000 guilders—enough for him to live a year in Bali."[93] Considering that he managed to convince Tj. Gde Oka Dalam, Sukawati's cousin, to rent him a plot of land by a spectacular ravine on which to build his house for only "5 guilders a month," Spies certainly had more than enough to spare for the year. At the goodwill of the Balinese, whose mode of transaction at that time was barter trade, Spies would retain the land subsequently, paying only a sum total of 175 guilders. "Well, Agung," said Spies to Sukawati, "I never asked the price of the land; I only know I want to pay rent for ten years and that is 600 guilders." In a classic settlement that upheld colonial entitlement, Sukawati, who refused Spies's request for a ten-year rental agreement at 600 guilders, was talked into an even lesser agreement. According to Sukawati, Spies had "insisted and so on and on and eventually I just took 175 guilders from him."[94]

Pointing to Spies's colonial stature as a white man, Sukawati reminisced that at the initial meeting of the rental negotiation, "my cousin (Dalam) was so nervous" that when Spies offered him the "Mascot No. 7 cigarette," he "took it in his trembling hand" and "it fell apart."[95] Spies's personal connection with royalty like Sukawati meant that he traversed freely in the realm of Balinese aristocracy and got what he wanted easily in spite of his civilian status. Even though the rental agreement was seemingly transacted in goodwill, the unequal terms of the contract determined, as it were, by Spies himself were a classic commercial maneuver that imperial powers have used to colonize much of Asia, from Bali to Hong Kong, with very different economic structures and ethics.

The stark difference in Sukawati's plain description of Spies is worth considering next to the unabashed exaltations accorded to him by his Western compadres:

Walter Spies had first lived with his father, an Ambassador in Moscow. He left Moscow for Holland and from there took ship as a cannoneer. As soon as he arrived in Java, he went to Djogja and he became a servant of the ninth Sultan of Djogja so that he could learn Javanese music. After staying one year in Djogja, my brother Tj. Gde Raka Sukawati asked him to come and live permanently in Ubud. At first he lived in the front courtyard of the Puri Saren. He brought a piano with him, a German bicycle, and a butterfly net.[96]

None of the dreamy language about Spies in Western biographies is evident from Sukawati's matter-of-fact account about his life on the island. Rather than seeing him as the "father of modern Balinese art," Sukawati noted plainly that Spies participated in Ubud's "Art Society" and helped in the construction of the Museum of Bali Modern Art. In passages about their hikes together, the landscape is less cosmic than utilitarian. They would be hiking from "valley to valley catching butterflies and put them in gold leaf boxes and send them to museums in Europe and elsewhere."[97] The unlaced characterization of Spies as a "servant" of the sultan also stands out as a counterpoint to Western accounts. Still, his treatment by the Balinese and Javanese sultanates was far from paltry. In fact, he lived grandly and comfortably under their patronage:

> The sultan . . . asked questions about the blond German and a few days later a carriage with princes and servants with *pajongs* stopped in front of Spies' humble boarding house. He was asked to be the conductor of the European orchestra in the *kraton*. Eagerly he assented and he received a pavilion in the *kraton* to live in. His wages were one hundred guilders a month plus food and rent and a young servant.[98]

From the simplicity of arriving with his personal accoutrement, consisting of only "a piano, a German bicycle, and a butterfly net," to the pomposity of being greeted with a regalia of royal honor, Spies wavers back and forth between a façade of high appointment, imperial connection, and everyday man. Notable in these accounts is his easy connection with the Balinese sultanates and his privileged status as a white man. The euphemistic "young servant" put under his charge points to the easy access he had to boys. So what kind of love for the Balinese people—as we are told over and over again he possessed—was Spies's "love"?

We might trace the history of Spies's love to a serendipitous visit to the Dutch Colonial Institute (now the Tropenmuseum of the Royal Tropical Institute in Amsterdam). There, Spies experienced a "call from the East," and decided the Dutch East Indies was to be his "new spiritual home." In Bali, his spiritual awakening moved him to renovate Balinese culture along the same axis of colonial ethnographic design that European curators do so well at museums like the Dutch Colonial Institute. According to the Balinese historian Ide Gde Ing Bagus, "[t]he Dutch wanted us to be a living museum," adding that this meant that

> Bali is not allowed to be modern, it is not supposed to be touched by new ideas. The Dutch tell us: education is all right, but it must be blended by tradition. For example, when I am in the primary school, I have to dance in the Balinese way. I have to draw the Balinese style. I have to do Balinese literature. They do not want us to be modern, because that is Western. . . . We have to be Balinized.[99]

Like the colonials, Spies wanted Bali Balinized. In fact, he was such an active proponent of this Balinization project that he wanted Bali to be his own living museum. He designed Balinized buildings such as "temple-style" primary schools, and would "rejoice" when Dutch colonials forbade "natives to wear shirts and trousers" and enforced the adornment of sarong for the governor-general's visit in 1937. Such a Bali was for Spies "natural" again, even for just one day.[100] Spies's support of colonialist beliefs is paradoxically mixed with disdain for colonial figures. In the book *Bali, the Imaginary Museum: The Photographs of Walter Spies and Beryl de Zoete,* Michael Hitchcock and Lucy Norris state, "He [Spies] disliked the pettiness and officiousness of certain Dutch civil servants, but was never entirely opposed to imperialism, and like many of his circle regarded Enlightened Colonialism as the way forward. They were united in their desire to preserve Balinese culture and saw the less sensitive colonial officials as a hindrance to this process."[101] In Hitchcock and Norris's sympathetic analysis, however, Spies was "never as overtly paternalistic" as others.[102] Besides, even if he had openly espoused these sentiments (as the novelist Vicki Baum did in her novel *A Tale from Bali*), he would merely be reflecting "prevailing European attitudes towards colonialism of the period."[103] By pitting Spies against "petty" Dutch officials in a relative scale of goodness, Hitchcock and Norris deflect from the real issue of colonial lordship by asking, Who's the better white man? If Hitchcock and Norris were reserved in their indictment of Spies's colonial ways, Tessel Pollmann was more forthcoming with her view that there is no contradiction between Spies's "love for the natives" and "quiet appreciation of colonialism" insofar as "colonialism [is] a paternalist protection against modernization."[104] But such subtle distinctions were not easy to make for the natives, since the "Balinese tend to see all white people as Dutch and all Dutch as civil servants. And they were very afraid of civil servants."[105]

Indeed, we are reminded from Sukawati's account that Spies profited from the Balinese and affected a colonial presence as a white man that sent even his cousin, a royal family member, cowering in fear. But Spies was German, not Dutch. The extent to which he was perceived as colonial and wielded control over policies of Balinization was complicated not only by this fact but also by the way he was thought to be a "friend" of the Balinese. Yet Spies's political influence was evident as he hosted such eminent figures as the Dutch viceroy, British aristocracy, and Hollywood stars. Regardless of his true intentions, Spies helped materialize the colonial fantasy of Bali as a land steeped in "traditions." For instance, his "beautiful photographs" of the mystic, agrarian landscapes and "nativized" practices of Bali were reprinted for the tourist brochures of a powerful Dutch shipping conglomerate, the Koninklijke Paketvaart Maatschappij (KPM).[106] Spies's influence in this regard is further inscribed in a new painting style that he helped create in Bali known as the Pita Maha, whose dominant subject matter was local everyday scenes.[107] In short, Spies was credited for putting the "profuse diversity of [Bali's] cultural riches" on the world map while reifying a Western exotic imaginary of the island.[108] Those who praised him note he was selfless, facilitating, and remarkably generous as a grassroots figure. Others tied him to Dutch colonialism as he determined what constituted "authentic" Balinese "traditions" and what kept the Balinese "happy."[109] In a telling discussion with one of his expatriate associates, Spies sought to preserve the Balinese way of life from foreign influences and even wanted legislation to "make of Bali a national or international park."[110]

The "international park" that Spies imagined for Bali in the abstract became concretized through his role as a "tour guide" and cultural attaché for a glittering constellation of foreign guests. Casting such a tropic spell, Bali became a legendary destination in the 1930s and thereafter for a primarily Western traffic of stars, scholars, millionaires, and diplomats. Forming a circuit of liberal bohemians and travelers, they lived complicated sexual lives even among themselves around Spies's residence in the Campuan area of Ubud. Spies's living compound is characterized as "open-door residences" affecting a blend of "the salon, the café, and the academic equipe."[111] He was said to have "led the life of a young Berlin homosexual in a Christopher Isherwood atmosphere of art and travel."[112] Hedonism and sexual excess were encoded in these conceptions. To further evince modishness, Spies's name routinely circulated in the "salons of New York, Paris and Berlin" at the height of his reputation.[113]

Neither tourists nor travelers, Spies's prominent guests considered themselves the "cognoscenti" of Bali and conveyed their "insider" knowledge throughout the world with their work and social connections. The effects of their individual and combined work in this regard are too large to cover here, but a famous example would be Margaret Mead, one of the most prominent anthropologists in the Western academy. Spies led Mead to field sites and served as her commentator and "local" contact. Under his guidance, she pioneered the use of photography for fieldwork and ingrained the trance character of Bali through such classics as *Trance and Dance in Bali*, *Learning to Dance in Bali*, and *Karba's First Years* from 1936 to 1938. Mead was just one of many who fomented Bali's trance-consciousness (promoted tirelessly by Spies) as the island's intrinsic character.

Such a "possessive" vision of Bali was central to Spies's curatorial work at the Paris Colonial Exhibition in 1931, when he was appointed by the Netherlands Indies Government to be in charge of the exhibits of the Dutch East Indies. This spectacular Parisian event was one of the last installations of this sort in the modern era. It took three years to build a festive "world stage" on 110 hectares of scenic land around a lake, and eight million people were said to have visited the exhibition.[114] Configured as an amusement park, it was also a cultural battlefield where imperial powers strove to outdo each other with ostentatious displays of colonial possessions, including "native" people. It was an opportunity to display the spoils from the colonies and to discover or learn all about native magic, from African "primitivism" to Balinese "mysticism." To facilitate this colonial pedagogy, Spies staged a medley of Balinese dances that included numbers called "Gong, Gong dance, Kebyar, Janger, Lasem, Legong, Baris, Rakshasa and Barong."[115] Significantly, the Calonarang dance was held up as the centerpiece for its trance and ritual value.[116] This was evidently an effort on Spies's part to promote the idea that native magic was quintessential to Balinese culture.

Notably, Antonin Artaud, an avant-garde French theater theorist and director, was among the audience in this colonial amusement park.[117] Artaud was unduly fascinated with the assortment of Balinese dances that Spies had carefully chosen for the event and would leave the exhibition to write the influential manifesto *The Theatre and Its Double*.[118] Using what he saw of the incomplete and decontexualized Balinese dances, Artaud would (in)famously consolidate the image of Bali as "mystical" and "exotic." He would also theorize Balinese dance as a metaphysical and ritualistic expression of "three-dimensional hieroglyphs" and "mysterious signs."[119] Another testament to Spies's influential legacy, Artaud's writing based on his fantasy mapped onto Spies's as well as the colonial projection of Bali would become a cornerstone for many influential Western performance theories and theater practices in the twentieth century.

Framing *Kecak* in *Island of Demons*

There is a sense, I think, in which it would be true to say that
all dancing in Bali is related to trance-consciousness.
—Beryl de Zoete and Walter Spies,
Dance and Drama in Bali

The 1931 orientalist film *Island of Demons*, directed by Victor von Plessen and Friedrich Dahlsheim, provided the occasion for Walter Spies to choreograph a dance section that would be subsequently known as *kecak*. Having arrived in Bali from German high society, von Plessen and Dahlsheim turned to Spies as the one who could provide them access to Bali. They were evidently aware that he wielded "considerable influence [even] on the Dutch authorities and was often called upon to give advice."[120] According to a Dutch civil servant, "Spies had been to the most remote and almost inaccessible villages, and since he always had a receptive ear for what the villagers had to tell, he heard of many things the administration was never told. But when the people saw me traveling regularly in his company, I too gained their trust."[121] For *Island of Demons*, one of Bali's exorcistic trance dances, the Sanghyang Dedari, or angel dance, would provide the spectacle for the island's possession by good and evil spirits.

The narrative in the film is based on a series of contrasts (terror/ security, sickness/cure, amok/balance) tied to the spiritual and integrative mechanisms of a well-ordered Balinese society. This silent, black and white film features a thin plot about a pair of young heterosexual lovers whose courtship in their serene village is temporarily disrupted by the evil witch Rangda, incarnated as an ostracized and bitter old woman. Rangda's exploits would wreak havoc on the village and cause disharmony, imbalance, and unhappiness. At the film's resolution, Rangda is purged when the villagers come together to enact a cleansing ritual, and a state of harmony and order is thereby restored. Notably, Bali's cultural and ritual landscapes are captured in this film with lush cinematographic visions of reflective rice terraces, blood-spilling cockfights, and verdant tropical foliage. These are juxtaposed with images of children who never stop smiling, contented bare-breasted women doing their domestic chores, and scores of happy naked men in natural bathing pools. Such a bright side to Bali is counterbalanced with the darker side involving trance rituals, witches, and epidemics.

As the film's "cultural adviser" and "ethnographer,"[122] Spies exerted a dramaturgical influence that can be perceived on a number of counts, from its spiritual themes to the cinematographic images of rice paddies and lush tropical forestry. However, the most lasting contribution he made to the film is in the ritual cleansing segment, where he purportedly made key changes to a Sanghyang trance dance that resulted in *kecak*. Scholars who write about *kecak* invariably cite the film as its germinating ground, arguing that Spies "remodelled the Kecak dance"[123] or engaged in the "invention of a completely new Balinese dance form."[124] Although accounts of *kecak*'s origins are clouded in conjecture, Spies figured solely in all of them as the "inspiration," "collaborator," "choreographer," "director," and even "inventor" of *kecak*. From I Made Bandem and I Wayan Dibia to Hans Rhodius, Adrian Vickers, Kathy Foley, Craig Latrell, Michel Picard, Michael Hitchcock, Lucy Norris, Claudia Orenstein, and Philip McKean, Balinese studies and theater scholars have all credited Spies as the principal or collaborating choreographer of *kecak* using the film as source material.[125] The fascination of these accounts is primarily centered on Spies taking liberties with notions of Balinese exoticism and concretizing them in a form of dance-drama.

It is important to note that credit for the development of this performance ritual has also been given to four different Balinese men: Ida Bagus Mudiara from Bona, I Limbak from Bedulu, and I Gusti Lanang Oka and I Nengah Mudarya from Bona.[126] In addition, there are also strangely perfunctory mentions of two women, Katherine Mershon and Rose Covarrubias, involved in the production. When mentioned in various writing, both women are given cursory attention with very imprecise descriptions of their work: "Some also believe that the American choreographer Katherine Mershon who was in Bali at the time, also helped to create this new dramatic form";[127] "One of the dances in the picture, the *kecak* dance from the *Ramayana*, was directed by Spies together with Rose Covarrubias."[128] Given the paltry records, the gendered dimensions of *kecak*'s staging certainly require more critical attention from these largely obliterated female perspectives.[129]

As for the four aforementioned Balinese men, each was said to have taken comparable and different artistic initiatives under particular circumstances. These include personal inspiration, royal commissioning, or collaboration with Spies. In some cases, the innovations were believed to be coterminous developments, so that inspiration for using the *Ramayana* epic, for instance, happened "at the same time" in different places.[130] With much debate about *kecak*'s discourse of "origins," there is simply not one site that is definitively "where it all happened." Importantly, however, the theater historian Claudia Orenstein has suggested, "the Balinese did not simply provide the materials out of which Spies constructed something new; they were actively involved in the creative process. The difficulty we encounter tracing the origins of the *kecak* derives from the strong desire of Spies, Limbak, Mudiara, and whoever else was involved that we view *kecak* as purely Balinese."[131]

Indeed, even Spies himself tried to veil his contribution to the form, noting in his coauthored *Dance and Drama in Bali* that while "certain Europeans" were involved in the "creative effort which established the astonishing ensemble," "*Ketjak* was of purely Balinese inspiration."[132] In her analysis of *kecak*, the Asian theater specialist Kathy Foley has pointed out that even though the performance genre of *kecak* would seem "prototypically Balinese" to most tourists, it is more accurately a "fusion" piece.[133] She means to highlight Spies's involvement in the development of *kecak* as a "spin-off of a collaboration" he undertook while consulting for the film *Island of Demons*.[134] Implying the intercultural roots of its formation, Foley suggests nonetheless that *kecak* has been "made by the Balinese in recent years as an indigenous art genre."[135] In contrast to Foley and others, there is a seal of Balinese authentication about *kecak*'s cultural identity that comes in I Wayan Dibia's authoritative claim, notwithstanding any intercultural encounter, that *kecak* is Balinese right from the start.[136] I Wayan Dibia is the rector of the Indonesia Institute of the Arts (STSI) and a master choreographer of *kecak*. One might identify this as a Balinese claim on a Balinese form. In this regard, Dibia exhorts readers of his book to view I Gusti Lanang and I Nengah Mudarya as "the Father(s) of Kecak Ramayana."[137]

While the controversy over *kecak*'s cultural identity is tied to complex questions of Bali's postcolonial cultural affirmation, Spies's work in *kecak* is nonetheless documented in *Island of Demons* as an example of an artist's exotic vision produced in collaboration with others. In the film, *kecak* was interpolated in a climactic Barong versus Rangda showdown through a series of phantasmatic frames. They depicted the trance exorcism taking place in the bodies and intercession of two young entranced Balinese female dancers incarnating the nymphs. The girls are the staple feature of the Sanghyang Dedari, and they are thought to channel demigoddesses for ritual purification. The name of the dance form is a tribute to the "Honoured Goddess Nymphs."[138] As proof that they are in the possessive spell of the nymphs, the girls tread on red-hot cinders without pain or injury.[139] In *Island of Demons*, the trance ritual appeared to be an excerpt or a close variation of the Sanghyang Dedari. It also functions as part of a narrative device to exorcise the evil spirit of Rangda channeled through the body of the old woman.

In the narrative of the film, the woman was portrayed as an outcast who goes to the "old, hellish temple" to make sacrifices. Her ominous identity as a long-haired local witch was signified by her wretched isolation and the hysterical cries of children who caught sight of her. This woman was believed to have provided a young man later identified as "the son of the witch" some kind of "magic oil" that was subsequently applied on the spur of a prized cock.[140] On the "day of the great cock-fight," Lombos, a male villager down on his luck, was gambling that his cock would earn him all the money he needed to recover from his substantial debts. The debt collector just visited him, and he was desperate. Unfortunately, his cock was killed by his nemesis with the "magic oil" in a spectacle watched by hundreds of bare-chested Balinese men. The men are clad only in their sarongs and huddled in crowded, expectant circles around the bloody cockfight. Lombos's misfortune and humiliation were quickly framed as the result of the witch's spells, and Bali became swarmed by darkness, demonic epiphanies, and all kinds of sick, dysfunctional behavior. Everywhere children were weeping and perennially smiling faces turned dismal. Such a terrible disharmony provided the context for the performance of Sanghyang Dedari, which is ordinarily performed in villages "to ward off or mitigate an epidemic or other disaster."[141] In the film, the female chorus sang the *kidung* to invite the goddesses as the girls were quickly induced into a trance while being purified by smoke. Once the trance was engaged, the male *cak* chorus took over with the vocalizations for the girls' trance dance and became the dominant spectacle. Evil is purged when the witch is exterminated by the ritualistic spell of the worshippers doing the Sanghyang Dedari, and harmony is once again restored in the Balinese village.

It is apparent that Spies wove documentation of various Balinese dances and ritual to highlight local witchcraft and exorcistic practices. This was clearly the thematic focus of a film with a title like *Island of Demons*. To intensify the chaos and mysticism of trance encounters, phantasmatic images of Barong and Rangda were superimposed on each other and enmeshed with the throbbing actions of the *cak* chorus as their chanting accelerated in volume. For a contemporary audience, the editing sequence during this climactic showdown appeared reminiscent of horror films, and the *cak* beats heightened its dramatic effect. In a way, Spies assured the authenticity of the scenes by choosing a highly sacred ritual like Sanghyang Dedari and exploiting the sickness/cure theme as a function of the island's spiritual culture. But the focus on the *cak* chorus and the effectiveness of its choreographic intensity appear to only obfuscate Spies's choreographic recomposition of this form into *kecak*. Nonetheless, these choices not only showed that he was privy to the most rarefied spaces in Bali, but also exposed the audience to the "real" Bali, as it were.

Conclusion

Ethnographers, tourists, and artists have all had their field day on the exotic Balinese landscape, and Bali continues to be called the island of dance, gods, temples, demons, and taboo. This is not just a discourse but also an art of the Balinese exotic. So prolific and powerful is this imaginary that it seems to subsume all accounts of Bali in its dominant narrative while purporting to be merely telling the truth of the matter. As I have shown in this chapter, the tropic spell of the Balinese exotic is at once a performative and a performance. Yet, much of the spell is obfuscated by the naturalization of certain colonial frames and even critical approaches toward Balinese performance. They continue to privilege patriarchal, heteronormative, and other such "proper" frames of analysis without addressing the possible appeal and complication produced by queer encounters.

The contemporary popular fixation on Bali as "paradise" is the legacy of Dutch policies as well as an influential enclave of Western "cultural colonists."[142] Spies's "glittering international orbit of artists and intellectuals" helped to suture this now deeply ingrained belief.[143] His expatriate "salon" and "academic equipe" were a tropic spell of anthropological work, high tourism, colonial cocktails, and artistic work that conjured up the island's seemingly indissoluble exoticism. In the years since, the Balinese themselves have turned the spells of exoticism into a global tourist and art industry, and even perhaps a "fact of life." Meanwhile, scholars grappling with the illusory and imaginary discourse of Balinese exoticism have queried about its representational cost: Is not the popular appeal of Bali as the blissful "last paradise" a colonial spell that negates native agency with touristic aestheticism? What histories, politics, and other imaginative possibilities are obliterated by the dominant visualizations and fantasies of Bali as hopelessly exotic and erotic? For whom does the constancy of this label serve, and at what cost? Is there a Bali outside this mythic discourse, or is the superlative performative—"Bali really *is* magical!"—part of the pleasure and ritual of knowing Bali? The epistemology of the Balinese spell is a site of frequent invocation in many critical discourses, but how do "we" know what "we" think "we" know about Bali?

Attesting to the power of this discursive enchantment, the anthropologist James Boon declares that "[e]veryone has heard of Bali, if not in touristic lore saluting this supposed tropical Shangri-La, then in news dispatches concerning either the devastating volcano eruption in 1963 that obliterated lives, villages, temples, and precious paddy, or the massacres during 1965-6 that eliminated tens of thousands of suspected Communist party sympathizers."[144] The 1965 military coup, for instance, was reported with an exotic flair: "The populations of whole villages were executed, the victims either shot with automatic weapons or hacked to death with knives and machetes. Some of the killers said to have drunk the blood of their victims or to have gloated over the numbers of people they put to death."[145] As the political historian Geoffrey Robinson notes, the massacre was written as if to corroborate the "proof of Bali's presumed exoticism or as an unpleasant anomaly that would be better forgotten."[146] Boon's and Robinson's observations are remarkable in the context of Bali's longer colonial history. We might consider the "calm and dignified manner" in which the suspected communists allegedly allowed their execution as an atavistic reference to the European narrative of *puputan* describing the "ritual" or "mass suicide" of the "heroic" but "tragic" Balinese in Badung in 1906 and Klungkung in 1908.[147] These recurring themes of slaughter, sacrifice, offerings to gods, uncontrolled emotion, and impotence point to the lasting reiterative logics of an exotic discourse that is also marked by the native boy's absent presence.

As my study of *kecak* demonstrates, the critical notion of Bali as always already magical unveils each truth-claiming experience of wonder as merely derivative of prior discourses. This colonial performativity of Bali precedes, constrains, and exceeds any representation that performs or partakes of Bali-ness.[148] Today, that discourse has become so dominant that its tropic spells are cast on every conceivable subject on Bali, and to all and sundry: from tourists who want a good time at its beach bars and spas, to global reporters and advertisers profiling the island, writers for Bali's tourist information literature, witnesses of Balinese animist-influenced Hindu practices, performers of its myriad entrancing rituals, and men wearing beautiful gender-bending sarongs.

Clearly, in this day and age, doing the deeds of exotica is no longer the domain of Westerners who want to talk and view things "Balinese." Today, the so-called Balinese natives fashion their modernity using the spells that first magically possessed foreigners and out of which Bali, now always already possessed, reifies its exoticism. In this regard, it is ever more crucial that the coupling of colonial white man and native boy in *kecak* be engaged as a queer, possessive trope hovering over the tropical landscape and performance cultures of exotic Bali.

2

THE GLOBAL ASIAN QUEER BOYS OF SINGAPORE

too long sentence

From Bali to Singapore, the transmogrification of the classic white man/brown boy configuration into the postcolonial father-state vis-à-vis its gay citizenry presents a conceptual iteration of the dyad with its own erotic, juridical, and performative spells. This "twist" involves unlikely bedfellows, the Singapore father-state and partying gay boys, intertwined in queer positions that are sometimes fabulous and sometimes bizarre. For both parties, these are often compromising positions that have a set of requisite, if also incriminating, role-play: the state is an unctuous but also leering patriarch, while gay men with sizeable disposable incomes are wild, promiscuous boys performing for him in rainbow gear. The dyad, to put it bluntly, is now ramified in the cultural policies, national legislature, and queer theaters of a postcolonial Asian city-state, particularly around issues of homosexuality.

dyad is moe politically charged and invested in the culture

This inextricable twosome has a long history, and is allegorical of the colonial coupling of yesteryear. Even as the differential power and erotic adjustments of this postcolonial scenario are unique for the dyad, the queer encounter of the Singapore father-state and its gay populace is curiously conjugated by the tropic spells of the dyad in new form. It is embroiled in the "magic" of religious, commercial, and state action at once catholic, contradictory, and world making for local queers. In other words, the queerness of the colonial dyad is regenerated as a complex of disciplinary and neoliberal sexual logics in a postcolonial and transnational site. And with that move from early-twentieth-century Bali to contemporary Singapore across the Java Sea, brown boys have also turned into global Asian queer boys.

The global Asian queer boy, or the native boy in transnational drag, is the trope at the heart of this chapter. Using Singapore as a test site, this chapter examines how the boy references colonial legacies in global/local iterations of erotic power play afforded by the tropic positions constituting the dyad, and thereby extends the book's assembly of queer reading practices of performance in the Asias. That is, the spell of the boy's exotic sexuality differently staged through queer scenarios vis-à-vis the Singapore father-state, like the brown boy on display for the colonial, serve as critiques of discursive formations about Asian (auto) exotic and erotic positions. These positions are tied to the state's as well as the boy's peculiar places in the transnational world.

On the Singapore Sling

Performance is particularly useful for parsing the dyad's impact on the sexual and representational politics of queer Singapore in national and transnational terms. It provides a critical vocabulary for the myriad spells hovering over local gay men as global Asian queer boys and abject homosexuals simultaneously. This peculiar Asian encounter and its postcolonial politics are vividly found in the country's English-language gay theater, a major venue of the boy's new middle-class struggles.

By the new millennium, the curtains are completely unfurled for the Singapore boy to come out with a paradoxical aura of sexual charge, commercial viability, and abjection by the state. From the pink stages of state-funded theaters, global city blueprints, and gay saunas, bars, and parties to a public pushback campaign by the local Christian right wing against the "homosexual agenda," queerness is seemingly ubiquitous, rising to a level never seen in public consumption, visibility, and debate before 2000. If one were to spotlight the boys sashaying their hips on the semiotic catwalks of Singapore's queering, one would see them swishing to one side as fabulous theatrical stars with their tops off, and then to the other side as sodomite-criminals caught in flagrante delicto with their pants down. I am referring to the saturation of queer theater and widely disseminated images of its often shirtless or naked male leads, on the one hand, and the retention of the colonial-era statute 377A (criminalizing consensual sex between men), on the other hand.

More than just a sideshow, the global Asian queer boy's movements on this tropical island are closely watched by politicians, censors, audience members, and religious activists, who view his pelvic thrusts and hip action—whether they be flouncing, sapless, or seductive—as part of the country's economic, cultural, and moral destiny. He is strapped, so to speak, on the Singapore Sling with chains of binding and titillating possibilities, not all good or all bad. His performance on- and off-stage, on the street or on the Singapore Sling (not the cocktail), is a crucial space for interrogating what is or is not allowable for queer representation imbricated in the dyad's postcolonial and transnational complex. The state's fatherly position on homosexuality is, after all, informed by the shifting valuations of the free market, Victorian penal codes, U.S.-style evangelical fundamentalism, Western gay liberation movements, and the discourse of Asian values. And the boy's compliance with this unequal role-play is based, in part, on an active reception of the state's control with a more or less consensual use of restraint, fantasy power, and mutual (economic) stimulation.

This give-and-take struggle is embroiled in the covert racialization of transnational imaginaries in unexpected ways. For instance, colonial racial anxieties about the perverse sexuality of natives are "sublimated" in contemporary religious (largely Christian) or cultural ("Asian") prohibitions about their sexual deviancy. One sees in this regard the evangelical, sexual panic of local public officials—predominantly Chinese—who regard homosexuality as a virulent form of contagion substituting for the colonial fear of buggery with or among male natives. Like the racial other, the boy is seen in this regard as diseased or dangerous, as if to uphold the heteronormative, regulatory mandates of an imagined adult majority (by numbers or moral self-selection). As a result, the Singaporean gay male (of any ethnicity) is routinely and "justifiably" infantilized as a boy in need of control or corrective guidance.

Crucially, the import of evangelical Christianity from the West accounts for much of the faith-based spells in the postcolonial state's sexual regulation, especially the heterosexual panic around gay sex. But East Asian cultural mores or ethical systems such as Confucianism are also rhetorically refurbished to nativize a moralist stance against homosexuality. Notably, there is no discussion of homosexuality in the analects of Confucius, apart from a few euphemistic references. It bears note also that Sinocentric Singapore indexed by Confucius often sits uneasily in the national ethos of multicultural cosmopolitanism, and immigration has become one of its symptomatic fracture points. The recent state-sanctioned influx of mainland Chinese immigrants, in particular, has exacerbated intra-ethnic (among local and foreign Chinese) and interethnic tensions.[1] But Singapore has always been an immigrant nation. Among its populace of 5.18 million, over 40 percent of its residents are foreigners and 23 percent of its citizenry are born outside Singapore. The indigenous Malays predates the migrants from China and India under British colonial rule in the nineteenth century, which accelerated trade and established a multiracial environment with Chinese (who became its majority at 79 percent according to the government census in 2009), Arabs, Europeans, Indians, Malays, and Peranakans (Straits-born Chinese). This makes the country's population almost entirely made up of migrants or transnationals, a demographic trend that is on the rise in many global cities. Hence, homogenizing claims by the conservative Right about a monolithic "Singaporean people" bound by tradition or united against homosexuality do not seem to make a lot of sense. In fact, such claims only cave in to right-wing Christian homophobia or a falsely "conservative" Confucianism, while fronted by nationalist notions of cohesion and cultural unity.

Singapore is distinguished from other postcolonial states in its determined efforts to emulate industrial advancements of the West while retaining Asian values. It exemplifies a capitalist—some say "philistine"—modernity.[2] English is the first of the republic's four official languages, which include Malay, Chinese (Mandarin), and Tamil. Singapore is one of the most prosperous countries in the world, and as in many global cities, a potpourri of biennales and arts festivals mark a distinctly postmodern, global, and cosmopolitan urban living. The city-state gained independence from British colonialism in 1965, and is incredibly commercial. Endless mega shopping malls, futuristic entertainment complexes, and financial services grow at a rate that does not seem to have a saturation point. This architecture of consumer control and hyperstimulation prompted the novelist William Gibson to call it "Disneyland with a Death Sentence." The government's official rhetoric and policies, anchored in economic rationality, have come to embody the national culture.[3] Its statesmen often point to and reiterate the five Cs—cash, credit card, car, condominium, and country club—as the touchstone of personal fulfillment in Singapore, and many citizen pursuits appear to follow the script.[4] Singapore's globalism is also eminent among Asian countries. It has one of the freest economies in the world, and is consistently ranked at the top or near the top of surveys about the world's most globally connected economies in the past decade. Surprising many of its critics, it also topped the list on the companion Cultural Globalization Index in 2004.[5]

Consequently, a paradoxical queer formation emerges at the intersection of multiple public spheres and (often) conflicting discourses, from the conservative/commercial, traditional/neoliberal, diasporic/regional to national/global. In an important study, Audrey Yue locates creative queer Singapore as a space that sanctions "the illiberal pragmatics of cultural production."[6] While inventive possibilities abound for the Singapore boy in these spaces, he is also haunted by the afterlives of colonialism. In other words, while he may play with the tricks of transnational capital as a sexy global Asian queer boy, he is also under the duress of Western colonial, moral, and religious dictates with a disciplinary Asian cover: the postcolonial daddy with a Sling in hand.

Glocalqueering   —definition of terms

The vicissitudes of queer modernity in Singapore revolve around the native boy as a problematic of gay sexuality in the cosmopolitan postcolony. For the Singaporean gay male, this condition is neither simply a sentence in the colonial daddy complex nor a form of agency that is wholly efficacious. Rather, he is caught between and betwixt a constellation of postcolonial, dyadic positions with different representational stakes, histories, and socio-erotic consciousnesses.

The boy's predicament, I argue, is transformative of observations about Singapore's queer politics (as solely derivative of the West), exotic authoritarianism, and insipid cultural consciousness. Furthermore, it uncovers how the queer erotics of colonial encounter inform Asian performance in global perspective, and makes a case for a different epistemology, what I call "glocalqueering" in performance. A glocalqueering matrix reveals complex circuits of mobility that follow neither a model of bilateral cultural transmission (West to East and vice versa), nor a contextual study of national productions that attempts to locate in this case a quintessential Singaporean queerness. It configures an inter-Asian diasporic framework that produces new models of cross-cultural understanding about queer sexuality aligned with recent studies that imagine alternative ways of conceptualizing traditions, affiliations, kinship, genealogies, and citizenship.

My use of the term "queering" in this global and transnational context refers to the theater of Singapore's dramatic if also dubious transformation from draconian father-state to Asia's short-lived gay capital at the outset of the new millennium. The act or performance of queering signifies a number of referents. In sociolinguistic queer theory, for example, queering may be said to be a performative act pronouncing or recuperating the visibility of queer lives. Singapore's queering encompasses the rise of the nation's gay and lesbian theater; the rapid development of queer social infrastructures like gay bars and real estate; the consequent media visibility of gay men and lesbians in the public eye; and transnational events such as the Nation Party, which for a few short years gained the reputation of being Asia's Mardi Gras. This process is further bolstered by the state's embrace of queer capital as a form of creative technology, the open employment of gay individuals in government agencies, and the profitability of pink-dollar industries in the form of gay and lesbian tourism, entrepreneurship, and consumerism.

Glocalqueering bears these conditions in mind while formulating an alternative way to understand the exigencies and efficacies of doing queer acts in a transnational site. One of the major theoretical gambits of glocalqueering is its disorganization of the dominant East-West comparative paradigm and its epistemic strongholds, which have tended to dictate a set of debates attuned largely to Western sexual contingencies. If we are to imagine otherwise, the rhetoric and ethos of discussion must involve a multidimensional shift (spatial, temporal, ocular, tactile, aural) that incorporates regional interactions elsewhere, other eroto-historiographic temporalities, and new analytic frames. For instance, is an "interesting" debate on transnational Asian queerness always only defined and thinkable in contradistinction to Western epistemic categories and their limitations? Can queerness be thought across lateral and proximate sites in and across Asia, the Middle East, and Africa?

Recent scholarship suggests that the study of global queer or same-sex formations is delimited because the dominance of Western homosexuality presumes a universal set of political or erotic preoccupations, an "uncorrectable" myopia, as it were. In the United States alone, the singular issue of gay marriage has come to epitomize its latest, rights-based, homonormative progress narrative.[7] For over a decade since the 1990s, critics have debated whether the global propagation of Western gay culture is a progressive development helping to liberate sexual minorities in Third World countries. Called "global queering" by some theorists, this neoliberal model of free market transmission, by which an emancipatory and often glamorized Western gay culture is transforming the rest of the world, presumes a primarily North American and secondarily European standard constituting what we think of as "'modern' homosexuality."[8] Those who take a celebratory stance often champion a "universal gay identity" as the basis for a rights-based struggle or community organizing against homosexual invisibility and oppression. In other words, homosexuals around the world will learn the language of political sexual movements, and articulate their sexuality through identitarian narratives (including but not limited to "coming out" stories, LGBT theater, Pride marches, and sexual identity markers) with the modernization or globalization of their societies. Those with a more skeptical view see this as a "reproduction of versions of U.S.-style gay/queer identities/communities" in countries of the "South" or "Third World."[9]

On some level, "global queering" theorists are expanding historical studies showing how industrialization and capitalism created the conditions that made possible "the emergence of a distinctive gay and lesbian identity."[10] These studies based on European and U.S. contexts are now globalized to encompass the world of developing economies, particularly in the "non-West." The international queer subject with an urban sexual identity and taste attuned to the middle-class white gay male—Broadway musicals, Equinox gyms, cruises around the world— is thus a prominent "marker of modernity" in world cities.[11] Bridging a universalist approach to gay identity and a modern way of life, emerging narratives of "global queering" are readily identified in a wide variety of places, from Buenos Aires to Tel Aviv to Singapore. They are often organized around a coherent or "respectable" sexual identity such as the middle-class gay or lesbian household or consumer base. In the world at large vis-à-vis the West, same-sex diversity is increasingly based on an international taxonomy that reinscribes (if inadvertently) divisions along Western/non-Western sites. Consequently, the world is calibrated by geographic and national distinctions constituting a global spread with a familiar Western political agenda for all sexual minorities: from oppression to liberation, from backwater invisibility to defined, modern sexual identity. Additionally, an enumerative list of "discoverable" terms, from *kathoey* (Indonesia) to *bakla* (Philippines), *mati* (Suriname), *litwa* (Middle East), and *tongzhi* (China), is offered as an alternative to the Western terms lesbian, gay, bisexual, transgender, queer, and intersex.

While inclusive in its nod to diversity, Western sexual exceptionalism and narratives are often left uninterrogated as the basis for organizing various ethnographic, historical, and literary studies of the other "gay." Though the term "gay" is a more or less defined and politicized sexual identity in the West, its usage in multilingual Singapore is less certain; hence, a short but crucial note on sexual terminology is warranted at this point. I use the term in its common local usage among English speakers as a polysemic, subcultural sign for homoerotic/ sexual practices of and between men. "Gay" and "homosexual" have been used interchangeably by the state in medical, criminal, and sexual classifications of men in this grouping. In contrast, I use "queer" as a root term to problematize any normalizing conception of sexual identity, and to indicate Singapore's turn to queer capital to further its artistic ambitions as the regional cultural hub. Notably, one or all of the three above-mentioned English terms—though not the colloquial and/ or pidginized terms in Chinese, Malay, Tamil, and their respective dialects—may be used to describe the sexual identity and/or practice of the nonheteronormative Singaporean male, depending on the context, class, ethnicity, personal preference, and understanding of these usages. Generally speaking, "gay" rather than "queer" is more commonly used in the local parlance for personal sexual identification or as a sign of male homosexuality. However, due to Singapore's complex linguistic situation and the inconsistency in usage, there is really no one definitive way to use each of these subcultural terms. There is also a plethora of local terms for queer identities and other shaming epithets. What bears noting is that the terminology for homoerotics in performance is complicated by postcolonial history, multilingualism, differentials in sociocultural positioning, the varieties of English used, and the rise (or end) of queer theoretical models from the West.

Attending to such nuances of cultural production in the queer Asias means that undoing vertical power relations with the West on top has to become *less* of a singular quest. This is particularly crucial as the politics of sexual lexicon and legibility—what terms to use, what issues are important or even intelligible to the so-called non-Western sexualities— have dominated discussions of transnational sexualities and intercultural performance. For instance, the liberal, Western slant of using a term like "gay" or even "queer" becomes a fraught issue when tied to narratives of sexual progress and Western modernity. Consider an all too familiar question about the simultaneously capacious and self-reflexive deployment of these terms, which often ends up reiterating Western biases or impasses of knowledge production just the same: Can we or should we call homoerotic sexual practices in Siberia, Sri Lanka, or Sulawesi queer, lesbian, gay, bisexual, transgender, or intersex, or should we use a less imperialist, local, regional, non-English term?

Rather than revolving around or reacting solely against the white ga(y)ze, a glocalqueering understanding works within the milieu of queer globalizations and diasporas while attending to the ways non-Western homoerotics are racialized by (auto)exotic and (neo)colonial epistemologies, ethnographies, histories, and different genres of queer performance.[12] While engaging in the logics, histories, and contradictions of pragmatic local practices that exploit the currency of queer globalism in myriad ways, it asks how we know what we think we know about the global transmission and formation of queerness in the face of national heterosexism, intercultural modernities, neoliberal regimes, and other critical contexts. In one way, it extends J. K. Gibson-Graham's observation that "[b]y querying globalization and queering the body of capitalism we may open up the space for many alternative scripts and invite a variety of actors to participate in the realization of different outcomes."[13] It is also to think alongside scholars working in the burgeoning fields of queer diasporas and globalization.[14]

If attending to the critical blind spots of existing paradigms necessitates a new set of questions that can be raised about Singapore's queer boys, we might begin by thinking along the lines of an inter-Asian analytic: Who is looking, speaking, or performing for whom? And how can the wagers of such a queer performance be modulated in service of specific political objectives and reading practices that have both local and transnational ramifications? Glocalqueering, in other words, is less a descriptor of identity than a queer politic for survival, and an alternative reading practice in an age of globalization. By "reading," I mean to also include seeing, sensing, hearing, feeling, crying, and thinking, all of which are markers of understanding attuned to performance scholarship. In such a reading, the native boy in transnational drag is like an epistemic emollient for queer feelings. He is an embodied guide who cracks open a set of glocalqueer inquiries tying the colonial to the present, the nation to the region, and the diasporic to the transnational. And he is particularly visible in Singapore's middle-class English-language theater, where gay representation is caught in the politics of the state's queer act(ing) and global mapping.

In the remaining sections of this chapter, I will first do a close reading of *Asian Boys Vol. 1*, by the Malay Singaporean playwright Alfian Sa'at, to elaborate on the significance and stakes of glocalqueering the Asian boy in performance. This groundbreaking gay male theatrical production is an exemplary site to understand the global and inter-Asian queer imaginary. Written in English with Chinese and Malay dialects, the play is cathected in Singapore's transnational economic matrix, performing a global city's highly mediatized queering within "New Asia."[15] It also belongs to a lineage of Singaporean theatrical productions that create "limited cosmopolitan [and sexualized] versions of regional Asia that are connected to but simultaneously contend with the global West."[16]

The chapter wraps up by considering the conceptual pairing of the postcolonial father-state vis-à-vis its gay citizenry as an iteration of the colonial dyad, and the performance politics of such a pairing. I do a historic flashback to the heady years of Singapore's national queering at the outset of the millennium (2000–2004), which established conditions of possibility for a gay public sphere. The father-state's gay awakening and the Singapore boy's cosmopolitan drag constitute a queer, disciplinary relationship that has several implications for queer love and politics, which I will examine using ethnography, the glocal media, and the parliamentary discourse on religion, penal code, and (homo)sexuality. These explorations sum up the possessive spells of the four titular terms of this chapter—"global," "Asian," "queer," "boy"—in a cultural, juridical, and sex war haunted by their binding Western definitions and competing ideologies. They present a different set of tropic spells of the dyad as cast in or through the intersection of theatrical and ethnographic, and postcolonial and religious interventions.

(Re)Making History with Asian Boys

The year is 2000, and a curious, queer spectacle is slowly taking over the theaters and tabloids of Singapore. Gay discos, websites, parties, and performances are sprouting up everywhere one looks. The new millennium is proclaiming an age of careful flamboyance for young professional gay men who have come out in droves to celebrate their public visibility in these new playgrounds. They are the country's global Asian queer boys with spending power and a lot of fabulousness, and the gleeful media is noting the excitement (their own as well as the boys') on the street. Of the shows that are a portal to this sea change, *Asian Boys Vol. 1* is easily the campiest standout, and word of mouth has made it the hottest ticket in town. The show not only marks a brazen turning point in queer theatricality, it also heralds a shift in the repertory of major theater companies; the city would soon be saturated with explicitly gay as well as lesbian and transgender performance. That the boys would drive the ticket sales of not one but multiple theaters seems rather out of place for a country widely perceived to be repressive and antiseptic, the Dullsville of global cities.

Like the boys cruising the streets of queer Singapore, the boys in this play are always shape-shifting, relocating, and never quite at "home." *Asian Boys Vol. 1* is a queer fantasy-extravaganza in an unmarked time and space evocative of the island-state. It tells a languid story of a "goddess sent to earth to save Asian boys from extinction."[17] The play is adapted from *A Dream Play* by August Strindberg, a work that exemplifies the playwright's surrealist experimentations. In Strindberg's conception, his play takes the "disconnected but apparently logical form of a dream: Anything can happen, everything is possible and plausible. Time and space do not exist." Conceiving the mind as a technology of transformative visions enacted onstage, this expressionistic dreamscape weaves "a blend of memories, experiences, pure inventions, absurdities, and improvisations."[18] Part of the enchantment of this dreamer consciousness is the way characters are freed from confining probabilities. Instead, they "split, double, redouble, evaporate, condense, fragment, cohere." A prime example is the play's main character, Agnes, the Daughter of Indra, who descends to earth and becomes embroiled in humanity's foibles. Significantly, *Asian Boys Vol. 1* uses the surreal if also magical transfigurations of such a freeing premise as a condition of possibility for local queers. In the play, Sa'at channels a different Agnes by turning Indra's daughter into a celestial and multicultural fag hag who makes a very queer journey across the homoerotic time-space of Singapore during two centuries, accompanied by a coterie of local gay males thinly veiled as Asian boys. Conjuring such a Strindbergian dreamscape is a way to make "everything (gay) possible and plausible" and to envision a queer history and space in the face of Singapore's ambiguous censorship of homosexuality.

The comparativity of the two plays, however, is limited, as Sa'at's work bears only a cosmetic imprint of Strindberg's surrealism. Rather, *Asian Boys* is emblematic of a "glocalqueering" technology that communicates and cross-codes a glocal and diasporic Asian homoerotics in this global city-state.[19] Told in nine episodes, *Asian Boys Vol. 1* foregrounds the queer underside of historic landscapes by turns fictional, fantastic, and distinctly Singaporean. As a fictional goddess, Agnes is supposedly an Asian queer construct in an international lineage of gay icons, divas, and fabulous beings. She is accompanied by a coterie of multicultural Asian boys (three Chinese, one Malay, one Caucasian), who adopt different gender and ethnic identities, while inhabiting various spatial and temporal zones in Singapore's history. Each of the nine episodes presents a gay site that Agnes and her chaperone, Boy, visit as detached observers, conspirators, disguised characters, critical commentators, intervening higher forces, or heterosexual fundamentalists working for the Singapore government. The historical backdrop of their queer journey runs the gamut from Chinese migration to Nanyang (Singapore) in the nineteenth century, Japanese occupation during the Second World War, the detention of several local presumed Marxists under the Internal Security Act in 1987, and the vibrant transvestite cultural scene on Bugis Street that was part of the city-state's queer past, to contemporary gay life both on the street and online.

Tracking this unpredictable itinerary, the audience follows Agnes's haphazard journey to discover a myriad of gay lives, all tentatively defined in colonial, global, and virtual Singapore. This self-guided tour is described in the program notes as a "happy ride through glorious holes to experience style, phallic monsters, stardust, and macho goddesses."[20] This is not far from the truth as seen through Agnes's eyes, since she meets only homosexuals, queer beings, and gay men on such an island. While the proclamation appears to be a fantastic conception set in an indefinable queer zone, Sa'at is evidently locating these Asian boys and their varied manifestations within the city-state's national history, ambiguous cultural policies, and postcolonial sexual mores. The reference to "glory holes" implicates the audience members as sleazy voyeurs looking through the kaleidoscopic peephole of an erotic history. Sex shops, by the way, are nonexistent in the country.

Staged in the blackbox of The Necessary Stage (TNS) in the symbolic heartland of Singapore, a housing estate known as Marine Parade, this production speaks to several issues raised about glocalqueering in this city-state. TNS is a not-for-profit professional theater company known for its eclectic programs and social consciousness.[21] One of six major arts companies recognized by the National Arts Council, TNS receives funding and support from the state as well as private corporations, and operates out of a performance and office facility at the Marine Parade Community Club.[22] The company was formed in 1987 under the long-standing partnership of the artistic director, Alvin Tan, who is of Peranakan Chinese descent, and Haresh Sharma, the company's Indian resident playwright.[23] In addition to its local commitment to new works and new artists, the company is also global in its outlook.[24]

In addition to *A Dream Play*, the production also credited Roland Barthes's *Fragments: A Lover's Discourse* as a source of inspiration for its many-layered intercultural queer encounters. Gay practices are signified in the play in ways that are reflective of the state's carefully choreographed queering and oblique cultural politics. Fostering a dialogue about history and queer politics in Singapore, *Asian Boys Vol. 1* stages a unique inter-Asian construction of global queerness by drawing on Indian myths, Chinese soap operas, Japanese popular culture, Malay folklore, and Singaporean urban legends, as well as Western gay male iconography. While the play's multiculturalism is arguably part of Singapore's enlightened, cosmopolitan culture, its form of gay critique and representation has to be viewed and understood in light of the country's Censorship Review Committee (CRC) reports in 1992 and 2003.

Both CRC reports state that homosexuality onstage may be explored but cannot be promoted.[25] There is, however, a crucial but ambiguous caveat in the 2003 report. Although "deviant sexual practices" that undermine the "core moral values of society" are disallowed in performance, the 2003 committee recommends taking a "more flexible and contextual approach when dealing with homosexual themes and scenes in content."[26] Some of the key factors influencing this change in policy are "globalization" and "attracting talent."[27] In this regard, the CRC cites the Economic Review Committee (ERC) report of 2003 as having identified talent as the key driver in the new economy: "To attract talent, there are calls for an environment with less restrictive censorship guidelines and more diverse choices."[28]

Notwithstanding the issue of global talent, the CRC report notes that the Media Development Authority of Singapore (MDA) continues to take a "cautious approach towards homosexual content" even as it gives theater "greater leeway" in dealing with "homosexual issues."[29] The concession given to theater is due to its perceived status as an elite form of "arts entertainment."[30] By definition, Singapore's authorities will accept homosexual portrayals as long as they are "non-exploitative" and "non-promotional."[31] In the matter of regulating "homosexual content" in performance, seven committees and ministries are potentially involved in the process of determining or influencing the standards of what is appropriate.[32] Hence, a certain level of bureaucratic ambiguity haunts the boundaries marking a proper portrayal rather than the "promotion" or "exploitation" of homosexuality onstage.[33] As Alvin Tan, the artistic director of TNS, remarks, "The report says that a work can explore but not promote homosexuality. Works that cover homosexuality must then always take the apologetic position. Art is about how a story is told and not having to be preoccupied with how content is managed."[34]

With guidelines about the staging of homosexuality written, relaxed, and written off, Singapore suddenly became the Asian country where "it's in to be out."[35] The influx of queer capital not only helps transform the gay landscapes of Singapore, but also facilitates the dramatic rise of English-language theaters saturated with queer themes. Testing the limits of gay representation in performance, *Asian Boys* actively negotiates the republic's changing and pragmatic governance as it pertains to sexual and cultural practices in a global frame. Singapore's much-desired "diversity quotient"[36] can be enhanced only if its own sexual minorities are no longer subjected to the kind of persecutory surveillance and crackdown that had earned the country such ignominious descriptions as "oppressive" and "authoritarian."[37] Given this context, Singapore's theatricalized Asian boys are participating in the country's sexy makeover and cultural liberalization as they carefully stake out their own places in its official discourses.

Asian Boys Vol. 1 is an example of an original English-language play that exemplifies not only the company's mission statements and transnational influences but also Singapore's multicultural and middle-class sensibility. Both the playwright, Sa'at, and the director of the production, Jeff Chen, are young and exciting new voices in the local theater scene. The play's queer representations are socially motivated commentaries that both produce and are produced by an audience as subcultural as it is thoroughly bourgeois.[38] Playing to nearly sold-out audiences and much media fanfare, *Asian Boys Vol. 1* attracted a mostly young, male audience from professional backgrounds and tertiary institutions. Using explicit images of men in bondage and S & M gear, drag, G-strings, and sailor costumes to advertise the production, the R(A)-rated show highlighted its "salacious elements" to signal that

TNC was not "selling children's theater," and also to indicate the presence of "alternative lifestyles."[39] While professing to balance between the conservative status quo and the marginalized, the production clearly appealed to a queer male audience with its laugh-a-minute anal jokes, queer gags, and overt displays of campy male homoeroticism.

At the start of the play, Agnes, wearing a tacky bridal gown, white feather boa, and tennis shoes, makes a symbolic descent to earth via a fixed, elevated platform set against a sky-blue cyclorama painted with white clouds. As she glides down the ramp used for transitions between scenes, Agnes is accompanied by five voguish Asian boys prancing around her like divine consorts. They are dressed immaculately in neatly pressed white shirts and pants. The mise-en-scène of the production remains basically unchanged throughout the show as the actors rely almost exclusively on gestures, costumes, and performative utterances to evoke new locations. For instance, to mark a scene change, the narrator, Boy, chaperones Agnes to the next historical site by whipping out an IKEA rug from his sling-bag, while singing "A Whole New World" from Disney's *Aladdin*.

Agnes and Boy can be seen as omniscient and global forces incarnated as translocal bodies in Singapore. As a sanctified authority figure that manifests in different forms throughout the play, Agnes is easily read as the transmogrification of the state. And like the Singaporean state, she is scrutinizing, gazing, interrupting, and participating in queer cultures with amusement and judgment. In contrast, Boy is the gay native informant who guides her to understand and accept different versions of homoerotic longings, affiliations, and practices, while wielding the power of subcultural knowledge. The state is exposed and queered in its manifold surveillance, immersion, and fascination with gay practices through Agnes's unstable identity, contingent behavior, and trashy ways. As Agnes and Boy survey the sites of queer possibilities, the viewer is taken on a rainbow ride that revises the epistemologies of truth about Singapore's history. The hidden queerness of historic landscapes—by turns fictional, fantastic, and distinctly Singaporean—is thus uncovered by Agnes and her boys in their acts reprising gay abjection and gay hope.

The boys in the play are scripted as Singapore's queer citizenry, with their own version of national and social histories. They are cast

variously as modern gay men, goddess consorts, migrant coolie work-
ers, Internet chat room addicts, soap opera leads, authority figures,
and drag queens in G-strings and negligees. In one of the more overtly
political scenes, the boys walk out of their roles onstage to take on the
roles of the actual director (Chen), playwright (Sa'at), and an actor of
the play, who are questioned by a puritanical government interrogator
on their gay production. Such instances of defamiliarization are augmented by the nonlinear structure of the play to make visible queer lives
in unexpected spaces and bodies within a context of social justice. The
play enacts stories lifted from the unwritten queer pages of Singapore's
official cultural and political history, and does so randomly because no
official account will acknowledge them. By imbricating gay labor in the
construction of national history, the heteronormative narratives of the
father-state are homoeroticized with a purposefully queer slant to show
that homoerotic attachments existed back then as well as right now.

The play's publicity shots transpose the Frenchmen Pierre et Gilles's
highly stylized and homoerotic fantasy photo-art into Singaporean versions of a sailor boy, S & M bondage boy, mermaid, and diva goddess.[40]
As the first play to use such a fabulous queer aesthetic, *Asian Boys*
locates Singapore through thinly disguised metaphors, multiple sexual
fantasies, and, as its program proclaims, intercultural "wet dreams."[41] In
the production itself, Asian narratives and popular cultures substitute
for the stylized constructions of the photo shoot as both resources and
inspirations for performing gay. There are hardly any props onstage; the
actors mostly use dialogue, innuendo, gesture, and, to some extent, costumes and songs. Mixing Asian religious icons, pop idols, and historical figures such as Brahma, Chage, and Aska, Meena Kumari, *samsui*
women, and Chinese rickshawmen, the play constructs much of its own
erratic montage of queer personages and references that have little or
no Western bearing. Indexing this inter-Asian construction, much of
the stage language is a local patois that cross-codes the country's four
national languages and their respective ethnic dialects. As different
accents interlace the dialogue, phrases in Japanese, Malay, Hokkien,
and even a ridiculous polyglot are also used to serve the dramatic exigencies in various scenes.

The transposition of Western inspiration within an inter-Asian complex of transnational references continues with Agnes as the daughter

Figure 2.1
Asian Boys Vol. 1 postcard publicity
shot of Asian Boy as Sailor Boy.
Reproduced with permission from The
Necessary Stage.

of the supreme god Indra by way of Strindberg's orientalist conception. Clearly, however, Agnes is reimagined from Strindberg's play as a modern-day fag hag with a visible "bad perm" and a poorly defined mission to "help gay people."[42] This bungling supposedly Indian goddess is hilariously performed by a well-known local actress, Nora Samosir, who adds to the role with a few more cross-cultural layers. Samosir is a Batak Indonesian Singaporean who graduated from a Canadian university and subsequently trained in voice studies at London's Central School of Speech and Drama. Code-switching effortlessly in her multiple roles, Samosir's Singaporeanized BBC–style enunciation, *pasar Melayu* (a creolized form of Malay), and Singlish foreground a mishmash of linguistic worlds and an inter-Asian flux of cultural signs.

Right from the play's beginning, the cultural reality of Agnes and the Asian boys is always already unstable. As the goddess slips from one time zone to another, her costumes change from the tacky bridal gown to a Malay sarong to the generic uniform of an official. The politics of transcultural queerness are thus encoded in the very being of Agnes. Her lofty mission to "save mankind from extinction" determines to some extent the visibility of Asian boys and their "originary" tales.[43] Facetiously, the universal referent of "mankind" points to gay men in Singapore, while "extinction" camps up the grave predicament of their cultural annihilation. The parallel construction of Agnes as the state adds yet another layer to this regulatory Divine Order. Agnes's clueless campiness points to the state's spectacular lack of knowledge about gay lives, on the one hand, and its own queering, on the other. With parodic effect, the goddess appears on earth as an overaged beauty pageant contestant who mouths such grand campy clichés as "I want to save the world and make it a better place." Her father, Indra, who speaks with a heavy Singaporean accent, presents her in U.S. cultural terms: "5 feet, 5 inches, and 110 pounds . . . has degrees in cultural anthropology, gender studies, and comparative literature."[44] Following Singapore's embrace of American industries, the goddess's vital statistics are presented in the English system of measurement used almost exclusively by Americans. It is also implied she has an American education, since her academic degrees in gender studies, cultural anthropology, and comparative literature are typical at U.S. research institutions but unavailable at Singaporean universities. These allusions to U.S. cultural and intellectual traditions are looked upon as a kind of divine standard, even as they are inscribed on the somewhat ineffectual goddess herself. Yet, unlike an absolute benchmark, the Americanized meanings mapped onto Agnes's body perform a contested relationship operating on many different levels.

Agnes is both out of this world and intrinsically part of it, a predicament charged with the global condition of interculturalism. This is enacted in the hilariously campy segment in which she answers the question of how she might "save the world" if she were crowned Miss Universe.[45] Despite speaking English fluently, Agnes requests an interpreter because having a translator is "Lagi Glam" ("very glamorous" in Malay and Singlish). A mishmash of influences, the pidginized speech she spouts, and the coterie of world fag icons or "false goddesses" that she ultimately wants to replace as the one to be worshipped (Barbra Streisand, Greta Garbo, Bette Davis, Madonna, Gloria Gaynor, Diana Ross, Ge Lan, Meena Kumari, and Anita Sarawak) point to the intersection of diverse linguistic and queer cultures that positions her uniquely as the new Miss Universe.[46]

In the overlapping worlds of queerness and Singapore, then, intra- and intercultural influences always already collide and congeal in remarkable ways. The Indian derivation of Agnes, particularly the *Natyasastra* legend that implicitly frames the entire dramatic journey, is itself an intercultural product that points to the consortium of Asian influences in the play.[47] In this appropriated Indian myth, the disturbances on "Brahma's perfect creations" on Earth are mapped onto Singapore, the cartographic "little red spot on the face of the Earth."[48] Brahma is the Hindu god of creation recognized for his invention of drama. Within this composite world, Agnes would come to know Singapore as composed of exclusively gay performative spaces spanning two centuries. Queer Singapore is thus created in this postmodern constellation of mythic worlds at once fictional, local, and universal. Since the Hindu mythological reference in the play is an inter-Asian marker of globality, Singaporean gay men are scripted into a larger history and recuperated from their national cultural banishment and discursive absence.

Crucially, Brahma is mentioned to gesture at the origin narrative of the *Natyasastra*. Both the *Natyasastra* and *Asian Boys* frame drama as a mythic site of redemption, inclusiveness, and possibility. In the original narrative of this myth, Indra is said to have commissioned Brahma to create drama as a form of diversion that would help rectify the immoderate sensual pleasure of humans. Drama (*natya*) would become the sacred text known as the fifth Veda. It is said that Brahma staged the first dramatic show with Bharata and his sons, members of the priestly caste, and specially trained actors. Following disturbances by demons at the inaugural show, the performance space was to be ritually cleansed and sanctified thereafter. Significantly, the conflict was resolved by a principle of global inclusiveness, and the greater good of mankind was thereby redeemed. Everyone, including demons, would now be welcome at performances. This tale of origin and new possibilities is related in most accounts of Sanskrit drama and it marks a site of invention, negotiation, and change.[49]

While the ritual and religious significance of this account from the *Natyasastra* is eviscerated in *Asian Boys*, Sa'at appropriates the dramatic frame of an originary Hindu mythological site, twice removed by way of Strindberg, for a deliberately queer purpose. *Asian Boys* retains the inventive possibilities of its Hindu progenitor but substitutes the invention of gay myths in Singapore for the Sanskrit story of dramatic origin. In a campy political maneuver, these gay myths and stories willfully revise Singaporean history and create a political in(ter)vention of male and homoerotic significance. This framing device around multiple queer origins in Singapore takes its cue from Sanskrit literature rather than from dominant Western sources, such as same-sex practices of ancient Greece or the 1969 Stonewall Rebellion in New York City. Such a move not only reclaims the Asian cultural myth of Indian mysticism from Strindberg's conception, but also breaks the myth of the Western origin of gay practices. The principle of global inclusiveness in the Sanskrit story is also an important consideration for the validation of the boys. In this regard, the fictitiously mythic framing of *Asian Boys*, including "all," intimates a gay beginning of Singaporean queer history veiled to avert charges of promoting homosexuality in the country. This implicit queering of the Indian myth itself is an interesting lateral move as its dominant characters—gods (Indra, Brahma), priestly actors (Bharata and his sons), and audience—are all presumably male. Crucially, the disruptive act in this vignette is also a space-clearing gesture for an Indian myth to emerge in New Asia.[50]

Such an alternate myth of queer origin imbues *Asian Boys* with a diasporic genealogy by means of a South Asian dramatic narrative. By uncovering this perverse diasporic history, *Asian Boys* produces a glocalqueering circuit exceeding the formations of the Singapore state, whose rhetoric of multiplicities (multiculturalism, multiracialism, multilingualism) is seen in this regard as being inadequate to or unrepresentative of alternate genealogies that fall outside the national rubric. This queer critique of the state is made manifest in the symbolism of the white costumes worn by the boys and in the spatial displacement of Singapore as the "little red spot" where uniformity is the rule of the day.[51] Red and white are Singapore's national colors. Members of the country's ruling political party, the People's Action Party (PAP), typically wear only white, so the outfit of the boys is an uncanny sartorial reference. Each year, the sea of PAP cadres in white sitting at the elite spectator podium to view the National Day Parade is a formidable display of the party's political success and power.[52] The dominance of PAP, which controls eighty-two out of eighty-four seats in the parliament, has been a sticking point with foreign commentators confounded by the total domination of a single party. As a patriotic reference of its national color, PAP's "whiteness" is used to signal its corruption-free and no-nonsense approach to governance. Yet it is also a paradox for the country's honest and yet unresponsive form of democracy. White is, in other words, also a blind(ing) color, signifying the party's homogenizing and heteronormative dictates, which put the uniform worn by party members—a crisp short-sleeve white shirt with a party pin and pressed, starched white trousers—in a new light. Adopting the same look for a clone effect of a different kind, the boys substitute for the politicians as groupie-like fans who vogue around Agnes. They are alternative white consorts for a queer but nationless Asian community.

The voguing boys lend their shape-shifting arms, shoulders, and hips to queer PAP's intractable policies and heterosexism. They are a queer people's action party with camps of followers out there in search of a more inclusive society. The audience may see their searching and dissenting voices in the context of Singaporean artists who have tried, mainly in vain, to challenge the disciplinary rhetoric of patriarchal officials in relation to art production. For instance, in response to the late theater doyen Kuo Pao Kun's commentary in the local press that state

domination is a "crucial impeding factor" in the development of the
arts in Singapore, Koh Peck Hoon, the deputy director of the National
Arts Council, replied that the "arts cannot be a sphere unto itself and
artists should not arrogate unto themselves the position of sole deci-
sion-makers and agenda-setters in the arts."[53] While the boys in white
are not directly attacking the government or its bureaucratic ideology,
their performative embodiment of PAP in an explicitly sexualized context helps to situate the particular location/localization of the play's
queer sexual politics. These coded markers are opportunistic moments
to queer the state and to enact an oblique political critique; they are
also notably facilitated by staging directions that are often fluid and
slip outside the purview of censors. Yet the political valence of such a
critique in the Singaporean context is also contentious, since it is the
state's investment in global capitalism that enables such a critique. In
this regard, the apparent failure of the state to recognize a queer critique appears to enable the performance of queerness; in other words,
it also performs the state's propensity to simultaneously accommodate
and disavow queerness.

While negotiating the line between a queer critique that is no more
than a celebratory gesture and one that is grounded in social content,
Asian Boys Vol. 1 points to the various modalities of queerness in Singapore that had until recently been all but invisible. In this regard, Agnes
and her boys are like social actors working their way through Singapore's histories, and they urge for more queer work to be done around
the problematics of a glocalqueer visibility. They do so without a fixed
identity, and their action pays no attention to chronological order, fac-
tual verisimilitude, or narrative logic as each episode is staged in rapidly
changing locales and anachronistic time zones. For instance, Agnes's
chaperone performs spells of transport while brandishing a dildo for
navigation. He leans on Agnes, the "Dildo Divinity," and the duo sings
"A Whole New World" as a kind of running gag every time they transport themselves on their IKEA carpet to the next queer scene. But the
couple does not in fact move at all, stationed as they are on the carpet
while the actors for the next scene take their positions onstage. No one
is ever certain where this "Whole New World" is or what its decontextualized "fantastic point of view" may be on the bare stage.[54] The eli-
sion or obscurity of these queer beings is foregrounded when Boy talks

about how he has no history or definable identity, generating only more questions about his unknown origin:

AGNES: Who are you?
BOY: I am a boy. . . . I have no name. You can just call me Boy.[55]

Similarly, none of the other boys has a distinguishing identity or is sustained by any of his gay deeds. The funny and celebratory Disney tune is thus burdened with a graver undertone: the queer longing for "A Whole New World" is perhaps no more than an animated imagination at this point, a perennial elsewhere. In 2000, when the play was produced, the public visibility of gay men was still a matter of careful negotiation with the police; the small but burgeoning subcultural scene of clubs and saunas was still at best an open secret in the country.

The queer use of Disney's soundtrack points to another cultural resource in this gay world linked to the metropolitan West. The boys in the production are sometimes dressed in the Western subcultural style of a sailor boy and display a savvy knowledge about kitschy consumer products like Disney's songs. Yet their relation with Western gay male practices is often a troubled one. For instance, Lost Boy makes the following observation to Agnes about what he has to do to be "gay" following his first outing at a gay pub in Tanjong Pagar:

That I must get a tan. That I should start working out. That I will become a gym-rat disco-bunny with a snake in my pants. No more ugly duckling with chicken legs and pigeon chest. That my one desire is to walk here one day with a tight pink T-shirt with the word "Gorgeous" on it in glitter.[56]

One could argue that the body aesthetic and fashion codes Lost Boy learned that evening are the bread and butter of those who identify as exemplary gay citizens of West Hollywood, Chelsea, and Soho. In any U.S. gift shop with a gay theme, muscle T-shirts emblazoned with "Princess," "Divine," and indeed "Gorgeous" are staple items next to tank tops, disco CDs, and cargo pants. Besides, images of hypereroticized men with buffed bodies and snakes in their pants have become part of Western gay male iconography through the work of such artists as Tom of Finland, physique magazines of the 1950s and early 1960s, and advertisements in just about any gay magazine, website, or bill-board.[57] The aesthetic to which Lost Boy alludes is a commercialized lifestyle, the commodity fetishism purveyed by white middle-class gay men. In dominant images of Western gay representation, the well-chis-eled white male often takes center stage as the model of masculinity.

Significantly, visual representations of gayness in these media are often concomitant with an erasure of individual identity, suggesting that a type forms part of a collective identity. Like the gay icons typi-fied in the West, all the boys at the Tanjong Pagar pub in the play are identified as types rather than individuals with names. Apart from Lost Boy, Agnes and Boy also encounter Bi Boy, Muscle Boy, Social Boy, and Old Boy. Notably, all these boys are somewhat dysfunctional, as if to raise the specter of restrictive identitarian categories of Western gay life. While the nameless encounters appear to be about a problematic Singa-porean sexual identity, they are also not simply about some allegorical Western gay references based on type, looks, and community. Rather, these Singaporean males are conveying the anonymity and secrecy of men seeking other men in the city-state under the threat of constant surveillance. They highlight the troubled visibility of gay men in Singa-pore as a condition of possibility, however fraught, for the Asian boys trying to collectively claim a viable subject position and wield control of their queer representation. At the same time, they signify a conten-tiously configured sexual community within a geopolitical economy that is at once modern, Asiacentric, and accessible only via the privi-leges of a New World Order.

The East Asian matrix of this New World Order is negotiated in the episode fusing Chinese and Japanese encounters in the construction of these theatricalized queer boys. Deftly combining a critique of the state with the queering of Asian popular culture, local Chinese tele-vision melodrama is used to turn the Imperial Japanese Army into a metaphor for state oppression and police surveillance in Singapore. In this segment, two brutal World War II–era Japanese military officers, Lieutenant Tarepanda and Sergeant Sanrio, become surrogates for the Singaporean authorities who had zealously hunted homosexuals in the 1990s, humiliating those entrapped by their undercover operations.

There is a concomitant queering of authority here, as Lt. Tarepanda and Sgt. Sanrio are facetiously named after the contemporary Japanese merchandising empires of a panda bear, Tarepanda, and a corporation, Sanrio Company Ltd., best known for the Hello Kitty line of products. In this way, the tough military identity of the Japanese soldiers is queerly and anachronistically conflated with cute Japanese pop-cultural products that flood the present-day market. Mimicking the unique grammar of short English phrases emblazoned on these pretty Japanese commodities, the officers mouth expressions like "This morning is precious time. You my friend forever. Happy melody."[58] By layering the consuming public's contemporary fascination with these products on the construction of World War II Japanese soldiers, and by inscribing the officers with bizarre qualities exemplified by the sergeant's cutesy excess, such a representation produces a displacement that deforms power. It also directly queers the aesthetic of cute Japanese products and engages an open secret of Singaporean gay men who grew up toting Happy Melody water bottles, My Friend Forever knapsacks, Hello Kitty pencil cases, and various Precious Time curios. Lt. Tarepanda and Sgt. Sanrio are also theatricalized references to the Singaporean police officers who pose as gay men in the antigay operations. The critique of the Singapore police entrapment of homosexuals is made explicit as they converse about the "12 men" in "Tanjong Rhu" whom they have captured:

> LT. TAREPANDA: We will publish their names and faces in the papers! Then we will shave off all their pubic hair and make them bow to the sun. And then we will cane them. Perverts![59]

The men in question directly reference an actual antigay operation in Singapore circa 1993, in which police planted their own boys—known as "pretty police"—around the known cruising areas of Tanjong Rhu.[60] In this infamous sting, twelve men were persecuted for touching or pursuing sexual offers with undercover officers. Adding to their criminal charges, the men also had their names, ages, occupations, and the graphic nature of their encounters published in two Chinese newspapers and one English tabloid-style daily. The offenders all received three strokes of the cane and between two and six months in jail. Such a sensationalistic police entrapment exercise was not new. In March 1992, another similarly well publicized incident occurred with eight arrests.

Four of those arrested had their pictures published in the newspaper and one of them later committed suicide. Following the widely publicized police entrapment operation in 1993, the local performance artist Josef Ng created a nuanced protest performance, for which he was also publicly arrested on grounds of indecency.[61] Officials and journalists who had not seen the performance had sensationalized an inconspicuous segment of Ng's piece during which he snipped off his pubic hair with his back to the audience. Their assessment became the basis for Ng's persecution. There is no doubt that Lt. Tarepanda's call to "shave off all their pubic hair" is a direct reference to this infamous incident. It appears that by decontextualizing these events of queer injustice as instances of Japanese brutality, The Necessary Stage was able to pass the censors of the country's National Arts Council (NAC) who regulate content presented onstage.

Vectors of Understanding Asian Boys

In negotiating the cultural predicaments of queers in this global city-state, *Asian Boys* subtly negotiates state ideology and prohibitions using a glocalqueering mode of production that exceeds such classic dualistic frames as East versus West. The diasporic and inter-Asian dimensions of the production are demonstrated by the boys' embodiment of and/or references to Indian gods, Japanese pop icons, Sanskrit literature, Chinese melodrama, *samsui* women, and Malay urban myths. The construction of queer Agnes and her portrayal by the Singaporean actress also point to yet another conglomeration of Asian influences drawn from Indian, Singaporean, Anglo-Canadian, Batak, and Malay cultural resources and experience that variously instantiate, undercut, and exceed binary structures and relationships. Neither a monolithic Eastern nor a Western framework can account for such a queer construction.

In pointing to the ways that the theatrical production relies on Asia's media, cultural traditions, and commodities to construct Singapore's queer realities, I am not trying to construct an Asiacentric model of queerness devoid of Western references. Rather, the glocalqueering model of analysis I have been advocating brings out the different circuits, affiliations, and practices that constitute Singapore's version of a diasporic, queer Asia. Besides, unlike Euro-American models that emphasize the affirmation of a sexual identity, one that gay social theorists like Dennis Altman rewrite for the world as a "universal gay identity," Singapore's queering manifests more prominently as a set of pragmatic homoerotic practices with many inter-Asian and diasporic resonances. In this regard, the terms of global queering dominated by the global English language, the Euro-American gay lens, and capitalism have to be reassessed not only as a global/local issue but also one that challenges their paradigmatic dominance. The major question is thus not about how well non-Westerners adapt these superoriginary gay identities and practices in making their own queer world; nor is it a politics of representation that reinscribes classic binaries in broad strokes of difference that are ultimately cast in a narrative of sameness.[62]

Significantly also, Singapore's postcolonial governance appears prominently alongside free-market forces and theatrical stagings to simultaneously regulate and carve out spaces for a particular kind of queer performance linked to the country's global economic destiny. Local artists, actors, activists, and gay boys on the street, together with censors, bureaucrats, and evangelicals, are all actively involved or invested in negotiating queer representations as they relate to the citizen-subject of Singapore's political, cultural, and social institutions. But the continental imaginary of "Asia" is always part of the conversation. It bears repeating, then, that "Asian boys" is a contested term in itself, and embroiled in complex models of queer representation. In their global transmogrification, Asian queer boys are figures caught on the cusp of epistemic and political possibilities and impossibilities while embodying Singapore's economic and cultural globalization. This raises many questions about the effectiveness of this kind of queer representation in the context of Singapore. Is the Asian boy an icon of resistance? Or is he no more than a racialized sexual figure dressed up and accessorized with the hip, sexy appeal of queer capital? Is *Asian Boys* a neoliberal production that purports to stage the predicament of queerness in Singapore's postcolonial and postmodern present, but that reduces the nonparticipating male citizen in the country's heteronormative projects of national production—including marriage and parenthood—to no more than a boy with dreamy escapades?

To answer these questions, we have to take a closer look at the conceptual coupling of the postcolonial father-state and its gay citizenry through the politics of the colonial dyad. The details of this dyadic relationship demand a closer look as both an allegory and a model of glocalqueer politics with no easy resolution. In the case of Singapore, the father-state's gay awakening and disciplinary postures toward his gay sons are also queer acts embroiled in the cultural and urban makeovers of a global Asian city. The relationship of the postcolonial daddy and the native boy in high cosmopolitan drag is, in other words, a performance in itself. Under the watchful eyes of the father-state, the boys are both disciplined and liberated by its capitalist ethos, pragmatic governance, and conditional patronage.

In spite of the fanfare around Singapore's "coming out" as a nation, there is little illusion that the patriarch has become altogether queer-friendly; yet the permission to party as consumer-citizens like everyone else in the global gay world is appreciated just the same. This consensual mutual withholding-stimulation is part of being on the Singapore Sling. But it did not happen overnight. The "sudden," performative visibility of a queer public has to be understood in the context of the state's imperative to transform itself from draconian father-state into a sexy, global city in the new millennium. Before we examine the postcolonial daddy's change of heart, let's consider what this all means in terms of what's happening on the street.

Ethnography of Love

Beginning in 2000, I would return to Singapore and see throngs of young people at hip, queer venues concentrated in the central business district and Chinatown areas. Popular gay websites such as www.trevvy.com, www.utopia.com, and www.fridae.com have "up-to-date listings and reviews of all gay places," including "cafes and restaurants," "bathhouses," "spas, masseurs and gyms," and even "public hangouts." A burgeoning critical discourse on sexuality is also gradually being published, including such works as *People Like Us: Sexual Minorities in Singapore* (2003), *SQ21: Singapore Queers in the Twenty-First Century* (2007), and *Queer Singapore: Illiberal Citizenship and Mediated Cultures* (2012). Before the country's perceived liberalization, there was hardly any such writing, and most gay venues were unlisted and operated cautiously underground by word of mouth. For much of the early 1990s,

Vincent's Lounge was the only covert meeting place for gay men in Singapore, and was subjected to numerous "routine checks" by the authorities.[63] In 2012, the people I approached at the bars talked about their sexuality openly, and were nonchalant when reminded about reported (though rare) cases of police entrapment or periodic raids at the saunas.

"The police only comes when drugs are involved," says a server at the bar of Cruise Club, a rather swanky sauna in the heart of Chinatown, "or when another competing sauna calls to complain."[64] At Backstage, a confident young Chinese Singaporean man said, "Things are changing," as we conversed on a balcony where a rainbow flag fluttered outside. Posters of American musicals line the walls of the atmospheric interior. The bar is popular with tourists, expatriates, and a mix of locals, some of whom are into white men, otherwise known as sarong party boys. Just a short walk away are more clubs and bars like the ever popular Tantric and Taboo, as well as spas and massage parlors catering to men by men in remodeled colonial shophouses in Chinatown.[65] Any man I approached at the bar would tell me with wild abandon all the different cruising sites in the area, and what the scene was like at each place. With lychee martinis in hand, young men huddled in close proximity at the bars reported what they saw at the theater or exchanged stories about the city's new sauna. At Tantric and Backstage, I noticed a wide diversity of men. I spoke to a Thai Singaporean, diasporic Chinese from Malaysia, Hong Kong, China, Taiwan, and Indonesia, a few local Malays, Indians, and Chinese, and a handful of white guys from the United States, France, Germany, and Australia. Many of them were flicking a cigarette in one hand while imbibing cocktails with the other in consummate style. It was a predominantly male scene and the men were well dressed, in either tight T-shirts or designer shirts, speaking exclusively in English, and completely at ease. While the crowd was diverse, most were Chinese, and noticeably "gym fit." An American once told me the scene is filled with "shrimps," a derogative term for local men with great muscular bodies but unappealing faces, and, like the crustacean, best consumed headless. What I saw, however, was rather attractive, as if the magic of the global queer had cast a spell to actualize a vision of Asian Adonises in the style of Abercrombie and Fitch. The air was hot and uninhibited, and men were embracing and chatting freely.

Absorbed in this queer space, I wondered whether there was not something strikingly similar between this gay bar and the ones I have visited in Paris, Los Angeles, London, Melbourne, and New York City. The music and interior design, the muscle boys and their dress code were all familiar, as if these boys transcended time and place with an Asian face. Consumption was an index of liberation, and, as if it were not any clearer, a clearly inebriated man from Los Angeles standing next to me chimed loudly, "Can you f——g believe it's Singapore? It might as well be Weho [West Hollywood]!" The drunken drollness of his remark summed up the Western gaze for me: it cannot help trolling the world for the signs of Western queer culture while expressing incredulity at what similarities can be found. Singapore's "coming out" party was a curious spell. One can't argue that the Broadway posters and rainbow flag are iconic of Western gay and lesbian culture. You could order a cosmopolitan or a Bud Lite in a flash. You could dance to Beyoncé and "Moves Like Jagger," said one of the boys.

The spell of queer decontextualization was alluring but ultimately untenable as I looked out the balcony at the local cityscape and saw the bar with different eyes. Nearly everyone was Singaporean or Southeast Asian, speaking English in local/regional accents; the rows of hyper-gentrified colonial shophouses in candy pastel colors were a cruel urban design that only Singapore could dream up and make it work. Also, unlike the West, the white guy is often undesired, particularly at the saunas, and he keeps to his own clique at the bars. More than anything else, having a gay Chinatown, let alone a Chinatown in a country where the Chinese are the majority, is itself a unique paradox. The contradictions are beyond the easy visual correctives that are made to uphold a global Western queerscape. Yet ocular markers have a strong hold on cross-cultural understanding of a global Asian city's queering: media reports on the father-state's gay awakening, for instance, have tended to focus on sensational images of gay male bodies wrapped up in feather boas and swimsuits. They rely, in other words, on the transnational traffic of identifiable queer images, from pink-dollar tourism to dance clubs to upscale saunas.

Any number of these reportages and visual references would seem to confirm the prophecies of "global queering." However, Singapore's newly visible gay was also fighting a different fight while this Eurocentric way of looking funnels critical inquiries into a narrow set of self-interest for the West with little at stake for the locals. And such circular inquiries around the sameness and difference of Western gay culture sound very much like the indifferent exclamation of the enchanted American tourist ("this might as well be Weho"), or other drunken spells of global and national queering.

This ethnographic anecdote, styled ironically after dominant narratives of global queering, stages the power of a compelling sound bite: All over the world in every modern capitalist society, global queer boys are coming out with a universal gay identity that both distinguishes and sets them free within a transnational Gay Pride world. The rise of this prominent performative trope makes it all the more imperative to ask whether such identitarian paradigms of global queering are applicable—or even should be applied—to global cities like Singapore, where the quotidian reality as well as theatrical representations of gay men continue to be policed in both overt and subtle ways by the state. But how did it come to be that the father-state would embrace queer capital by sanctioning the proliferation of explicitly gay-themed theaters, gay bars, and other pink-dollar commerce in the first place—an unprecedented development? Is the queer visibility of the gay Singaporean as a global Asian queer boy a new form of nativization vis-à-vis the new dyad?

"It's In to Be Out!"

On September 14, 2003, Agence France Presse reported the meteoric rise of Singapore as "Asia's new gay capital," and quoted one of the nation's gay entrepreneurs as saying, "The pink dollar in Singapore definitely exists. It is not a myth, it is a fact."[66] News of Singapore's queering had been spreading in rapid media like fire. A month earlier, *Time* magazine declared, "it's in to be out" in Singapore, and tantalized its readers with a teaser, "Got pink dollars to spend? Then head for the Lion City."[67] Its endorsement of Singapore as "a hell of place to party" was quite a departure from "state-inspired dullness and conformity."[68] From the *International Herald Tribune* to the *South China Times*, news agencies around the globe reported Singapore's (homo)sexual liberalization. Amazingly, the magazines went as far as to claim that the "republic's gay life is more open than that of most other cities in Asia, even Hong Kong."[69]

Much of this excitement had been generated after Singapore's incumbent prime minister, Goh Chok Tong, noted, pre–Lady Gaga, that gays are born this way: "So let it evolve, and in time the population will understand that some people are born that way. . . . We are born this way and they are born that way, but they are like you and me."[70] This announcement was significant as it effected a policy change in the country's civil service, which began employing gays even in "sensitive" or high bureaucratic positions.[71] This stunning conversion of policy on local "gay people" would come to be a pivotal, transitional point of their visibility in the country and around the world. The public appeal for their common humanity became a lightning rod for the city-state's gay awakening. Perhaps with wished-for effect, this biological-essentialist "apologia" for gay people was channeled through the international newswire swiftly and with much fanfare.

The theater of Singapore's national queering was opening several new acts for its queer denizens. Multiple gay awakenings became public events within and outside the theater as alternative notions of filiation and sexual citizenship were configured. The gay Nation Party was, for instance, conceived as an expression of alternative patriotism to the National Day Parade celebrating the republic's birthday (August 9, 1965). To the international media, it was "Asia's Mardi Gras," attracting thousands of "pink-dollar"–spending tourists from all over the world, including Taiwan, Hong Kong, Malaysia, Thailand, Australia, Japan, Germany, and the United States.[72] Organized by the "leading regional gay website," Fridae.com, founded by a Chinese Singaporean entrepreneur, the revelry was spread over three days at the country's major tourist attractions. These attractions included the Musical Fountain at Sentosa Island and the Big Splash, a water amusement park with rainbow colored slides. Using the government's language of "diversity," the event touted itself as a "celebration of our diverse communities in Asia, coming together on Singapore's National Day weekend."[73] It was also billed as Singapore's "coming out" party, and endorsed by the government with public licenses. More than 4,500 local participants as well as gay and lesbian tourists from all over the world reportedly joined in the revelry of "Nation:03" spread over the long weekend of the National Day celebration.[74]

The father-state was on the fast track to becoming, if it was not already, a queer nation. Its rising prominence as "Asia's gay entertainment hub"[75] was so notable that an editorial in neighboring Thailand cautioned that the "previously homophobic city-state [of Singapore] . . . will take more gay-tourist money from less gay-friendly Thailand."[76] With characteristic efficiency, the city's queering was augmented by or, some say, saturated with theater productions. Three major gay-themed English-language productions, *Mardi Gras* (by the local theater company The Necessary Stage), *Bent* (by a bilingual local theater company, the Toy Factory), and *The Wedding Banquet: The Musical* (jointly produced by the local production company Fiction Farm and a New York–based Asian American theater company, Second Generation), were staged to sold-out audiences in July and August that year, continuing a trend of hip new productions featuring gay and lesbian lead characters in years to come. In the publicity posters of both *Mardi Gras* and *Bent*, nearly naked men were pictured in explicitly homoerotic poses, evincing a new queer confidence in the theater. These productions theatricalized the postcolonial daddy's queering into a fabulous nation. For many months after that, newswires and regional papers would report how Singapore was "loosening up," turning "pink,"[77] or becoming the gay capital of "Asia"[78] and "Southeast Asia."[79]

Queer capital was now suddenly hip and desirable. With one fell swoop, gay saunas, spas, shops, bars, and discos that were once under the radar became part of the local entertainment geography, and seamlessly integrated into the Chinatown area of the central business district. As a commentator noted in June 2003, the "seven saunas catering exclusively to gay clients" were simply "unthinkable even a few years ago."[80] But less than a year later, there were at least thirteen such saunas or massage centers, and twenty-two venues listed as gay bars and discos online. In 2012, eight gay saunas and countless massage centers continue to operate. At 274 square miles or 710 square kilometers, Singapore is less than six times the size of Rhode Island—the smallest state in the United States—or three and half times the size of Washington, D.C. The plenitude of gay saunas, for example, compared to Rhode Island or Washington, D.C., is, to say the least, rather remarkable.[81] The gay awakening of the father-state was carefully choreographed to link the emergence of global queer boys in its theater, nightlife, and public spaces with the city-state's embrace of queer capital. As the state "acted up" as a queer agent, the insouciant and diffused gay action on the street was also energized and even legitimated in commercial venues and the theater.[82] More and more stories about Singapore's trendy gay night-spots would headline pages of the city's weeklies. Before too long, perfectly coiffed Chinese gay men with their tops off became iconic of the country's cosmopolitan flair. The nation was certainly looking queerer than it had ever been, with the Asian boy as a poster child.

This queer turn with the boy as a proxy of the daddy's makeover is necessitated by a wave of economic exigencies whose currents are never predictable. In 2003, the city-state had not fared very well for many years in the global market, and was reeling from the effects of its frenetic courtship with globalism in the past three decades. The small city-state "relies heavily on the global network of cities where successful corporations of advanced countries have established their businesses."[83] In particular, its economic and social progress is contingent upon the "stability, enterprise and links with the West."[84] Such a structure of global dependencies has meant that its economy is subject to any number of hits as a world trade center. From the Asian financial crisis in 1997, the technology bubble burst, the 9/11 terrorist attacks in New York City in 2001, the bombings in Bali in October 2002, SARS in 2002,[85] the millennial rise of China, and the tsunami earthquakes, to the continuing wars on terrorism, Singapore's electronics-based, export-driven economy and its tourist, retail, manufacturing, and oil refining industries have all been hit by these various crises. New growth paths less vulnerable to external business cycles than the export-driven model on which it had relied had to be imagined.

To the Singapore government's added chagrin, many top talents have passed on chances to work there ostensibly because of its poor standing in cultural freedom and tolerance for sexual diversity.[86] Making matters worse, many accomplished Singaporeans have also left the country for the same reasons. A continuing "brain-drain" is proving extremely costly to a small country where the versatility and talent of its labor force are economic fundamentals—Singapore has virtually no natural resource. Moreover, the economic imperatives that had transformed the colonial outpost to an "Asian Tiger" were no longer as effective in stimulating the development and growth of the wealthy nation-state. Even as it was admired in some quarters for the clockwork efficiency of its governance, critics have also routinely criticized the republic's leadership tactics as negative practices of "corporatism," "hegemony," and "neo-Confucianism," and have described the leadership as an "authoritarian regime" and a "dressed-up dictatorship."[87] They point to the state's continuing legal persecution of oppositional elements and voices of dissent as evidence of state repression. These have attracted widespread media attention on issues of human rights, freedom of expression, and censorship control.[88] Homosexual persecution in the early 1990s via highly sensationalized police entrapments only reiterated the state's surveillance and unprogressive governance.

Constructed in part by queer abjection, Singapore's conventional image as a frighteningly harsh and boring city-state was now read by its leaders as an economic liability and something of a sore spot.[89] Noting its complex challenges, the incumbent prime minister, Goh Chok Tong, called the milieu "one of the most critical periods in our history." Not only was it facing a crisis of "economic relevance," Singapore's appeal for the cosmopolitan citizen was also being tested.[90] The father-state needed to remedy these economic and image problems with a double investment—to position itself as a "global arts city" while refurbishing its capital base. Queerness is a fundamental component in that makeover. As the founding prime minister, Lee Kuan Yew, noted, "They tell me that homosexuals are creative writers, dancers. If we want creative people, then we have to put up with their idiosyncrasies."[91]

The deployment of the arts and the influx and propagation of queer capital were a vital growth plan for Singapore to transform into a sexy and creative city-state. The decriminalization of homosexual sex is an important first step toward that goal. According to Pierre Bourdieu, there are four primary kinds of capital operating semiautonomously in relation to class and taste—economic, cultural, symbolic, and social.[92] Singapore's simulated taste for queer cultures was an explicit attempt at reflecting and reproducing queer capital in these dimensions. The boys are in that sense embodiments of queer capital and chaperones of global cities with a local agenda. In other words, they had become hypervisible for many reasons other than an implosion of American gay identities. As the country's minister of national development and Remaking Singapore Committee chair, Vivian Balakrishnan, has said, "Singapore will do 'whatever it takes' to attract talent."[93] Homosexuality will not be a stumbling block but a production factor of Singapore's economy as it strives to retain and attract both local and foreign gay talent to its diverse workforce.

To complement this growth plan, Singapore ushered in a new era in which citizens will be able to "make more decisions for themselves" and have autonomous choices in a "derring-do society." More than ever before, the prime minister announced, this is *the* time for "some risk-taking, and a little excitement," which translates into (the legalization of) all-night bar-top dancing, the HBO series *Sex in the City*, bungee jumping, *Cosmopolitan* magazine, and chewing gum. The radical "link between raucous nightlife and international competitiveness may puzzle students of classical economics," as an amused journalist at the *International Herald Tribune* notes, but Singapore's determination to be transformed into a "throbbing metropolis with innovators and entrepreneurs" is as unwavering as its stolid will that raced its development from among the poorest countries to the richest in three decades.[94] Besides, the conflation of bungee jumping, chewing gum, and queer culture as prime examples of zippiness in a capitalist state only adds to the bewilderment of the nation's attitude toward its sexual minorities.

The native boy in cosmo drag is part of the city's stolid will to be a creative city. In a much-touted book, *The Rise of the Creative Class* (2002), Richard Florida, a U.S. American professor currently based at the University of Toronto, posits that the economic growth of cities is contingent on their ability to attract a creative class identified as "a fast-growing, highly educated, and well-paid segment of the work force on whose efforts corporate profits and economic growth increasingly depend."[95] Rather than being drawn to employers, the super-creative core of this new class is drawn to *places* where there are, among other things, vibrant arts and cultural scenes as well as a high tolerance for diversity. Significantly, Florida's thesis points to a substantive gay population as an indicator of tolerance that will help generate this appealing city buzz. San Francisco, in fact, tops his list of creative cities. "If Prof. Florida is right," observed a columnist of the *Straits Times*, "Singapore could do with a hard look at itself."[96] Ultimately, "[i]t's not about gay rights, it's survival." In other words, the tolerance of sexual diversity is linked to the question of livability for global talents and expatriate professionals. A remark by a U.S. neurosurgeon exemplifies this sticking point: "Singapore may be a fine place to work, but why would I want to live there? . . . [it is] a rigid society with an authoritarian regime."[97] If such an insipid image was compromising the country's "relevance" in the new global economy as a medical, business, or research hub, a queer makeover could at least take some of the edges off. Besides, for too long, Singapore has been seen as a "nanny-state" where people were stifled, materialistic, and disciplined by government and economic design.[98] Queer capital was, in the father-state's calculations, a fair gamble for the next phase of national development.

With the decline of manufacturing industries, cities find themselves competing against the dominance of what social scientists like Saskia Sassen call "global cities" such as New York, Tokyo, and London, which concentrate centers of technology, networks of production, and a signature labor force of "white-collar worker-consumers." To be competitive, globalizing cities have to market themselves not only as "postindustrial, postmodern places, locations appropriate for the high-tech, financial, and service industries," but also as places of culture and consumption.[99] Without missing a beat, Singapore formed various committees to remake itself as one such competitive city. It wants to be the "London of Asia,"[100] a "Renaissance City,"[101] "Switzerland of the East,"[102] and a "Global City for the Arts,"[103] a world-class cosmopolitan city standing next to London and New York in terms of its cultural appeal.[104] This aspiration is documented in the *Renaissance City Report*, released by the country's Ministry of Information and the Arts:

> We want to position Singapore as a key city in the Asian renaissance of the 21st century and a cultural center of the globalised world. The idea is to be one of the top cities in the world to live, work and play in, where there is an environment conducive to creative knowledge-based industries and talent. . . . We should aim to reach a level of (cultural) development that would be comparable to cities like Hong Kong, Glasgow and Melbourne in 5–10 years. The longer objective would be to join London and New York in the top rung of cultural cities.[105]

Singapore's queering as a global arts city is the country's link to creativity and a sexy new image. Since the boys are pivotal to issues of creativity and diversity, they must be allowed to thrive in designated spaces. As many social scientists have further argued, queer spaces in globalizing cities serve as a "marker of cosmopolitanism, tolerance, and diversity," marking them as "participants in the global economy of the new millennium."[106]

In Singapore's case, queer management was adopted as an ambivalent component of the city-state's wide-ranging commercial and self-protection plan attuned to changing trends in the region and the world. While the state's semi-clandestine, semi-open efforts at queering were not part of any official directive, its queer outlook was indexed by the father-state's pragmatism in embracing queer capital. The ploy was and still is characteristic of the state's political savvy: it will pursue policies that work and toss out those that do not ensure its "survival as a nation."[107] For instance, queer was insinuated into the country's language of meritocracy as gifted sexual minorities became a recognized human resource in Singapore's government agencies and, by extension, in its global economy. The pushback by local evangelicals, however, was to mark a return of the colonial with an obsessive moral rhetoric against homosexuality.

"Anal Sex Is Like Shoving a Straw up Your Nose"

The twist in the story is the figurative return of the colonial white man in the form of a vocal evangelical Christian Right minority leading the backlash against the country's millennial queering. I am referring to the campaign of intolerance against an imagined "homosexual agenda," which culminated in a media event of both local and global proportions. One of this campaign's public figureheads is a conservative female law professor and nominated member of Parliament, Thio Li-Ann. She stands out for channeling U.S. megachurch male pastors like Jerry Falwell and Rick Warren to argue for the abjection of homosexuals. With Thio as the antigay white man in Asian religious drag, the perverse alterity of the native boy returns to haunt a postcolonial discourse on hetero-human rights and national self-determination filled with ironies.

Statistically, only about 15 percent of Singapore's population is Christian (mostly Protestant), and the trend of conversion has been among the "English-speaking" or "better educated."[108] In this regard, the vociferous Christian backlash was an interesting moral barometer aligned with Singapore's postcolonial Victorian statutes against homosexuality. It was also revelatory, on some level, of the power base in the country. As William Peterson observes, "Christianity has increasingly become the religion of educated, English-speaking, upwardly-mobile Chinese Singaporeans, and a disproportionate number of individuals at the highest levels of government and industry are Christian."[109] Accordingly, the National Council of Churches of Singapore (NCCS) chose to speak on behalf of "all Singaporeans" in its emergency plan to recuperate the country from the morass of a gay rights agenda:

> Stress: all Singaporeans are valuable but we should not promote the homosexual and gay rights agenda as this is contrary to the cornerstone values that sustain and protect the welfare of our society. Our values include a pro family approach and racial and religious harmony. What values do we want to impart to our children?[110]

The NCCS public "Statement on Homosexuality" stands against homosexual practices, refutes genetic claims of gayness, and emphasizes the need to enforce existing laws against homosexuality. The directive also urges the Singapore government to maintain policies of "not permitting the registration of 'homosexual societies or clubs,' and 'not allowing the promotion of homosexual lifestyle and activities.'"[111]

The Christian Right's imagined gay menace in Singapore is classic homophobia under the cover of a "caring community." The vehemence of its public antigay stance is in sharp contrast to the other major religious communities in Singapore, Taoism, Buddhism, Hinduism, Sikhism, and Islam, who were all unopposed to the change in the government's administrative policy to employ gays. These religious groups also did not foresee an organized "homosexual agenda" that would be deleterious to the moral fabric of the society. In the drama of doctrinal directives, town hall meetings, online missives, and public statements, the church's performative indictments substituted for the father-state's wagging finger against "homosexuals" in the past. This kind of social homophobia is, of course, part of the British colonial legacy.

Homosexuality remains a criminal offense in the country to this day. Men seeking other men in contemporary Singapore continue to face criminal charges under the same colonial statutes from the Victorian era, similar to the way sodomy laws were upheld in many states in the United States until recently. While such a contradiction of terms for Singapore is only one part of its many postcolonial, multicultural, and global dilemmas, it is a necessary one to consider. Singapore's rulers had been quick to point out that, as a postcolonial nation-state, its legislature is inherited from British colonizers. Britain's views on homosexuality may have changed, but social attitudes in Singapore about the same issue have to "evolve on [their] own."[112] Although the actual cases of people being charged by these "British 19th century laws on homosexuality" are very rare, the republic's will to retain these penal codes has been contentious.[113] Both Senior Minister Lee Kuan Yew and his son, Deputy Prime Minister Lee Hsien Loong, have given interviews to the international media defending the relevance of these penal codes even as they also sound very open to decriminalizing homosexual sex in the future.[114]

But in defending these statutes written under the appellation of a white, colonial, Christian order, both Lees viewed them to be in sync with the moral and cultural values of the Singapore public. This is the case even though the city-state is, as Deputy Prime Minister Lee observes, "multi-religious" and "multi-racial." Besides, as the Lees asserted, the "social mores and norms . . . are balance[d] not so much by the Government" but by the Singaporean people, who are, in their determination, "very conservative," "orthodox," and "traditional." The mutually corroborating statements of such a Singaporean society by both Deputy Prime Minister Lee and Senior Minister Lee are rhetorical moves. Even as the state disavowed its interference in the business of the citizens' sexual lives, the state would not allow political organizing of any sort because its hands are tied by a "conservative public." For example, state officials repeatedly asserted that they did not "encourage or promote a gay lifestyle" and were opposed to anything that smacked of a "gay rights movement." These positions were reiterated even in Prime Minister Goh's more queer-friendly administration.[115] The question of what is a "gay lifestyle" or "gay movement" remains open-ended. Meanwhile, "a new gay sauna is opening up every six months."[116]

The unresolved contradictions in the Singapore state's rhetoric and attitude toward homosexuality were and still are ongoing features of its pragmatic governing strategy. Hence, while imported Victorian statutes from the legacy of colonial white men pertaining to the "fear of buggery with natives" are seen as reflective of Singapore's social and cultural mores, "homosexuality" was framed as an entirely "Western issue" when presented as a human rights matter.[117] The "East/West" binary charge of the latter driven by an "Asian" culturalist standpoint was nowhere to be found when its officials justified Victorian statutes as effectively Singaporean laws. Under the rule of Lee Kuan Yew, Singapore has consistently invoked the rhetoric of "Asian values" by way of a Confucianist-inflected rhetoric to defend its brand of democracy.[118] Western liberal ideas and practices (homosexuality being a prime example) were seen as inappropriate to Asian societies like Singapore due to their emphasis on individual rights and adversarial politics. Moreover, these elements were thought to cause "the social and economic decay in the West." Indeed, if Singapore embraced a "Western-style democracy," Lee has said, "we'd go down the drain, we'd have more drugs, more crime, more single mothers with delinquent children, and a poor economy."[119] Apart from the intricate political motivations of these powerful positions in crafting nationhood, the direct effect of such discourses was also to limit the appeal and acceptability of gay practices in Singapore.

Notably, in the copious public and official discourse on homosexual activity, there is often a lot of passion in describing how the "bad" behavior of gay men can be disciplined. The illicit pleasure of interested parties, expressed through righteous outrage and voyeuristic speculation, continues in a recent debate about repealing the sodomy penal codes. The Christian conservative is a prime example of an interested party who would link gay sex to pedophilia, drug abuse, incest, bestiality, and a higher incidence of HIV infection. Much of this moral repulsion is also a finger-wagging exercise about the unthinkable and unspeakable sexual practices of gay people. This Victorian-style prudery, which Michel Foucault has famously called the "repressive hypothesis" in the history of sexuality since the eighteenth century, is consummately restaged in the country's discourse on section 377 of the Penal Code.[120] Sure enough, the debates demonstrate how sexual repression actually puts sex into discourse within mechanisms of power, and facilitates the multiplication of perverse sexualities.

Notably, the penal code on sodomy (broadly defined as anal and oral sex) has provisions for both heterosexuals (377) and homosexuals

(377A), but conservatives were advocating for the law to be repealed only for heterosexuals, and they succeeded in doing so by channeling the rhetoric of U.S.-style right-wing Christian fundamentalism. 377A is a provision inherited from the British colonials that criminalizes gay sex whether it is consensual or not. Offenders who are caught with the intention or act of "gross indecency" in public or private spaces can be imprisoned for up to two years. In her 2007 parliamentary speech against the repeal of 377A, Thio Li-Ann, a Nominated Member of Parliament, constitutional law professor and member of the local Christian conservative, enumerates a long list of gay sexual practices she finds objectionable. In one section of her long speech, she details how gay sex is painful and diseased:

> Anal-penetrative sex is inherently damaging to the body and a misuse of organs, like shoving a straw up your nose to drink. The anus is designed to expel waste; when something is forcibly inserted into it, the muscles contract and cause tearing; fecal waste, viruses carried by sperm and blood thus congregate, with adverse health implications like "gay bowel syndrome," anal cancer. "Acts of gross indecency" under 377A also covers unhygienic practices like "rimming," where the mouth comes into contact with the anus. Consent to harmful acts is no defence, otherwise, our strong anti-drug laws must fall as it cannot co-exist with letting in recreational drugs as a matter of personal lifestyle choice.[121]

Thio's voyeuristic gaze on the anus both channels and exceeds the pornographic fantasy of explicit anal sex by staging the scene of insertion as a kind of torturous, medical nightmare. Anal sex is thus like "shoving a straw up your nose," as the forcible entry causes "the muscles [to] contract and cause tearing," creating a reservoir of "fecal waste, viruses carried by sperm and blood." Worse still, it spreads various diseases and causes cancer. The mixture of misinformation, righteous outrage, and sexual fantasy is spectacular in itself. Yet it is only by sensationalizing gay sex acts as a dirty little secret that the campaign to inspire moral revulsion against sodomy can have traction. Thio's gratuitous description of "rimming" as "where the mouth comes into contact with the anus" is a case in point. But since there are two statutes with regard to sodomy, the crux of her argument must hinge on sexual preference, and a baffling assumption of heterosexual hygiene and morality. According to Thio, sodomy between homosexuals has a high "price tag" for society, whereas comparable sex acts between heterosexuals, however objectionable, have a protected moral base: family, procreation, decency. Besides, they are (for heterosexuals) a precursor to vaginal penetration as a final, procreative act. Homosexuals, in contrast, are unsafe, promiscuous, nonreproductive, and dangerous radicals with a long list of agendas. Thio warns that repealing sodomy laws for same-sex partners portends the rise of the militant gay.

There is a lot more in Thio's long and garbled cry for an Asian-style Victorian decency, but her conclusion is that gay activists and their perverse agendas must be tightly policed or they will grow into a U.S.-style lobbying group for rights and marriage, and lead to the crumbling of society. Following the successful lobby by Thio and others, the sodomy penal code was repealed only for heterosexuals, and retained for homosexuals. This stunning, discriminatory move was ironically endorsed as a referendum on the country's conservative Asian values. Together with 377A, a moralistic condemnation by the country's vocal Christian right wing against the carnal gay reveals another staunchly Western-style homophobia in an explicitly "Asian" context. A banner outside a local church declared, "Homosexuals can change." This conversion therapy is accompanied by calls to retain any legal prohibitions against same-sex practices based on the "love the sinner, hate the sin" doctrine propagated by U.S. megachurch pastors such as Jerry Falwell and Rick Warren. The preponderance of Western religious-moral discourse and the ubiquity of the pornographic-orientalist gaze add a bizarre colonial specter to local gay male subjectivity. In many ways, this social and religious backdrop haunts the performance of local gay men as Asian boys.

Conclusion

As a pornographic trope, *Asian Boys* straddles white colonial desire for ethnic men on the one leg, and autoexotic display of Asian sensuality on the other leg. In such a position, as queer straddling practices go, the paradox infuses the fantasy of the "legs wide open" native boy with the overachieving ethos of a modern Asian state trying to be sexy. Two versions of this global queer fantasy come to mind. In the PG version, we see Asian Mardi Gras boys on the streets, between the sheets, and up on stage attempting to rewrite the national marketing machine of "Surprising Singapore!" with a gay perspective. The R- or X-rated version involves the gay boys strapped on top of the postcolonial daddy, moaning and groaning for national ecstasy on the Singapore Sling with all the requisite tools and toys. This daddy-complex is both a shaming and sexual relationship, manifesting itself in the paternal surveillance of a gay community that is held hostage by 377A but otherwise given free rein to be global Asian queer boys.

The term "Asian" in the theatrical trilogy is thus an ironic deployment, since there is nothing particularly Asian about British colonials, U.S. evangelicals, and the sexual fetishism of "native" boys in cosmo drag. Rather, it calls into question the stability of entrenched terms like "Asian values," "Asian city," and "Asian conservatism," routinely sanctioned by the state in myriad campaigns, reportages, and speeches as the sensibility of all Singaporeans. The boys undercut the monolithic assumptions that make the city-state "Asian" and "Singaporean" by adding queer time, queer thought, and queer space into the mix. The trilogy is one of many theatrical examples that demonstrate how "acting gay" in this global city has many inter-Asian dimensions that are not accommodated by Euro-American models. The boys in the country's English-language theater are not merely replications of Western gay culture on the one hand or local homoerotica affirmed through national difference on the other hand. To put it another way, my goal here is not to merely refute the universal gay identity routinely foregrounded by those who herald commonalities over difference in the global gay world, nor am I interested in disaggregating Asia or Singapore into its discrete cultural and linguistic constituents and provide a sort of auto-orientalist anthropological account of queer heterogeneity. Rather, it is to fundamentally displace how we look at emergent global queer cultures and performance. Why, for instance, are ubiquitous images of protein shake–drinking gay boys decked out in designer tank tops and feather boas necessarily proof that Western queer cultures are the signs of progress and modernity in globalizing cities around the world? Such presumptions elide the local and regional histories as well as the intracultural and class differences of queer practices in any global city. More than that, such a limited viewpoint based on Western standards of understanding often results in a reduced sensitivity to acts considered political or interventionary at each queer site.

In the case of Singapore, we saw a new threshold for gay theater with its flamboyant fabulations as well as its fun and bold experimentation with queer forms. The queerness of the boys is a constitutive part of "Singapore" and "Asia." More than titular titillation, *Asian Boys,* with its faux-pornographic, touristic, and disciplinary references, brings to bear the complex pleasures and regimes that both regulate and enable the city-state's cosmopolitan gay life. The Asian boys of Singapore's postcolonial Anglophone theater marked a city-state's tentative foray into a new, queer millennium; it was a pink explosion with the proliferation of gay-, lesbian-, and transgender-themed shows, websites, saunas, and parties that dwindled as economic imperatives of the state shifted alongside a conservative backlash. Yet the dyad's postcolonial encounters rethink what is inherently "Singapore." The father-state's gay awakening and the native boy's cosmo drag are not merely passive conduits of global forces. Rather, they show how this city-state's national consciousness is always already glocalqueer, multiply split, inclusive of myriad influences, and diverse not just in cultural but also sexual makeup.

3

G.A.P. DRAMA, OR THE GAY ASIAN PRINCESS
GOES TO THE UNITED STATES

The acronym G.A.P., which stands variously for Gay Asian Princess, Gay Asian Pacific, or Gay Asian Performance, is a mock assemblage of puns, wayward Asian identifications, and queer acts on improper routes and cartographies. Neither a fixed genre of theater nor an identity marker of Asians writ large, G.A.P. is a set of performative cruisings made by the native boy in at least three cognate fields: queer studies, ethnic studies, and theater studies. These cruisings ride on G.A.P.'s polysemic *P*—Princess, Pacific, Performance—which signpost each of the three aforesaid fields with recent, transnational turns. They connect the discursive gaps between them in understanding the white man/native boy dyad in the Asian diaspora.[1] I am using the metaphor and practice of cruising to bridge different fields of study that are of interest to this iteration of the native boy as G.A.P. Moreover, the twists and turns of cruising between and beyond the epistemology-affect, collective-community binarisms binding G.A.P.'s search for pleasure are manifold, and follow no path of inherited doxa. They foreground the different meanings and stakes of theorizing queer Asian masculinity based on the native boy's transmogrification into an Asian houseboy, Suzie Wong in drag, and a butterfly gone berserk in the face of whiteness.

G.A.P.'s most basic theatrical modality involves playing with the requisite affect, speech, and identification of the Asian male as the native boy in love with the white man around the world. It begins by summoning the tropic spell of the dyad in the United States, where the native boy has arrived as a point of departure to the Asias. G.A.P.'s play with racial codes is a way to unravel the genre, geography, and gender of "Asian performance" that are set up by orientalism. It is in this regard a drama of unfixing old lies. G.A.P. drama also indexes the theoretical uprising of Asian Pacific American studies in the late 1990s against heterosexist cultural nationalism on the one hand, and the centrality of queer inquiries and coalitions in the field's transnationalization on the other hand. But more than merely a passing reference, the princess's drama parodies the dominance of U.S.-national(ist) epistemologies and ethnographies based on (or singularly against) straight white male chronopolitics and representational logic. It ups the ante of queer and diasporic pathos using the affect and narratives of Asian and Hollywood cinema, Korean and Japanese television soap opera, and random orientalist myths and motifs, like kabuki makeup, chop suey font, and Chinese godheads. With the spread of such cultural flows into the United States, it bears note that the performatics of G.A.P. drama is an American mode of glocalqueering using the vast visual, sonic, and mnemonic archives of Asian encounters.

Butterfly Gone Berserk

Perhaps the best-known illustration of the encounter in the context of Asian America is David Henry Hwang's *M. Butterfly*, which I read as a precursor to G.A.P. drama. The play won the Tony Award in 1988, and was said to be the "single event that put Asian American theatre on the national and international cultural map."[2] Since then, *M. Butterfly* has had a long afterlife in academic discourse, particularly in the 1990s. Its story, which continues to be something of a curiosity, is essential reading for American drama. I think the play is worth a brief revisit to understand an iconic version of the tropic spell in the U.S.-Western context, especially since a Chinese native boy is, as I will argue, central to its drama.

As is well known, the play is based on a court case involving Shi Pei Pu, a Beijing Opera diva-spy who is said to have fooled the French diplomat Bernard Boursicot, his lover, into believing he was female for nearly twenty years.[3] Part of the controversy is at the level of dramatic representation: Is Hwang giving carte blanche to the Boursicot-Shi story of sexual subterfuge to reiterate or break a persistent orientalist fantasy in theater? Moreover, are structures of understanding delimited by epistemic strongholds that enforce an evaluation of the play's theatrical representation based on either reinforcing or breaking U.S. racial stereotypes and the Western cultural imaginary? The politics of deformative legibility are in such a model contingent on conventional orientalist tropes and embodiments organized by the heterosexual dyad in the West, and centered on the white male. They are, in other words, restricted to binaristic positions of identification. Rather than taking an either/or position, we might see both Shi/Boursicot and Song/Gallimard (the characters in the play) as queer couplings with a signature Asian encounter traversing the slippery boundaries of fact/fiction, real/theatrical, male/female, East/West. What if Song was read explicitly through the queer tropic spells cast by or cast on the white man/native boy dyad across East Asian, Southeast Asian, and Asian American iterations of the native boy? Would his new centrality be at once an amalgam of autoexotic display, ethnic intervention, and colonial perversion?

In one of the most talked-about scenes at the end of the play, the French diplomat René Gallimard commits ritual suicide in native drag while ostensibly "possessed" by the spells of the orient.[4] The possession is made manifest by his theatrical transformation into a queer Butterfly, which he stages before his cellmates, donning a kimono, a wig, thick white makeup, rouge around the eyes, and red lipstick. It is a tragic scene because it marks an unseemly downfall: a white man turning into a Japanese female and a doomed one at that. In the film version, he is the centerpiece of the climax, with his white running makeup an indictment of his failed heterosexuality and of a manifest whiteness losing its cover.

What remains intact is the orientalist *scène à faire* with the suicidal geisha as a tropic identification of exotic, fatalistic, and infantile trappings. The transgression marks both the West's colonial obsession with and fear of enchantment by tropic spells. Gallimard's suicide in native drag suggests that the East's feminized barbarism, backwardness, and godlessness was/will be the downfall of Western civilization, particularly during the Vietnam/Cold War. Hence, rather than a transgressive act, the seppuku in drag "seals the erotic power of the dying Asian female body and its aura of redemptive sacrifice."[5] But the contentious interplay between (the potential and limit of) gender crossing and racial performativity is also partly a question of whose story is being told.

In the case of *M. Butterfly*, the play's narrative focus is on the orientalist/white man, which is additionally signified by its mise-en-scène: the incarceral space of Gallimard's mindscape and physical jail cell. He is entrapped in a set of spellbinding dilemmas, chief of which—to be or not to be nativized—is a classic predicament facing the white man on the road (literally or figuratively) in the non-Western world. This dilemma stages a version of what the anthropologist and poet Renato Rosaldo calls "imperialist nostalgia," a yearning for the traditional culture that colonialists have altered or destroyed.[6] A spectacular example of this nostalgia is captured in the documentary filmmaker Dennis O'Rourke's 1988 film *Cannibal Tours*, which features Italian, American, and German tourists going native after visiting "ex-cannibals" in Papua New Guinea. With a Mozart string quartet playing in the background, the tourists paint their faces in white striped Sepik designs and become playful savages on a luxury cruise ship. Unlike Gallimard's tragic native drag, this is a light-hearted show. As the tourists dance in slow motion, their fun masquerade is rendered "authentic" by the props purchased from the natives, including wooden masks, penis sheaths, and spears that they gleefully display. In a standout performance, a heavy-set male tourist stripped to the waist strikes a hackneyed pose for the camera with his fucated face; clearly a bad actor, he attempts to reenact the pose of a fierce savage flexing his muscles with the requisite props for an embarrassing moment.

The cultural sociologist Dean MacCannell suggests provocatively that such a performance "may be the creative cutting edge of world culture in the making," since "parody and satire are at the base of every

[handwritten note at top: "if it's important to be made fun of; enough to be made fun of, it must be actually important"]

cultural formation."[7] Moreover, there is "so much mutual complicity" between the postmodern tourist and the performative primitive who act the part of noble savage; both are striving toward an "impossible economic ideal."[8] For MacCannell, the more pertinent question has to do with calibrating the "interesting balancing mechanism" between groups that inhabit unequal spaces, and finding the positive technology of postmodern dramatic forms such as "satire, lampooning, and burlesque." Hence, the tourist trying to be a savage is in fact taking a risk by inhabiting the insecure space of bad theater, or a parody that misses its mark, which in its failing becomes self-parody. He becomes nothing but a bad actor, and "potentially raises the consciousness of an audience that is the butt of it."[9] Written at the height of postmodern discourse, which coincided with the play's rise in the late 1980s and early 1990s, MacCannell's critique is articulated from a Western perspective about modernity's universal drama. But the drama is often lost where the basic premise is not some spectacular primitive crossing made by the white tourist. Consider the insignificance of natives in T-shirts wielding Coke cans or speaking a smattering of English. They are hardly ever theorized as performative moderns, or even as parodic agents risking their primitive self-identity with postmodern techniques.

Between the white painted face of Gallimard and those of the old European tourists, the cultural logics of Western imperialism are foregrounded as dominant but not infallible. Yet they also index a nativized world at once wanton and magical, colonized and symbolic. Since racialized fantasies are "a field of symbolically structured meaning (the unconscious) that shapes and regulates our desires, our modes of acting 'in reality,'" fabulations of exotic probabilities are par for this course.[10] Given this "reality," the native boy is at once fascinating and ordinary, a thing of wonder and a thing of everyday life. He is the secret butterfly and the butterfly gone berserk. These dramatic tensions and undramatic turns are at the heart of his predicament. Hence, beyond a surprising reversal of gender (female/male) and nativized affect (the white man as geisha and the Chinese opera diva in a Prada suit), the biggest "revelation" of *M. Butterfly* turns out to be a mundane conceit: the native boy is like a native girl. And all the other characters, from Gallimard to Comrade Chin, are simultaneously spellbound and repulsed by this Asian boy in drag.

[handwritten margin note: "the boy, representing Asia, is both controller + controlled; all others only exist in relation to him, but he is natural"]

In an important queer reading, David Eng combines a Freudian psychoanalytic framework with Asian American studies to argue that Gallimard's fetishism of Song is an act of racial castration sanctioned by the colonial, symbolic order. This order is regulated by an impenetrable white male heterosexuality where tropes like the "cruel white man" and the "submissive Oriental lotus blossom" abound. For the fetish to work, Song must be a native boy in drag, which means he lacks the penis and changes seamlessly from boy to lotus blossom, thereby remaking the "unacceptable Asian body into an acceptable female form for colonial consumption, enjoyment, and privilege."[11] For Gallimard, this performative sublimation of rice queen to yellow fever relieves the taboo of homosexuality while creating a privileged context—a sexist old boys' club trafficking in the possession and exploitation of the native brown woman—for shoring up his "flagging white masculinity." The suspension of Gallimard's "state of divided belief" points to a peculiar dilemma dealing with a version of the hetero/homo opposition: "a failed heterosexuality in the face of whiteness and an occluded fantasy of homosexual desire."[12]

Eng's reading targets colonial psychology and its collusion with compulsory heterosexuality and whiteness as "veiled and undisclosed" protocols of social discourse.[13] Laying bare their operation then enables us to see the normative sexual and racial stipulations of the symbolic order, and by extension, the homosexual and racial anxieties occupying the abject margins of this domain. It also analogizes the management of Asian American masculinity by the U.S. nation-state. The assumption here is a powerful one: the structural integrity of this order, with its matrix of sexist fantasies, racialized anxieties, and homophobias, will be maintained at all costs, consciously or not. For Eng, making the whiteness and (hetero)sexual limits of this structure visible is thus a central undertaking. This focus on the white man is both strategic and imperative, since the burden of difference or "racial problematic" is always borne by the nonwhite, or the Asian male in this case. Hence, the colonial psychology of the white man is put in the critical spotlight to discuss what is sometimes not discussable, enabling in the process a rich exploration of the symptoms, reactions, and acts that result from this state of mind. Clearly, as Eng convinces us, race and (homo)sexuality are intrinsic components for understanding the white man's symptoms, reactions, and acts vis-à-vis his native other.

[handwritten annotation: even though he is minimal / natural, he has agency of his own]

But what of the Asian boy? Is he always to be the white man's fetish or symptom, the one who is a point of critical interest insofar as he triggers the white man's complex of defenses and reactions in a racialized state of mind? In such a colonial scenario, his supporting role is around the white man or "me" with a singular but messed-up subjectivity. What would it mean then to engage the native boy as "Asian American," "Asian diasporic," and/or "postcolonial" in a queer, national, and transnational context? Would it only reiterate the critical interest on the complex white man and relegate the native boy to different states of erasure, mediocrity, or even unrecognizability? Conversely, would his visibility only perpetuate the stereotype of an emasculated Asian male in the U.S. context or reinscribe the colonial notion of Asian nations as underdeveloped and needing guidance? These familiar questions resonate in the gap of discourse upholding the easy prominence of white man/white modernity, and the many difficult challenges engaging the native boy. Yet it is precisely the native boy's disconcertion, particularly his berserk queerness around the white man, that has to be engaged as the basis for understanding Asian encounters and Asian performance in a wide range of relationships and artistic collaborations that are simply taken for granted as the way things are. Caught between a rock and a very hard place, the Gay Asian Princess sashays her way onto center stage and declaims in mock anguish, "Are you diasporically fucked in the United States? Well then, bring on the drama!"

[handwritten annotation: really? / I am not amused.]

Theorizing the G.A.P. *[handwritten annotation: definition / explanation of terms]*

G.A.P. drama is all about self-conscious effacement, murderous rage, emotional excess, fake yearning, and insipid pleasure. In the U.S. context, we might identify these moves as ethnic camp, or a way to screw up with irony, bad taste, and other brazen acts the overdetermined and yet altogether vague associations of being "Gay Asian Pacific" or doing "Gay Asian Performance." Such a performative tactic typically attends to the diasporic woes of the East Asian male as an effeminized celestial, forever foreigner, or obsequious houseboy in the West. These tropes speak to the predicament of myriad and often irreconcilable geographic, cultural, and identitarian regimes in Asian/America. But G.A.P., as I propose here, is neither a corrective nor shorthand of this American

predicament; rather, it is simultaneously a queer episteme with resonances of ethnic camp, a performance intervention, and an alternative
reading practice that merges the United States and the Asias as a critical region of queer encounters and colonial imaginaries. Importantly,
these G.A.P. moves are essential for opening a space to think about performance in the Asias as a region of circum-Pacific formations with its
own set of queer chronopolitics and inter-Asian cultural mixing. These
are in turn saturated with old and new orientalist desires, presenting a
new model for thinking about ethnic and intercultural performance, or
a way to bring together Asian and Asian American theater as performance in the Asias. To put it differently, G.A.P. moves connect the gay
U.S.A. to the Asias as a region of circum-Pacific formations with a long,
colonial history documented by ethnographers, artists, tourists, thinkers, and migrants who carry that history across the world.

The contingencies of G.A.P. epistemes and interventions bear some
elaboration as they traverse and bridge several fields and methodologies, from Asian/American to transnational/postcolonial, as well as area,
diaspora, and ethnographic studies with performance studies. I use the
pluralized Asias not only to foreground the multiple mappings and orientalist fantasies at play about Asia and its diasporas but also as a setup
for G.A.P.'s performative navigations across their requisite visual, temporal, and affective landscapes. This cartography of the Asias is, in other
words, a counterpoint to straight colonial modernities and their narrow
chronopolitics of development. G.A.P.'s deviant temporality takes off
from Elizabeth Freeman's notion of erotohistoriography, or "a politics
of unpredictable, deeply embodied pleasures that counters the logic of
development,"[14] while its spatial configuration follows Gayatri Gopinath's
"cartography of a queer diaspora [that] tells a different story of how global
capitalism impacts local sites by articulating other forms of subjectivity,
culture, affect, kinship, and community that may not be visible or audible
within standard mappings of nation, diaspora, or globalization."[15]

By broadening the coordinates of encounter, G.A.P. changes the
forum of understanding from one that is exceptionally about the white
male U.S. citizen and his Asian other in its fifty states to the queer and
racialized transmigrant's predicament in interregional, transcolonial,
and cross-historical perspectives. G.A.P.'s body is in that sense a figure
for relations between nativized bodies past and present in a spectrum

of locations across the Asias. On G.A.P.'s transnational cartography, the United States is neither the singular focus nor the final destination; rather, it is a nodal point of multiple diasporic pathways and temporalities shaped by colonial desire, neoliberal economies, and new technologies of mobility. It is a space for enacting various sensorial and (de)familiar encounters between the East and West, and the Asias thus generated.

Navigating the Asias also requires that G.A.P.'s campy enactments be staged in contradistinction to the straight Asia of Cold War–era area studies and orientalist imaginaries. This is partly a critical response to the "objective" methodologies of their cognate studies, which numerous critics have charged as work justified in the name of Western progress, science, and rational knowledges. These cross-cultural forays in anthropology, theater, and history, to name three relevant areas, have generated some of the most exotic spectacles and narratives of Asia in national frameworks with largely heterosexual perspectives. Their factive power in spite of their exoticism has partly to do with the dominance of Western chronopolitics and spatio-temporal mapping based on straight white male logics. In contrast, G.A.P. drama in the Asias actively queers these areas by bringing out the fiction of orientalist constructs embedded within them, and thereby distends their carefully structured rationality to the point of excess and ridiculosity. That is, it mimics their truth claims and shores up their grand presumptions only to reveal them as implausible, incoherent, and incommensurable with current realities.

Performance is once again central in this case, particularly to G.A.P.'s mission as a transversal modality of (un)knowing and (un)doing queer acts attuned to histories of colonialism, diasporic perspectives, and contemporary forms of racialization. Casting G.A.P. as an alternative storyteller of entrenched gazes, orientalist routes, and queer erotics introduces a logic of disassembly around the power differentials of such relations while fostering lateral (rather than vertical) comparative frameworks and political solidarities. Such a critical move is crucial for linking U.S. queer of color critiques to the emergent field of glocalqueer studies grappling with the stakes of queer production in national and transnational contexts.[16] These links bring out scenarios of crossings that can potentially disorganize the positional lines and relational gridlocks that privilege a Western standpoint in many fields of understanding. This is why the princess's cruising, which constitutes a transcolonial zone of contact in the Asias, needs to be a signature scenario; it is a way for G.A.P. to stage a new comparativity of the gay Asian male's nativized predicament in various postcolonies and diasporas.

In what follows, I will be doing a close reading of Justin Chin's queer adaptation of Richard Quine's 1960 orientalist film classic, *The World of Suzie Wong*, into a solo 1994 performance, *Go, or The Approximate Infinite Universe of Mrs. Robert Lomax*.[17] Chin is a Malaysian-born, Singapore- and U.S.-educated Chinese American who has published five volumes of fiction, poetry, and essays, including an anthology of all his solo performances from 1993 to 2001, *Attack of the Man-Eating Lotus Blossoms* (2005). The campy irony of G.A.P. drama is fleshed out in Chin's performance as an Asian boy who takes on various shapes and forms, including the signature role of a fictional Mrs. Lomax, in different locations. Rather than dismissing the dyad as irrelevant, untenable, or old news, G.A.P. lets the Asian (house)boy and his white daddy sashay onto the semiotic catwalk as a queer iteration of the colonial order with its attendant homoerotic orientalism. Drawing from a cultural matrix of queer resources, its signifying contours frame the coupling in overtly performative terms while broadening the spatial and relational coordinates of their queer encounters on a shifting cartography.

In place of provincial Euro-America, the gay Asian male is placed in the conceptual space of the Asias, which enable a comparative encounter of the dyad across minor landscapes and transcolonial borderzones. This includes, in Chin's performance, Hong Kong, China, Singapore, Malaysia, and Thailand as one configuration of the Asias vis-à-vis Asian America. Part of the contrivance of these reconfigurations is the new focus on the native boy or gay Asian male as a leading character. These moves begin to stage what I have been calling G.A.P. drama, an epistemo-affective register that vacillates between hysteria and sentimentality, repulsion and longing, and a space for navigating the temporal and geographic dislocations of the Asias.

Queering Suzie Wong, the Desperate Asian Housewife

At Josie's Cabaret and Juice Joint in San Francisco, home to such performance artists as Lipsinka, Karen Williams, Pomo Afro Homos, and Monica Palacios, the performance artist Justin Chin is putting on a solo performance that picks up where Quine's movie *The World of Suzie Wong* ends. Chin's show has no central plot and is organized as episodic vignettes around the multiple identities of the native boy in the Asias. Chin takes on each of these roles with queer insouciance and disaffection. Throughout the show, each of the three principal characters, Suzie Wong, The Boy, and Justin Chin, come out with a set of related stories that connect them fictionally and diasporically across time and place. These characters also represent the prototypes of gay Asian boys who have overlapping encounters (physical or conceptual) with a white male lover across Hong Kong, Bangkok, the United States, ancient China, and other fictional geographic and temporal landscapes. The boy's transnational cruising under the dubious moniker of "Mrs. Robert Lomax" is a facetious reference to gay Asian males trolling for love. They include the Americanized but deformed Suzie Wongs; Thai male hustlers in pursuit of *farang* fortune; teenage gay Asian boys writing love letters to their European pen pals; and the militant queer and Asian *personae non gratae* with a "vendetta" against the colonial daddy.

The citation of Suzie Wong lays the groundwork for the performative and theatrical contrivances of G.A.P. drama. Imagine then, the audience hearing these closing lines of the film at the start of Chin's show:

ROBERT: Suzie, please, will you marry me?
SUZIE: Robert, I stay with you until you say, "Suzie, you go."

In this marriage proposal, which occurs somewhat inappropriately at the funeral of Suzie Wong's child in the film, the familiar scenario of a heterosexual, East-West romance is reprised. Robert Lomax is the white male protagonist from the United States, and he bears an unquestionable entitlement to love. Suzie Wong is the submissive and self-sacrificing Chinese woman unconditionally devoted to him. Ever ready to attend to his desires, she accepts his marriage proposal while grieving, and professes to stay with him no matter the circumstance until she is dismissed or asked to "go." (Hence the title of Chin's show, *Go, or The Approximate Infinite Universe of Mrs. Robert Lomax*.) By quoting this key passage, Chin's show invokes two of the most familiar tropes of the late modern orientalist imaginary that are instrumental for "a plotline of choice in East-West romance narratives produced in the West"[18]—the slavish, lovelorn Asian female and the gallant, if also callous, white knight. As is well known, the quintessential example of this plotline is Giacomo Puccini's *Madame Butterfly* (1904), which sets up the tantalizing and tragic premise of Asian women forever encumbered by their brief sexual liaisons with white men. But unlike her fatalistic female counterpart in the *Butterfly* narrative, Suzie Wong is neither suicidal nor dead in the end, and even marries her white lover, Robert Lomax. Moreover, it is her illegitimate child who is "sacrificed" (killed off by a squatter area landslide) for her passage to the United States. This happy ending lifts her from the morass of female Asian corpses of the *Butterfly* narrative as she heads to the Land of the Free to live her American Dream.

The story of *The World of Suzie Wong* is based on the British novelist Richard Mason's semiautobiographical 1957 novel, in which Robert Lomax, a forty-something white male banker from Britain, goes to Hong Kong to become a full-time painter specializing in native women as his subject. Significantly, Lomax becomes an American in the Broadway play (1958) and Hollywood film (1960), pointing to the seamless transferability of white male privilege. With Hong Kong's seedy exoticism and colonized charm as its backdrop, Lomax finds his Asian muse in the form of an alluring if also beguiling twenty-three-year-old Chinese woman with multiple identities. She is Wong Mee-ling, a self-professedly rich, virgin girl when he first encounters her on a ferryboat to Wan Chai, and a feisty hooker who goes by Suzie Wong by night. Much of the action happens at the hotel, where Lomax lives on the top floor. Incidentally, the infamous Nam Kok bar/brothel is also located at that hotel. With its sea of slinky Chinese women in cheongsam entertaining inebriated British and American sailors, military men, and business executives, Hotel Nam Kok stages the smoky fantasy of Eastern sexual permissiveness with exotic aplomb. But it is Suzie Wong who stands out among all the girls with her exquisite beauty. Taken by her irrepressible charm and solicitous demeanor, Robert recruits Suzie as a regular model for his paintings, and tries to reform or educate her in the privileged ways of expatriate life, such as fine dining at Western restaurants. Meanwhile, their lives are separated by a mixture of conflicting business and love interests, but their fraught and enchanted encounters continue to cast a spell for both parties, who defy different odds to eventually become lovers.

To more fully understand the historic and fictional composition of this fantasy, we have to take a deeper look at Mason. His notions of the East would help to peel away the layers of the dyad's cultural inventions explored in Chin's show. According to Mason, the fictional premise of the book was based partly on his own experiences as a tourist in Hong Kong, where he stepped off the Star Ferry at Wan Chai, just as Lomax did, in search of a muse for his next novel. Felicitously, the hotel "recommended by a friend" turned out to be "a brothel," and "[c]hecking into a Hong Kong brothel was probably the luckiest decision Richard Mason ever made in his life."[19] As he recalls in a 1994 *South China Morning Post* interview, "I went down the first night to have my chow fan and saw all these women in the bar and I realized that it was virtually a brothel. I was absolutely thrilled. From that moment I knew I had my book. I thought that was unbelievable—like a gift from God."[20] Mason disavowed any premeditation on his part for going to the British colony to write *The World of Suzie Wong* by using instinct as justification: "Something in me said Hong Kong was a place where I would immediately find material. . . . I simply bought a ticket. I didn't know I was going to write a book with that sort of background, or that kind of subject at the time."[21] But the cryptic "recommendation" by a friend reveals the network of patronage already established by a Western clientele. His "surprise" at being in a brothel was very much a fake revelation of what he already knew or came to expect using "instinct" as cover and "luck" as his charm. It was a moment of discovery where there was nothing to discover. Such a "gut feeling" about the fabled lures of the East was, if anything, an artistic embellishment that added to his innocence or desirability as a good colonial. The availability of sex was a self-fulfilling prophecy, and a romantic story about a Chinese bar girl in love with him would only make it all the more palatable. The book, in other words, was already written.

What is remarkable about this encounter is the way that sex tourism, ethnography, self-interest, and fiction converged in Mason's account to create "a gift from God" to the Western world. We might specify this sacred "gift" of the white man a little more explicitly as orientalist inspiration and nativized sex. Mason's touristic encounter in Hong Kong staged a path already trodden by friends, and his book is but a restaging of that well-oiled, white male fantasy. In fact, in Mason's godlike recollection thirty-seven years after his book was published, Hong Kong continues to be that timeless, exotic destination. But beyond one man's fictional fantasies, the sexy, eastern accents of Hong Kong standing in for Third World Asian exotica were already deeply ingrained in the West. And Mason was, for better or worse, just one historic and prototypical occurrence of the white man that constitutes one half of the colonial dyad and its fabulations. Meanwhile, an established set of tropes for this kind of encounter, including the ones Mason provides—aspiring English artist falling in love with Chinese prostitute—continued to gain greater transnational circulation from the 1950s onwards.

With an eye on the commercial value of such tropic spells, Mason's publisher jumped in sheer excitement on first reading the manuscript: "The minute I read the opening chapter I knew this book was going to work and be a best seller."[22] Indeed, it has come to be regarded as a popular "classic," and its appeal quickly made it into a Broadway stage play in 1958, a West End production in 1959, and a Hollywood film in 1960. A handsome income from the royalties of the book have allowed Mason "to live a comfortable existence ever since," including retirement in Rome with three rooftop terraces where he gardened, studied languages, and sculpted before his death in 1997. This is in stark contrast to the actual, anonymous Suzies, including one who attempted to sue him for using her name but failed because "it wasn't her."[23] Instead, as Mason saw it, "I just thought Suzie was a good name; rather like naming a pet, you look for a good name. Then the Wong came."[24] The invention of Suzie Wong was thus predicated on the crudest denominators of familiarity: a house pet and a common Chinese family name. That level of triviality has not stopped her from becoming not merely a fictional character but a mobile cultural imaginary as the white man's pet, an endearing nativized other, as it were. It bears note that the Asian pet trope is also found or readable in Carlos Bulosan's *America Is in the Heart* and Jade Snow Wong's *Fifth Chinese Daughter* to mollify anxieties of both the pet and master over racial difference. In other words, the postwar metamorphosis of white American and Asian American social relations into a master/pet relation mandates that the Asian pet become an emotional laborer producing feelings of benevolence in those in power. From this standpoint, the interplay of what is real and fictional, what fantasies pay off, and what pet liberties can be taken in the name of love is deeply embedded in the dyad's regulation of what is possible for social interaction as well as cultural representation.

Suzie Wong, like Madame Butterfly and Miss Saigon, has long become a fetishistic icon perpetuating the myth of docile Asian femininity and Western heroism through the frame of an interracial love story. Chin's show, *Go, or The Approximate Infinite Universe of Mrs. Robert Lomax*, cites this "traditional" romance deeply entwined in the sexual and cultural politics of (Asian) America. But rather than focusing on its heterosexual realism, the show brings out the queerness of Suzie Wong through a correlative dyad, white man/native boy, hovering over the same landscape. This denaturalizing move turns Suzie Wong into a queer sign as well as a transmutable identity, "Mrs. Robert Lomax," who is without a stable gender or racial essence. As one facetious identity of G.A.P., Mrs. Robert Lomax is an ironic moniker for all nativized boys who are coupled with the white man as if they were ineluctably "married." But if "you can't have one without the other," as the song goes, the performativity of this dyadic lovin' is nonetheless subject to the checkered possibilities of queer and theatrical execution. Dancing between the poles of reiterative and deformative embodiment, G.A.P. drama positions the native boy within and against various discourses—orientalist, colonial, and ethnic, for example—and methodologies—filmic, anthropological, literary, theatrical—that have attempted to cohere the histories of his queer encounters with personal narratives of love or flimsy accounts of postcolonial agency. Its critical gambit is, in other words, neither liberatory nor transgressive in terms of a measured "outcome" or identity, but rather functions as an epistemic irritant to self-evident telling, to uncritical desires, and to fixed identities. Its transnational cruising for love turns Suzie Wong from sex symbol to desperate Asian housewife, a queer deformation that wrests the native woman out of her false, colonial romance while providing a platform for G.A.P.'s exposé of the white man's dirty and bestial love.

G.A.P. v. U.S.A.

But what does it mean for the native boy to go to the United States of America as the desperate Asian housewife? In U.S. queer studies, the gay Asian male often identifies or is identified as a racialized stranger or exotic other in the utopic West modeled by a community of white gay males. From Mardi Gras and Stonewall anniversary parties to marches for gay marriage equality, the mythologized histories of sexual liberty and rights-based liberation fashion a very gay gateway to the capitalist paradise of the United States. Gay initiates of this American Dream would be lost without iconic deities like Bette Davis, Judy Garland, and Joan Crawford. Its narratives of inclusion are, however, both mythic and neoliberal. They promote an American mentality of exceptionalism and commodification that also parochializes queer, ethnic cultural production in the conventional terms of non-Western otherness. Hence, the kitschy appeal of Suzie Wong cafés and the oriental excess of *Flower Drum Song* on Broadway translate seamlessly into pleasurable cultural gaps for American consumption. The provincialization of gay Asia within the United States is particularly egregious, producing what we might call queer chop suey, a persistent rendering of Chinese or other national-ethnic exotica as most "interesting" insofar as it is spectacular and foreign. The costs of this reiteration are manifold. As Jasbir Puar has argued, the normativizing zeal of such exotic frameworks has tended to veer toward homo-nationalist formations with an uncritical racist bent.[25] Such an exceptional homo-globalist United States with racialized myopias is a colonial legacy with a performative force. It turns glocal theories on their head in the form of a reverse glocalism, whereby the village of white gay United States sees itself in global terms, exporting Pride parades and pink-dollar products to the rest of the world, even as it generates a limited or even homogeneous set of gay Asian issues under its liberal banner.

Chin's turn as Mrs. Robert Lomax (a.k.a. Suzie Wong) takes on these delimitations with G.A.P. indignation. He first appears onstage in a headless bear suit, signifying Suzie's semiotic deformation into a half-bear, half-(wo)man in the United States. Her name and hence her identity have notably been taken away from her. There are fourteen episodes all together in the act, each of which is announced by a slide projected on the wall, including the one at the start of the show, "Suzie Wong, as worn by Justin Chin, Performance Artist. $10.00." These slides serve as axiomatic announcements, scene titles, or commentaries framing the action. The low price tag at the end of each slide points to the cheapness of U.S. orientalism and invokes a racialized history of consumption.

While the ticket to Chin's show costs, incidentally, ten dollars, the price is also a reference to the infamous haggling by a Vietnamese prostitute with two U.S. soldiers in the movie *Full Metal Jacket*, and reproduced in the 2-Live Crew rap song "Me So Horny." To quote the native prostitute, "For $10, you get everythin' you want, because Me So Horny, Me Love You Long Time," phrases now etched in the popular imaginary of Asian sexual decadence.[26]

Meanwhile, the Suzie Wong clip pops back on the TV screen and loops like a videotape gone awry, scrolling forward and backward erratically in jump sequences that break down to frame-by-frame fragments. The audience hears a "nails-on-the-blackboard" screech, marking a terrifying shakeup in Suzie Wong's world and heralding the entrance of a different Suzie Wong.

As the lights come on, we come face to face with a queer-looking bearish "wo/man" many years after the film:

SUZIE WONG: He said Go. So here I am, stuck in Anytown U.S.A., finally able to speak, read, and write English correctly and still, my life is one goddam tragic TV melodrama movie-of-the-week. HOOKER WITH QUINTESSENTIAL HEART OF GOLD DUMPED FOR LITTLE THAI BOY.

As the story goes, Suzie Wong's marriage to Robert Lomax is anything but a honeymoon. Lomax has become a rice queen in his sixties and a sex tourist infatuated with a Thai boy. Their trip to Bangkok to begin their lives together happily-ever-after quickly fizzled. Suzie recounts, "It all seemed like being in Hong Kong all over again, except the language and the food." And we might add to her list of exceptions, the boys. The new Mrs. Robert Lomax is, after all, "the Little Thai Boy." This nameless but generic euphemism refers to a local sex worker instantly recognizable as a purchasable or disposable erotic interest for the older white male tourist.

Chin speaks in a continuous drone throughout the show, as if to lull the audience or to foreground G.A.P.'s indifference to identity politics. I viewed the video at the Franklin Furnace archives in Brooklyn, New York, and found Chin's monotonal "nonperformance" campy in its insistence on unpleasure or undoing of exotic pleasures. But the campy affect is hardly the same kind of funny we might associate with drag queen camp. In fact, there is nothing particularly amusing about Chin as he is stuffed like a life-size plush toy with an indeterminable gender to parody the overladen artifice and soft appeal of "Suzie Wong."

The toy animal role-play also brings to mind the idea of diminutive Asians, particularly the gay Asian boy, as sweet but disposable little playthings without real emotions. This reference to cartoon Asians is, however, undercut by four large mason jars, each containing a stuffed animal pickling in vinegar. The pickled animals point to the unnatural preservation and display of Asian "tenderness," which Chin rails against later in a segment titled "Robert's Lesson on How to Be Tender." Raging against colonial dictates on Asian decorum, Chin proceeds to stab and skewer the stuffed animals with barbecue forks and knives, holding them up like stick puppets to enact the violence of this enforced affect. The visual defamiliarization of Suzie Wong as a strange, furry mascot portends the show's meta-critiques and narrative disjuncture of conventional East-West romance that are constitutive of G.A.P. drama. The defacement of Suzie Wong is partly a narrative device to bracket the allegorical fantasies of her filmic "World" and its afterlife, chiefly of the American white knight coming to rescue the Asian prostitute-damsel in the Third World. It rewrites this myth of liberation and its paradisal happy ending (heterosexual marriage, cultural assimilation, and U.S. citizenship) by exposing the unromantic and ugly fate of Suzie Wong in his hands. The affair was quickly consumed like a can of Coke, and the white knight, the artist-hero Robert Lomax, has not only moved on to his next exotic destination but has also turned gay. While once the ultimate embodiment of the sexy, nativized yes-girl from the 1960s, Suzie is no longer the vixen in her aging, Americanized state. She is, if anything, an old commodity and fantasy recorded by the sonic and televisual remnants of the film, which loops like a broken videotape on the TV screen. Abandoned and alone, Suzie Wong has turned into a desperate housewife in middle America. The myth of Suzie Wong, as it were, is shattered; it is over.

The substitution of "The Boy," an agreeable Asian houseboy, for Suzie Wong, the archetypal Asian bargirl, is thus uncanny on a number of gender, sexual, and contextual expectations. On first blush, he functions much like the filmic Suzie Wong, who was half the age of Lomax, and clearly signified by the casting of the eighteen-year-old actress Nancy Kwan opposite William Holden, whom a reviewer called "a somewhat weathered" forty-one-year-old actor.[27] On Broadway, the part was filled by "an exotic 19-year-old French-Chinese girl,"[28] France Nuyen, whom her costar, William Shatner, characterized in his 2009 autobiography as a plastic beauty who would have been a "great star in still pictures or a wax museum."[29] He thought Nuyen was "absolutely gorgeous," but as good as a mute or a wax figure. He also equated her lack of English proficiency with emotional illiteracy as an actress. Shatner's patronizing slip five decades after he worked with Nuyen belies a deeper racialized current in the perception of "foreigners" in the United States. Like Suzie Wong, the young, "barely legal" Asian actresses who speak little English are all emotionally and intellectually vacuous. Moreover, they index the unquestioned virility of the white male who is able or entitled to have his way with the choicest native youth.

The native boy functions like the native girl in that sense, particularly in the way he is "programmed" to desire or love the white man. Notably, the age disparity is even greater, as in the case of the Little Thai Boy, who is a quarter of Robert Lomax's age. The predatory rice queen/nubile Asian boy coupling comes to mind, but regardless of age, the native male is infantilized as a beautiful but incomprehensible child who should be seen more than heard. He doesn't, after all, always make sense, linguistically and emotionally. This colonial disparity is underscored by the implausibility of the reverse encounter: young, white Adonises, for instance, are not within the reach of any old Asian queen. In the world of G.A.P., however, these seemingly binding designations are both invoked and denaturalized, producing a tension and ambiguity around the stereotypes that populate the dyad's colonial body politic. In a way, the tension and ambiguity evoke the performative bind of the racialized dyad in G.A.P. drama, but the layers of queer contradictions and uneven power play also actively undercut any easy legibility or judgment.

For instance, out of the slippage between Chin's Suzie Wong and the filmic role immortalized by Nancy Kwan comes The Boy, a character who performs the role of Lomax's fresh-faced artistic muse and sweet native fetish. He is not unlike Suzie Wong in a sense, but he is also a foul-mouthed critic who sees through the white man's art as a form of fetishistic patronage. He is a speaking and completely self-conscious subject. On first blush, The Boy appears to be the submissive, erotic subject of Lomax's painting who also doubles as his sexual and romantic interest. But unlike Suzie, who is a totally willing native poser—"Me lying on his bed. Me on the veranda holding an apple. Me fishing. Me in silk"—The Boy is a cynical participant who calls out Lomax's lascivious intentions: "He wants to paint me, but I tell him that I don't want to be painted. He says, Paint to draw a picture of you. He thinks that I think that he wants to *paint* me. I tell him I know what the fuck he means, and he laughs." The exchange points to the explicit role-play of Lomax as the white man and The Boy as a native boy while inversing the power structure assigned to these positions. The Boy may be subject to Lomax's exotic gaze, but he is also in control and speaks out against him. He is, in other words, crossing the protocols of his subjection and wielding power as a critical agent. In contradistinction, Lomax is a non-speaking, non-present role, and a helpless old man. Returning the favor of colonial condescension, The Boy enumerates Lomax's powerlessness, from his senility—"he doesn't ever get hard anymore," all those "pathetic attempts to overcome his impotence"—to his irrelevance—"shitty has-been career." From The Boy's perspective, Lomax is full of phony clichés culled from rice queens, which are repeated "a lot as if he's trying to convince himself":

> He likes everything from my cultures, he says. "The people, the places, the atmosphere is just so nice . . . I mean, it's just so different, so easy-going and open and friendly . . . people are so beautiful, not like model beautiful, though so many are. . . . But you, you are beautiful both inside and outside."

Lomax's professions of love for The Boy, like the pickup lines of rice queens at U.S. gay bars catering to Asians and their admirers, are turned into the sound bites of every Western tourist under the spell of destination exotica. They conflate the white male's love for his Asian other with a random assemblage of Asian art, artifact, and aura, from Chinese water painting and origami flowers to an accessible friendliness. For the rice queen, his collection of Asian paraphernalia also functions as an arsenal of seduction props—"Do you want to come to my home to see my Buddha?"—and proof of his serious adoration of Asians in general. It presumes that the white man's essentialist idea or taste of Asian culture and traditions is acceptable and even shared by all the Asians he fancies. Both the rice queen and Robert Lomax are in a hyperbolic state of self-induced Asian possession. Lomax, for instance, has to constantly "convince himself" of liking "everything" Asian, including positive thoughts on the beauty of Asians—"people are so beautiful, not like model beautiful, though so many are." Put another way, the spell of destination exotica or "Asia" by which he is taken is the spell of colonial magic that once created the captivating display of nativized objects and people at museums, world fairs, circuses, and entire colonies-for-excursion.

The politics of these erotic expectations and emotional transitions, as well as the histories of racialized display, have been explored by American playwrights and artists such as David Henry Hwang, Cherríe Moraga, George C. Wolfe, Coco Fusco, and Suzan-Lori Parks in such plays as *M. Butterfly, The Colored Museum,* and *Venus,* to name just a few significant works. G.A.P. drama extends these performance interventions with queer and ironic reprisals while calling for comparative critiques beyond the American landscape, as well as the use of other intertextual references. The Boy's so-called love for Lomax is thus both allegorical and performative of a range of colonial encounters. Apropos of such a scenario, at once historic and fabled, G.A.P. presents the love of the dyad as the afterlife of scattered colonial circumstances, and always already mediated by a varying set of spells. Hence, The Boy acts like an avatar of exotic desire with no authentic feelings. He is apathetic and yet plays along as Lomax's lover—"he makes me put my head on his lap, rolls his eyes back in some tantric state between nirvana and psychoneurosis . . . says he loves me . . . he can't live without me." Chin intensifies these aspects of the character by forestalling any emotional or erotic identification with various incomprehensible acts that have no words. For instance, in the monologue about Lomax's senility, The Boy interacts with the images from the television sexually, first as a gawker, and then with his tongue as he tries to lick every character appearing on it.

An unnatural character, The Boy appears to be from a different era, devoid of tenderness, and fixated on the television (substituting for the white man) as a source of desire. He gives no explanation for his pleasure in licking the screen, but he is evidently enjoying it. He does not know why, and for that matter, we do not know why, the act seems so pleasurable. The disconnect of form and desire, romance and pleasure, helps to denaturalize the dyad's love story as a matter of pure feelings between two human beings. Rather, the jarring act of The Boy "tonguing" the television uncovers the objectification of the dyad's loving desires, and demands that such a love be plugged into a larger discursive framework. From this point of view, The Boy's mercurial coldness and rapid loving are partly a filmic and theatrical formation, as in *The World of Suzie Wong*, and partly a requisite affect of the native boy whose senses are or must be evacuated of content.

Extricated from the transcendental or redemptive love of the white man, The Boy is a conscious and articulate queer subject who is cognizant of the colonial political economy in which he is trapped, and for which he has a performative critique. For instance, the unmistakable sexual connotations of *"painting"* the Thai boy bring out Lomax's dirty secret as a traveling artist and link him to a fraternal lineage of white male tourists or expatriates in Asia. It connects him, for instance, to the German artist Walter Spies (discussed in chapter 1), who photographed and painted a number of transfixed Balinese boys while choreographing a ritual performance, *kecak*, with the same boys, who served as the *Ramayana* monkeys in the ritual. The boys were also his muses, houseboys, and sexual objects in 1930s Bali. This encounter constitutes one iteration of the classic white man/brown boys dyad in the early twentieth century. Significantly, both Lomax and Spies are artists, indicating the blurry convergence of art and patronage, romance and exploitation, fiction and fact. In this regard, the generic term "Boys" is both a historic reference to and an update of the nativized brown boys in Bali and other exotic locations for Westerners like Morocco, Africa, Sri Lanka, India, and Japan, to name just a few of the most famous sites.

Literary luminaries, the likes of Gustave Flaubert, Roland Barthes, Lawrence Durrell, Paul Bowles, and André Gide, have traveled to all these destinations in search of male companionship that often manifests in the form of native boys. And unlike their white male counterparts, the native boys are etched in memory as visual remnants, either as sketches or untitled photographs; otherwise they are an indistinguishable or sexualized mob that is unpredictable and even threatening. In Tennessee Williams's classic example, *Suddenly Last Summer*, a band of dark-skinned beggar boys on a sunny island, Cabeza de Lobo (literally "head of the wolf"), became a cannibalistic orgy that devoured Sebastian Venable, the play's gay white male protagonist who took vacations there in search of boys. Indeed, where documentation of such queer encounters exists, whether fictional, theatrical, or ethnographic, it is invariably focused on the white male's conquests, misfortunes, dilemmas, or secrets during his travel. The native boys are there in service of his narrative, often as a secondary but colorful, conceptual entity—menace, love, beauty, muse—offering some kind of insight to the white male psyche, subjectivity, or fascination with otherness. But they remain invisible, absent, or a mystery.

Citing this history of erasure, The Boy stands in for other such nameless native characters and boys living in the "infinite universe" of anonymity, and whose best shot at history is the title of Mrs. Robert Lomax or its "approximate" honorific. In Chin's performance, this includes the allegorical "Tragic Teenager," who hopelessly yearns for "The German" who never returns for him, and the "Eversmiling Thai Boy," who smiles automatically on Lomax's demand but is somehow unable to satisfy his criteria for racial authenticity and love. The switch from barely legal girl (as exemplified by Kwan's and Nuyen's Suzie Wong) to boys of indeterminably young ages (Little Thai Boy, Eversmiling Thai Boy, The Next Unfortunate One, and Tragic Teenager—all allegorical) is a performative slippage in the show that points to the native's infantilism and female gender assignment. This theatrical transfiguration from the native girl to boy also highlights the fluidity of an orientalist gaze across gender roles and sexual orientation, and accounts for a way the native boy (adult or otherwise) is very much like a girl. In other words, the interchangeability of the woman and the boy brings together an intertextual Madama Butterfly—M. Butterfly. The gendered disparity of the colonial heterosexual dyad is thus invoked as an analytic for same-sex encounters between the white man and the native boy. Hence, the queer "inversal" of Suzie Wong sustains the native girl myth for Robert Lomax's rice queen fantasy, so that in Chin's meta-performative iteration, the gay Asian male or native boy is at once a citation of and a foil to the white man's native girl. This play with gendered, ageist, and physical designations enable G.A.P. to occupy several identities and positions that both invoke and exceed the primary expectations of the colonial white male.

Such a critical role-play is necessary since next to the Euro-American man, the native boy is the youth or "minor" in stature regardless of his real age or standing. His perceived childishness, mischief, cuteness, and caprice are a major part of his appeal. The valorization of cultural difference based on uninterrogated Western ideologies of gender and race helps to validate the claim or impression that the manly man with authority is always the older, bigger, and taller white guy. When the exotic other is feminized as an immature youth, a relational dependency is established to justify or even encourage the affection and patronage of colonial desire. In other words, the guidance and benevolence of the white man is crucial for the native boy's well-being, growth, and development into a man. This dynamic is not merely about personal relationships but allegorical of bilateral relations between the United States and Asian countries.

The characterization of the Filipino president Ferdinand Marcos as "America's Boy," postwar Japan as "a boy of 12," or "all [of] Vietnam" as "not worth the life of a single American boy" points to the heteromasculinist and paternal logics governing the American modernity project.[30] Tellingly, it views "stasis, resistance, or barriers to 'proper' development" of the nonwhite nation through the figures of "an inept, incorrigible child or a naïve, foolish woman."[31] The conflation of "child" and "woman" activates in one stroke the phallic and adult glory of U.S. modernity and its ideology of maturity. Within the United States, this form of colonial racialization manifests most clearly in the Asian houseboy stereotype, a form of ethnic terror that enforces servitude and infantilization in the popular representation of the Asian male. Chinese houseboy servants, for instance, are a designated role-type for Asians in early U.S. television series such as *Bachelor Father* (1957–1962) and *Bonanza* (1959–1973), much like representations of native boys in earlier colonial photography, art, and performance. As is clear, these houseboys in the popular American imaginary are linked to the colonial dyad with a latent homoerotics.

More recently, the logics of this exotic gaze have also produced Matt Sun, an Asian houseboy figurine modeled like a superhero in the toy market. When the doll is paired with the snapshot of a gray-haired white man from the *pictures of you* series by Viet Le, an Asian American scholar-artist, we might arrive at a different moment of gay erotica invented by the dyad.[32] The "untitled" picture features a nameless daddy with a blurry face looking emptily into the distance. He has an austere gaze and looks emotionally ambiguous, but another more explicit shot in the series reveals that he has just masturbated, leaving cum on his own thighs. The juxtaposition of the two images locates his paternal gaze as a sexual fixation on the doll, a first step toward uncovering the unspeakable locus or addiction of racialized desire.

To put it another way, this visual pairing of a plastic Asian boy toy and his fictional daddy owner makes explicit the artifice of the dyad and its sexuality. Like Chin's turn as Mrs. Robert Lomax looking for love, this pairing also conjures up another spell of the dyad's circum-Pacific cruising: The houseboy is now a chiseled and upbeat American doll while his daddy owner is stripped naked, anonymous and washed out, as if reversing the colonial dyad's identity prescriptions. One has become undistinguished while the other is no longer part of a nameless mob. But if the tables are turned for the native boy as the modern Asian male, the "upgrade" is only plastic. Matt Sun's superhero persona, for instance, is a gay joke as a fulsome doll. He is quite literally the Asian male made into a plastic plaything, not unlike the muscle clone of any gayborhood striving to be the next Tom of Finland pinup. But if Matt Sun has attained a new class status like the upwardly mobile Asian American, he is also no more than The Help.

The racialization of his toyness as a superboy supplements his designated domesticity as a modern houseboy. This is a perverse colonial legacy with a neoliberal cover, since the facetious reinvention points to the spells about the native boy's adaptive allure in the market, and celebrates his new visibility or "coming out" with popular or commercial appeal. While one connects the gay Asian male's diasporic predicament in the West to circum-Pacific formations of queerness linked to colonialism, it bears note that this queer twist is at once a critique and a cackle. G.A.P.'s ethnic camp is crucial, in that sense, for a different staging of the gay Asian male (G.A.M.) in the United States. As G.A.P. sees it, G.A.M. is burdened with a consortium of dissembling cultural signs, identities, neuroses, and dysfunctions. As we are wont to know, his subjectivity is incurably fractured or multiply split as a diasporic or migratory subject: He is neither "over here" (in the United States) nor "over there" (in Asia), and carries a baggage full of "oriental" woes through such limited roles in the U.S. media and in everyday life as geisha girls and exotic houseboys; he is bound and sexualized by tradition; he has a bit of an identity and gender crisis; he is part of a mob of angry Asian boys who hate the white man, or he is a potato queen who only sleeps with the white man; he is a boy toy in need of white, paternal discipline; he is Miss Saigon, he is not Miss Saigon; he is either an exotic trick to the rice queen or a sticky rice-cultural nationalist; he is trying to find his penis and he does not want to be the bottom; he's found his penis and he wants to be the bottom . . .[33]

This schizophrenic list of gay Asian issues parodies the kind of drama we have come to expect from some of the most representative gay Asian and Asian American performance, visual art, and critical discourse. These issues show how the spells of the dyad continue to have far-reaching effects in Asian performance broadly defined. They foreground the performativity of racialized affect in Western contexts or whenever the Asian male is paired with a white male. At the same time, the list points to the centrality of performance in the casual and critical reiterations of the dyad in various ethnic, touristic, and ethnographic contexts. The oeuvre of Asian/American performances that are read this way often suggests that there is one dominant affliction: the Asian guy is infantilized, criminally rattled, or psychosexualized as an exotic other in a white male (gay) universe. The cultural logics organizing this trope seem to permit no other possibility but either resentment toward or pity for the Asian guy. Moreover, it essentializes his "disorientation" as an inherent defect. In contradistinction, the white (gay) male is a universal prototype of the male ideal. He is the Adonis, the standard bearer of beauty, the one for whom good food and entertainment are made. If the gay Asian male is left out cold from the Adonis order, he is invariably coupled with older white men as a younger, fetishized other. He has, as they say in gay American lingo, fallen prey to the rice queen.

In G.A.P.'s geography of desire, however, the erotic locus is shifted from the singular white man as the originator or innovator of desire to G.A.P. as a beleaguered and indifferent star wielding a queer cartography. Traipsing across the United States, she has a checkered memory rather than a biography. Hence, the trans-embodiments of G.A.P. as the other Suzie Wong in Anytown, U.S.A., are connected to their colonial precedents in Hong Kong and other comparable sites, such as sex tourism in Thailand. They point to the dyad's lasting effect across diasporic circuits and transnational maps in our present era. As the fate of this "forgotten" Suzie Wong demonstrates, coming to the United States has not improved the lot of the native boy. The same set of bad options and cruel fate awaits him as he is transplanted from the Third World to the Land of the Free. Not only has he to contend with the ubiquity of the rice queen syndrome in gay America, he is also mired in the politics of cultural nationalist masculinity by Frank Chin et al.

G.A.P. drama expresses mock anguish at such a fate, in which "marriage" to the white man is the top prize, as if the quest to be Mrs. Robert Lomax will always be the Asian boy's lot. If nothing else, it is his chance to occupy a desired subject position even as a fictive Asian mistress. The high stakes of such a matrimonial quest are of course ridiculous. For the turn from *The World of Suzie Wong* to *The Approximate Infinite Universe of Mrs. Robert Lomax* is a ridiculous move, not unlike Charles Ludlam's or Charles Busch's drag shows. The performance idiom of ridiculosity, or the Theatre of the Ridiculous, includes the parody of Hollywood B-movies, film noir, camp, drag, grand opera, and classics by Marlowe and Molière. Its wanton deformation of the canonical repertory, in particular, brings out the bizarre and ludicrous in heteronormative codes and regimes. Chin's show borrows some of these ridiculous theatrics to rework the racialized naturalism of "Suzie Wong." Her tight-fitting cheongsam, her wily, hustling ways, her poor living quarters, her bad English, her submissive and sexual charge are thus turned into queer, parodic, and cross-gender scenarios that render these realistic markers preposterous. They bring out, in other words, the ridiculousness of the original premise, and suggest that the "World" of Suzie Wong does not belong to her at all. Rather, they reflect the skewed impressions and expectations of the West, which demand that Suzie Wong be realistically fictionalized during such overdetermined encounters.

We gather at the end of Chin's show that the imperative utterance "Go" is a pointless vector (go where? America?), since there is no real destination or place to be. Hence, G.A.P.'s transnational cruising is both inestimable (approximate infinite) and ubiquitous (universe) at the same time. Besides, "the story" of Suzie Wong is transposed and implicated not only in the character's life but also everyone else's: "Me: I am Suzie Wong. You are Suzie Wong. He/She/It is Suzie Wong. You are/ They are/We are Suzie Wong." These fraught tensions—the inestimable/ubiquitous, approximate/cosmic, real/imagined, native girl/native boy—that G.A.P. must negotiate indicate that an oscillatory sense of the world is part of every gay Asian male identity and being. It is also through this unstable position that the artifice of his requisite masquerades as the docile and yet feisty, loving and yet tragic native boy is exposed.

Conclusion

G.A.P.'s setup positions the white man/native boy dyad as central to the queer expression of gay transmigrants in the Asias. But rather than merely performing the queer flip side of heterosexual affect, gay Asian artists confronted with an Other complex (native girl/native boy, insider/outsider, subject/object, participant/observer) are testing the performative limits of their queer expression in ways that draw on and exceed U.S. national history and jurisdiction with alternative histories, identifications, and contact points. They are cruising in the borderzone for possibilities and imagining a different futurity while making lateral connections across sites in minor locations or postcolonies, such as the ethnic United States, Asian diasporas, and the queer conduits found therein.[34] This transcolonial complex is elucidated through a study of circum-Pacific formations in the Asias in the work of performance artists such as Justin Chin, who defies any easy categorization in discrete national, diasporic, or postcolonial terms.

Read through G.A.P.'s cultural matrix, Chin's show points to a way Asian American theater and performance may serve as a queer interchange of Asian encounters with colonial histories. What the audience and/or reader sees in G.A.P. drama is an ethnic in(ter)vention of queer time and space that invites an alternative reading practice of the Asias.[35] In other words, G.A.P. drama serves as both a site and method of analysis using the native boy, the native girl, and/or the colonial dyad to arrive at a different set of questions, encounters, and histories in the Asias. At the same time, it foregrounds how queerness stemming from such a dyadic form (and its performative transmogrifications) is constitutive of transnational modernities in many ways. This approach to queer production in the Asias is an Americanist application of glocalqueering, which I argued in chapter 2 is a way to recalibrate the Eurocentrism of global queering as well as the coordinates of queer diaspora and globalization with circum-Pacific and inter-Asian viewpoints. In this regard, G.A.P.'s dramatic oeuvre has to be understood not only as an Asian American performance in the United States, but also as memory traces of queer diasporas tracked through the circulation of colonial imaginaries in major Asian global cities. And it is on these improper and queer routes that G.A.P. cruises the common circum-Pacific worlds of the United States and the Asias with a queer, colonial bind in drama.

CONCLUSION

Toward a Minor-Native Epistemology in Transcolonial Borderzones

In her now classic essay "Where Have All the Natives Gone?," Rey Chow likens modernity's preoccupation with nativizing cultures to a colonial visual technology in which the native becomes useful and falsely knowable to her onlooker. Using photography as her key example, Chow argues that the reproduction of the native as the visual other presents a set of tricky conundrums about our relationship to the technology of this enduring image: do "we" critique the image itself, expose the machinery of its truth-effects, or call for a substitute? The native, as concept or body, image or historical experience, thus becomes a shifting ground for "more general questions of exploitation, resistance and survival."[1] Chow's interventions may be traced to a lineage of postcolonial criticism from Gayatri Spivak to Homi Bhabha that wrestles with the colonizer's construction of indigeneity or nativized otherness, and the contested conditions of possibility around the native's representation, speech, and self-identity vis-à-vis the gendered histories of colonial subjection. Yet her formulation also points to the transnationalization of the native in the market as well as across nations by implicitly bridging the racialized discourse of nativism to a politics of ethnicity widely applied. In a way, the native has gone ethnic.

Throughout this book, I have explored this intersection primarily through the native boy and his transmogrifications in the queer Asias attuned to orientalism, colonial homoerotics, and dyadic performativity. The ethnic queerness of G.A.P. drama, for instance, provided a campy critique at the intersection of the native and the ethnic vis-à-vis the white man in a transnational context. By way of a conclusion, I turn to a one-woman show, *Details Cannot Body Wants* (Singapore, 1992; New York, 1997; Australia, 1996), by the Peranakan (Straits Chinese) American performance artist–scholar Chin Woon Ping, to conceive an allied reading practice with the native woman back on center stage and the native boy witnessing from the wings.[2] It is a way to account for the shifts that are occurring around the native with the analytics fostered by this book's gambit on the tropic spells of Asian performance. Simply put, how is the native woman queered by the native boy in the postcolonial Asias?

Chin's show broadly examines the plight of nativized women and women of color in various parts of Asia and the United States, and is based on the cultural assumptions of East/West configurations commonly applied to intercultural performance projects. I argue that it is also a classic case study for how a minor-native interpretive framework afforded by the native boy may change the way we think about the figures, encounters, and points of reference traditionally cast for related feminist performance projects. The convergence of critical methodologies outlined above can yield a different set of questions about Asian performance and Asian encounter, or in a broader sense, racial and nativized performance in multiple locations. Importantly, it can also bring about minor coalitions (Asian American, Native American, diasporic minority) in criticism.

In what follows, I will elaborate on the logics of my two proposed spatio-epistemic reconfigurations for a different intelligibility and politic about the native/ethnic located outside or at least unhinged from the overdetermined frontier of the imperial West, particularly the United States. The frontier includes diasporic configurations that presume a rigid two-point ("over here" and "over there") mapping, with the West as the final and present destination, and the East as the point of origin and the past. My reconfigurations, however, enable the (Asian) native/ethnic to speak and signify differently in or through transcolonial borderzones where the United States is a nodal point rather than the center of the world. In doing so, I hope to add to discussions about the transnational turn of American studies on race and sexuality (concentrating on what critical approaches travel and what do not) while emphasizing the continuing need for Asian studies and its cognates to consider diasporic and migration links to the so-called West.

Notably, "Asia" has come to be a category for a particular approach to queer studies that seeks to reify intra-Asian connection, often from a deracialized vantage point, that ignores or even disparages Asian diasporic and migration links to the West.[3] The critical matrix of race, sexuality, and empire, however, demands a reading practice of Asian performance and Asian encounters that brings together different permutations of cognate fields and extends critical inquiries beyond the impasses or blind spots of each field. One such reading practice is proposed here by bridging the native and the ethnic using the *minor-native* and the *transcolonial borderzones* of queer Asias as its model epistemes.

From Native to Minor-Native

The overlap between the native and the ethnic is evident in the way the native functions as a classic racial form in the West, and continues to ghost contemporary understanding or misunderstanding about Native Americans, ethnic women, queers of color, or even entire populations in Third World countries. The French-Senegalese Muslim woman wearing a boubou with lightweight Mauritian voile in Harlem, New York City, is said to carry herself like an African native even if that is a statement of "every fashionable woman."[4] She is a native woman, a diasporic African ethnic, and a fashionista simultaneously. The logics of these intersections are found in a curious set of racializing queries that are often reiterated in quotidian or critical discourse: who is the real native among the ethnics?[5] Is the native real only insofar as she fits within the racial-ized order of the colonial West? Must the ethnic minority display some nativized attributes such as traditional sartorial flair in order to be con-sidered authentic? Such queries belie the discursive disconnect in post-colonial and ethnic studies that scholars have only started to address in transnational frameworks. Broadly speaking, postcolonial studies on the native have focused on the ocular, aural, and ethnographic (native as/in image, rhythm, field subject), while the study of the ethnic is orga-nized around citizenship claims, imagined communities, and the dias-pora with discrete relational structures. If the disconnect is protracted by the location of the native and the ethnic in seemingly disparate fields of study, their exotic, racializing imaginaries are nevertheless connected or conflated across time and place.

Chow's work begins to align the different critical investments and locations of the native vis-à-vis the ethnic as a productive starting point to rethink the analytic contours or limits of comparative frameworks (postcolonial, ethnic, border, diasporic) for transnational racial perfor-mance. But can performance shift the terms of recognition around the native, the ethnic, and their transmogrifications using a set of spatial and relational coordinates other than the colonial dyad (for example, white man/native woman) and its related topographies (such as the exotic East)? How might Native American scholarship help to recon-figure the perceptual strongholds of an orientalist gaze that has in many ways dominated Euro-American cultural production of the other? Such a theoretical gambit is staked against what many critics have noted as the recursive limits, blind spots, and impasses of analyses organized by one or the other term.

One might ask, why return to a term like "the native" at all, the antithesis of the European, with particular histories in colonial and anthropological encounters as the basis for imagining alternative per-ceptions of difference in transnational contexts? Part of it has to do with the longevity of the native as a flexible, racial form that undergirds the logics of (self-)exoticizing display and understanding in an age of glo-balism. Besides, as a signature legacy of colonialism, the native is often used as an icon or ruse for racial mastery or racist alienation; we must therefore invoke such a history in order to attempt a different model of analysis that begins to efface her easy recognizability, whether in her primitive, indigenous, or ethnicized form.[6] In the United States alone, the legacy lives on in a smorgasbord of nativized encounters with Asian and Arabic orientals in the form of spies, terrorists, and prostitutes. The native is thus a repository of emotional effects and a sign of history's violation that demand persistent historicizing and critical embodiments. These moving embodiments demand the use of performance and its vocabularies as well as a critical shift from imagistic native to epistemological minor-native.

In Chow's interpretation of the native as a model, she warns against what she calls the "cultural corporations" of scholarly tools that purport to render the native less exotic and less denigrated by supplying an arsenal of original "contexts" and "specificities" that only brings about the visibility of the scholar while neutralizing the "untranslatability of the native's experience and the history of that untranslatability."[7] The root of these reservations can be traced back to the politics of postcolonial critiques emanating from First World academies, and the performability of silence. According to Chow, the native cannot be "saved," her voice and body can never be restored to her authentic context, and in the absence of witness and discourse regarding her victimization, silence is "the most important clue to her displacement."[8] There is, in other words, no simple replacement, corrective, or hidden interiorities to the native-image, one that substitutes "a 'correct' image of the ethnic specimen for an 'incorrect' one, or giving the native a 'true' voice behind her 'false' image."[9] While resonating with Gayatri Spivak's provocative statement "[t]he subaltern cannot speak,"[10] what is striking here is the way performance is central to Chow's characterization of the native's silence:

> That silence is at once the *evidence* of imperialist oppression (the naked body, the defiled image) and what, in the absence of the original witness to that oppression, must act in its place by *performing* or *feigning* as the pre-imperialist gaze.[11]

The possibilities and limitations of embodying nativized silence as evidence of oppression present a potentially radical alternative in the form of a scenario: the native is actively gazing at the colonizer as witness to her oppression prior to her becoming image. As witness, image, and a form of critical gaze, Chow's native exposes the phantasm of colonial fetishization. This shift is crucially moving from the literary and visual to the realm of performance, where we are encountering the emergence of an epistemological native with a critical gesture and gaze. She is pointing to a new context, embodiment, and methodology. In Chow's study, however, the native is always already stuck in an imperialist setup, which necessitates a postcolonial critique structured around vertical power relations. As critics have noted, speech, translation, and intelligibility in such a setup often occur unidirectionally, from Third World to First, from subaltern to imperialist. As urgent and vital as are the critiques of this approach, they are stuck in the scope of postcolonial intervention. The native, for better or worse, will always be bound by a classic set of colonial problematics.

Bridging the gap between postcolonial and U.S. ethnic studies, Victor Bascara demonstrates in *Model-Minority Imperialism* that the native figure is also found in Asian American studies. Using the "Oriental" as a nativized figure, he bridges postcolonial cultural studies, critical American studies, and Asian American studies to tell the story of U.S. empire and imperialism through its theater, drama, novels, government speeches, and film. Part of his argument is that "struggles over the meaning of difference" have to be studied across interdisciplinary fields and objects of study.[12] Importantly, Bascara's work cracks open the relational fields of American culture vis-à-vis the United States as an imperial nation by reading against the grain of the American Dream and its Big Brother role in world "peace and progress."[13] This critical move is emblematic of the transnational turn in Asian/American studies, and productively uncovers the continuities of racial subjugation in imperial and national projects. The prominence of the United States as a locus of study, however, appears to be unquestioned. This is not so much a critique about Americanist projects in general as much as it is about the way that the United States is not reducible to periphery or nodal status. Without such a critical gesture, the native will be forever stuck in the dominant, U.S. progressivist narrative as a remnant of the past; her critical iteration as the minor-native would also be deemed irrelevant and implausible.

Following the leads of Chow and Bascara, I propose pushing their critical work further by considering the minor-native (here, an intersection of the native and minority referenced in their work) as a post-disciplinary episteme of racial performance in the queer Asias. The minor-native can fundamentally change the way we think or look at the native in mobile contexts, and shift the discourse from one about complicity, resistance, or subversion to one about comparativity, lateral relationality, and coalition. Put another way, I am interested in an articulation of othering or difference that resonates beyond the colonial white male and his exotic others. As is clear, the latter is a familiar, some might even say naturalized, setup within the discrete confines of a dominant Western nation-state (the United States) in relation to another outside the West.

Rather than focusing all critical energies on this apparently exhaustive and exhausting setup, it behooves us to turn to Native American studies and its transnational cognates to consider the manifold origins and connections that constitute the borderlands occupied by Native Americans and nativized immigrants around the world. Chin's biography and show point to this aesthetic of distance and affiliation in the Asias, where individual and collective identities are always embroiled in a complex of diasporic, culturally hybridized, and cross-national histories on the move. In other words, the United States may be the third or fourth point of contact in the history of transmigrants with multiple national or ethnic identifications. Native (native to what, whom, or where) is thus a fraught and mutable concept with different sets of racialized markers and encounters. This means that the worldview or subjectivity of many has been shaped elsewhere or produced in a matrix or cross-section of experiences that exceed the local. For instance, the Filipino immigrant in the United States may have worked in Southeast Asia as well as the Middle East as a foreign laborer, and cultivated a particular form of transnational sensibility mixed with the history of Spanish-U.S. colonialism in the Philippines before arriving in the United States to become an Asian American. A Chinese Singaporean may have family and relatives in Malaysia, Taiwan, Canada, Australia, and China with whom she spent parts of her childhood years. She may have a "cosmopolitan" outlook, but her encounter with Filipinos may be largely shaped by their ordinary presence in Singapore as domestic live-in maids. These diachronic and cultural borderzones invoke the regional memories and resources of their contingent class geographies, and shape a polyracialized sense of place that exceeds the

Western/other model. It also suggests that there are several other ways the nativized or racist gaze is composed.

Chin's show encapsulates these varied depths of knowledge as an uber–case study of Woman as the minor-native in the transcolonial borderzones of Singapore/Malaysia, Japan/China, Asian/African/America, and their geopolitical surround. But what is meant by the transcolonial borderzones of queer Asias?

Navigating the Transcolonial Borderzones

By "transcolonial," I mean the different relationalities among minorities or former colonies that share affinities and animosities that are primarily defined in relation to each other rather than or only to their respective (former) metropoles in Europe and the United States. This way of thinking, advocated by scholars working in such fields as minor transnationalism (Francoise Lionnet and Shu-mei Shih),[14] border thinking (Walter Mignolo),[15] and hemispheric performance and politics (Diana Taylor, Jill Lane, and others),[16] adopts "an-other logic" in our critical study of performance and writing outside the Western canon, archive, and epistemic organization. For example, in her study of Mauritian-Creole theater, Lionnet asks,

> How might we theorize this other logic of writing without simply seeing it as "a reconfiguration of the [European generic] content"? . . . How do we highlight the transcultural dimensions of their [writers from the Indian Ocean and the Caribbean] work and their intellectual contributions to the shaping of new contexts of understanding in which familiar questions of theory and practice, form and content, knowledge and understanding, politics and culture, are brought to the fore?[17]

Lionnet conceptualizes "the links among the varied cultures of the so-called 'peripheries'" so that we begin to articulate "Creole texts (oral, written or visual) not just with their European generic 'models' but also with postcolonial creative texts and performances."[18] The transcolonial approach is therefore neither a disavowal of the West and its colonial legacy nor an articulation of cartographic contiguity among former colonies as a condition of exchange. Rather, it is a multi-sited and mobile configuration of thinking and feeling that organizes the issues of the West, including the white United States, as a "minor" function of writing and performance while foregrounding gendered and/or minority issues in comparative perspective.

Among the many articulations of "borderzones," one can begin with the cultural anthropologist Ed Bruner's concept of "touristic borderzones," which stages the interactional exchange between natives and tourists "in an ever-shifting strip or border on the edges of Third World destination countries."[19] He elaborates, "although the borderzone is located in an actual place in the world, what is created there is a cultural imaginary, a fantasy, in itself not a real-life culture but a theatrical one."[20] This particular iteration of the borderzone presumes theatricalized encounters, the touristic gaze, and an "ever-shifting" spatial dynamic as conditions for playing out a confluence of imaginaries, conflicts, and exchange. I use performance as an actual and exemplary site of "borderzones" to address a multiplicity of gazes with different assumptions of race and otherness vis-à-vis the broad question of nativization in the transnational era.

By "transcolonial borderzones," then, I am thinking of nativized encounters in a spatial configuration not contained by the established logics of postcolonial, diaspora, and border studies: center/colony, over here/over there, bi-national metroplex. With a center, origin, or nation as pivotal factors, comparative analyses often result in "the usual comparison of the margin with its hierarchical other that becomes inevitable in studies of intertexuality, literary influence and cross-pollinations."[21] Being situated in a position of vertical power relationship has direct ramifications on an intercultural understanding of otherness. Put another way, the dominance of the West means that the encounter with the native, the way she is looked at or defined, is often overdetermined. The epistemic logic and space of transcolonial borderzones provide the opportunity to simultaneously unthink the generic native and our natural recourse to a binary-center complex (the idea that Western binary configurations, such as civilized/savage, modern/primitive, center or verticalize all thought and exchanges) for critical interventions. Less a corrective than a tactic, reading the minor-native in transcolonial borderzones enables a syncopated interpretation that combines and moves across various critical positions while focusing on lateral comparisons and performative elucidation. The colonialism undergirding such an approach may emerge, for instance, from within Asia, such as Japanese colonialism. As Leo Ching posits in relation to Japanese colonialism, "Japanese or Japaneseness, Taiwanese or Taiwaneseness, aborigines or aboriginality, and Chinese or Chineseness—as embodied in compartmentalized national, racial, or cultural categories—do not exist outside the temporality and spatiality of colonial modernity, but are instead enabled by it."[22]

The Details of Epistemic Relocation

Chin's show, *Details Body Cannot Wants*, provides a way of relocating the native woman or woman of color in the transcolonial borderzone of Southeast Asia and Asian/America. A generic character "Woman" functions as an embodied guide to a nameless roster of women being subjected to endlessly sexist, infantilizing, and misogynistic treatment. On first blush, *Details Body Cannot Wants* is situated in a matrix of cultural imaginaries, languages, conflicts, and practices that appear to relate to postcolonial Singapore-Malaysia on the one hand, and the Chinese diaspora in the United States on the other hand. But describing the show as a diasporic production of Southeast Asian America is inadequate in accounting for the other cultural coordinates at play. Neither does a postcolonial or binational study in the context of Malaysia and Singapore fully cover its critical contours. Moreover, the amorphous— if also fictional—category of "cosmopolitan native woman" slips in and out of her show, further complicating its cultural identity.

A Chinese-Malaysian émigré, Chin resides in the United States and teaches at Dartmouth College but has a tri-national cultural background that informs her Peranakan Singaporean, Malaysian, and Asian American identification. The Peranakans are the Chinese and mixed-race (Chinese and native Indonesian or Malay) descendants of mainland Chinese immigrants who first arrived in the Indonesian archipelago in the late fifteenth and sixteenth centuries, and adopted local Nusantara customs to create the creolized language of Baba Malay containing many Hokkien words as well as cuisine, religion, and clothing. They have come to be known as Straits Chinese, as many relocated along the Straits of Malacca, and were largely English-educated. Many are at least trilingual, speaking Malay, English, and Chinese, though later generations have become less proficient (if even at all) in Chinese so as to assimilate into the Malay Peninsula.

The multiple sites of Chin's cultural if also contested "origins" are uncannily reproduced in the reception of her show in Singapore and New York City (and broadcast as a television show in Australia), where at each location, she was read as an Asian woman from "over there." This pointed to a way that national location, ethnic status, and diasporic coordinates were not necessarily congruent with the show's identity, just as dominant racial expectations are often incommensurate with the actual identification of a minority person. Is the show Singaporean, Chinese- or Peranakan-Malaysian, American, or Asian American? The conundrum raised by this question is not so much about parsing cultural authenticity by national origins as it is an issue of cultural formations that both precede and exceed the contours of current transnational configurations and Western thought.

In the show, the title character Woman is not one person but a performative abstraction of multilingual women who are nativized in the context of Southeast Asia, East Asia, and the ethnic United States, and connected through their differential nativization. The show is in the form of a choreopoem with dance and choral elements, and its overall structure mimics an improvisational music score or dance movement. As meditative vignettes, each section covers the travails of womanhood around a thematic tapestry. The "Details" section plays out her servitude to a set of gendered expectations, from makeup to speech to sitting posture, which also shames her into compulsory womanliness. "Cannot" continues along the same axis by enumerating the myriad prohibitions she faces as a girl, but her own refusal to acquiesce—in other words, her own "cannot"—is not tenable. In the "Body" section, the didactic norms of the female body as a locus of male power and desire are detailed in sexual and violent terms. The cumulative effects of the three dicta result in "Wants," or the performativity of gendered pleasure; she is both socialized and built to please.

This four-part performance art piece is episodically organized around each of the broad concepts in its garbled title, *Details Cannot Body Wants*, which is also a facetious reference to the native woman's incomprehensibility. The Woman reorders patriarchal rationalities purveyed by colonial English by making sense out of this seemingly disparate and ungrammatical set of words. At the same time, she brings to bear the incongruous elements of a modern feminine identity. Anti-realist in its form, the show has no linear plot or stable character, and it uses multiple languages, including Mandarin, Cantonese, Japanese, Malay, and African American English. In addition to linguistic diversity, the sonic environment is a syncretic array of performance and popular music culled from China, Japan, Indonesia, Malaysia, the United States, and Singapore. A small chorus accompanies the action with background noises or instrumentals. The music runs the gamut from Chinese er-hu, Japanese bamboo flute (shakahachi), and solemn choral sounds like Noh voices to Elvis Presley's "I Wanna Be Free." Costume-wise, she is just as eclectic, and appears in an expressionistic "naked" outfit, a 1950s circular skirt with rock and roll motifs, a Chinese samfoo, and a Vietnamese peasant costume. To accentuate this random getup, she often appears with mismatched makeup and accessories. The agglomeration of these visual, linguistic, and sonic elements provides the backdrop for sampling the memories, affect, and motifs that recur in any random, nativized encounter with the Woman. There is neither a coherent narrative to account for her background nor a clear relationship between the sounds and sights (or her environs) and her identity. Part of and yet unhinged from an orientalist and sexist landscape, the multifaceted, sensorial encounter sets up a polyvalent gaze from a spectrum of positions and encounters that also deflect a pointedly Western look on the Asian woman.

One might note that the politics of Chin's intervention are clearly legible to a U.S. audience familiar with other female performance artist of color such as Denise Uyehara, Carmelita Tropicana, or Robbie McCauley. As Helen Gilbert points out, Chin's show is deeply aligned with contemporary U.S. feminist performance art in its "conscious foregrounding of the body and its physical functions, the explicit treatment of sexuality, the direct audience address, the satire of patriarchal power, the rapid shifts between dialogue and song, and the intentional instability of the persona's stage persona."[23] But in contrast to its form, Chin's references are nearly all from Southeast and East Asia, and the Woman signified in her show is also visualized through her own body as an "Asian woman," which carries a set of nativized markers. From the perspective of a Singaporean audience, however, her show appears in a foreign format, and signifies as "American," or at least a transnational U.S. perspective on women's lives. A diasporic reading of the show might consider how U.S. feminist strategies are adapted to resignify exotic femininities in the Asian American context while a postcolonial critique from Singapore/Malaysia might focus on undermining "Western stereotypes of passive, submissive, hyper-feminine Asian womanhood."[24] But the circulation of the show in Singapore (1992), the United States (1997), and Australia (where it was broadcast in 1996), as well as Chin's tri-national, multicultural background, exceeds the parameters of such analyses, and demands that we think through the performative encounters she stages not in one or the other location but in the transcolonial borderzone.

It is within such a spatial imaginary that Chin brackets "native woman" as a colonial construction while foregrounding the motifs, qualities, sounds, and gestures that nativize the Woman in her show. Refusing to give coherence to the universal category of either native woman or Woman, the racialized female figures in her performance are all channeled rapidly, which has the effect of both expressing and undercutting their allure in a kind of strategic obfuscation: "So why are you fascinated by the native woman?" This first move, which turns native from an object to nativizing as a comparative act, involves defamiliarizing the guiding principles of Western looking. If splintering the gaze "we" use on the native woman involves an initial perambulation, after Chow, around the epistemic trappings of "the West and First World" –first thinking, this move asks that we leave that critical framework as a backdrop rather than the mise-en-scène of our critique. For instance, in theatricalizing patriarchal sexism, Chin weaves in an encounter that has to be read in relation to colonial disciplining. For the woman in question, shame is encoded in her "show-in-your-dimples-but-not-your-teeth smile"[25] as she learns to "primly" and "demurely" respond to a preordained set of questions as though she were in an elementary English lesson:

WOULD YOU LIKE ANOTHER PIECE OF CAKE?
(primly, demurely) No, thank you
DO YOU WANT TO GO FOR A RIDE?
No, thank you.

DOES IT HURT?

No, thank you.

CAN I SHOW YOU MY SHAME?

No, thank you.

WOULD YOU LIKE TO GO?

No, thank you.

WOULD YOU LIKE TO COME?

No, thank you.[26]

The lesson of shame is a disciplinary encounter in which the native woman learns the proper ways of speech, body etiquette, and English. This classic colonial lesson is continued with a seemingly celebratory song-and-dance sequence that sets her free in the Western world. To demonstrate this freedom, she yodels "I love to go a wandering" and then sings Elvis Presley's "I Wanna Be Free" in an almost maniacal display that is capped by a ridiculous rendition of a Chinese song, 何日君再来 ("He Ri Jun Zai Lai" [When Will You Return?], first sung by the mainland Chinese singer 周璇 Zhou Xuan for the soundtrack of the 1937 film 三星伴月 [*Three Stars and Half Moon*], and later popularized by the Taiwanese superstar Teresa Teng 邓丽君), with accompanying meowing sounds.[27] She explains, "I had to have a voice like a meowing cat, like the greatest meowing cat in the history of Chinese pop music, the adorable, inimitable, eternal Miss Zhou Xuan."[28] The conscious disorientation of the Woman, as played by Chin, a Peranakan-Chinese-Malaysian-American, singing a Mandarin song to meowing sounds after a yodel and rock classic juxtaposes colonial disciplining and Asian transculturation with diasporic alienation in the United States. Hence, rather than correcting what Chow refers to as the "pornographic gaze" of the West, this opening segment stages the complex effects of nativizing forces through a ridiculous sequence of an amnesiac performance where China emerges alongside England and the United States as a zone of power vis-à-vis Southeast Asia: she does not know why, but she wants to be like a meowing Chinese cat; she does not know why, but she will repeat the same answer to every question in clipped English; she does not know why, but she will yodel and rock like an American. And she will, it seems, continue to act in the ways sanctioned by her conscious and unconscious nativization.

The symbolic prominence of China is reiterated at the end of the section, when the Woman paints half her face in the traditional colors of the Chinese opera heroine and the other half in the black colors of the male warrior in full view of the audience, forming an unknown composite figure with an aura of the authentic native. She then pulls out a mirror from the heap of domestic objects and finds herself looking back at her image, an ephemeral reflection with curious expression and life as "she primps, she grins, and she makes faces of all kinds."[29] The disfigurement of the Woman using the brush strokes of a traditional Chinese opera stages the (self-)exoticizing logics of the nativized woman in a predictable and yet alienating environment. We hear the chorus simulating the cymbal, *pipa,* and bamboo noises of traditional Chinese opera while the transfigured native woman sings an aria from *Madam White Snake,* 白蛇传, based on an ancient Chinese legend. In her state of defilement, nakedness, wonder, and beauty, the woman gazes back at herself as the transnational audience gazes at her. The multiple gazes zeroing in on her, from her own curious self to the publics represented by the different audience in Singapore, the United States, and Australia, create an extraordinary convergence of looking that raises many questions. Is she performing the quotidian exoticism of native cultural shows or the way that Chinese women are readily nativized by a few cosmetic and gestural strokes? Is she staging a pre-imperialist gaze or an ethnic gaze with a cultural nationalist fervor? Is this about the rise of China and a critique of Sinocentrist chauvinism? Is this an embodied articulation of a Sinophone gender that is in conversation with Asian American feminist discourses?

Disorienting the Gaze: Visual Sovereignty and Minor Epistemes

The questions uncovered amid the enactment of *Details Body Cannot Wants* point to the productive epistemic intersections in the transcolonial border zone. Yet the critical lens most readily applied to an understanding of Chin's performance is focused on "the power relations masked by orientalist images."[30] This often involves a singular focus on the myth of cultural authenticity or the politics of assimilation into the dominant culture of a host country. But such a familiar, major-resistant strategy tends to homogenize the encounter "we" have with the Woman by invoking East/West paradigms as the critical bait, while foreclosing the transcolonial encounters of nativized women who are differentially gendered. Rather than looking at the minor solidarities that are potentially forged on a lateral plane, the native woman becomes a stick figure, victim or otherwise, for recuperation by a "feminist postcolonial sensibility that traverses Asia, America and Asian-America."[31]

I want to suggest that the politics of Chin's show may be more productively analyzed in conversation with Michelle Raheja's notion of "visual sovereignty," which provides an alternative way of dealing with the gaze of the Western viewer vis-à-vis Native Americans, particularly as they are represented in ethnographic or mass-mediated images. Using the Inuit film *Atanarjuat* as her case study, Raheja explores "what it means for indigenous people 'to laugh at the camera'" in the context of "often absurd assumptions that circulate around visual representations of Native Americans, while also flagging their involvement and, to some degree, complicity in these often disempowering structures of cinematic dominance and stereotype."[32] Visual sovereignty is, in this regard, a filmic technique as well as "a reading practice for thinking about the space between resistance and compliance wherein indigenous filmmakers and actors revisit, contribute to, borrow from, critique, and reconfigure ethnographic film conventions, at the same time operating within and stretching the boundaries created by these conventions."[33] As notions of sovereignty are embroiled in "creative self-representation" and the "intellectual health" of a community wiped out by genocide and colonialism, the Inuit filmmakers "operate as technological brokers and autoethnographers of sorts, moving between the community from which they hail and the Western world and its overdetermined images of indigenous people."[34]

While the historical specificity and stakes of visual sovereignty in this regard pertain to the Inuits as a focal point, the film also stands in facetiously for the "Primitive Everyman."[35] In addressing the gaze on the Inuits, Raheja identifies the multiple audiences the film is addressing, and points out that their varied understanding of the film's Inuit episteme or cultural references calibrates their access to its wry or self-reflexive play with indigenous signifiers. These levels of address are pegged with different aims of serving their "home communities," and "forcing viewers to reconsider mass-mediated images of the Arctic."[36] A knowing Inuit audience, for instance, would see the film differently than non-Inuit Native Americans "who may read some of the cues from the film and place them in dialogue with their own tribally specific oral narratives and discursive contexts." A third group consists of non-Inuits "who do not understand Inuktitut or the cultural practices represented in the film but who may be aware of the stereotypes surrounding Inuit in literature and film."[37] With these three prototypical ways of looking, Raheja rereads the iconic smile of an Inuit hunter portrayed in Robert Flaherty's *Nanook of the North* (1922) from "putatively naïve" to "laughing at the camera"[38] to "laugh[ing] at the audience" in *Atanarjuat*.[39] This play with the audience is exemplified in one of many instances of the film's visual sovereignty where the filmmakers "take the non-Inuit audience hostage" by refusing to edit the 161-minute film to conventional length or narrative style.[40] The "slowness of the sequencing," allegorizing "the wait for hours at a seal hole," for instance, forces us to "alter our consumption of visual images to an Inuit pace, one that is slower and more attentive to the play of light on a grouping of rocks or the place where the snow meets the ocean."[41]

One of the lessons of visual sovereignty is the political solidarity of Inuits and Native Americans anchored in the common exigencies of their communities' claims to misplaced or suppressed cultural identifications. While this particular intervention is specific to the Inuits and Native Americans as subaltern groups, its transcolonial convergence presents a model for framing and conditioning the ways of looking at indigeneity or nativeness in other minor contexts. Chin's Woman enters the fray of this transcolonial borderzone to address the comparable issue of nativization in the Asias. Like Native Americans on film, the native Asian woman is an overdetermined concept in performance with several ready tropes. But as Raheja demonstrates with visual sovereignty, destabilizing Eurocentric principles of looking is not necessarily predicated on the Western gaze as a structuring episteme. Besides, the political stakes constituted by a reaction to the dominant way of looking at otherness would always serve "the dominant's sense of entitlement" and "produce in the minor a reactive notion of authenticity."[42] A transcolonial understanding of the native Asian woman forges visual sovereignty with queer minor-native tactics to address multiple audiences while foregrounding how a minor episteme can be a central and effective critical strategy. It calls, in other words, for another way of looking at the nativized females in Chin's show as more than simply deconstructing or subverting the orientalist stereotypes of Asian femininity for an audience who can only see through the Western lens. The latter approach is encapsulated by a postcolonial, feminist critic's summation of the show: "*Details Cannot Body Wants* plays with—and up to—Western stereotypes of passive, submissive, hyper-feminine Asian womanhood."[43]

The limitations of such an optic have to do not only with its sole focus on the vertical power relationship between colonizer and colonized but also the inadvertent reinscription of stereotypes even where they don't apply in order for the critique to make sense to a Western audience/gaze. Consider, for instance, this excerpt of the "Cannot" section of Chin's show:

> Hello Doll. Where are you from? I'll bet you're lonesome, aren't you? I bet I know what you want. I know *all* about you. How about some hunky chunky company? How about it, lovely dove?
> And you're supposed to reply,
> (*In docile, 'Oriental' voice and posture, with white profile to audience*)
> Hai. Watashi karimatsu. Arigato gozaimasu. Me China Doll, me Inscrutable Doll, me sexy Miss Saigon, me so horny/so so horny/me so horny, me love you long time (etc. from 2-Live Crew rap song).
> (*The Chorus can pick up the beat and song.*)
> BUT WHAT YOU REALLY WANT TO SAY IS,
> (*Use loud, sassy black mannerisms and tone, with black profile to audience*)
> Hey Muthafukka. Quit messin' round with me and mah sistahs you hear? We don't want yo jive talk an yo bullshittin. You know what's yo problem? You ain't got no RESPECT, that's yo problem. Pick up after yoself! Go wash yo *own* goddam underwear! Clean that toilet seat after you take a leak! Take yo goddam inflated inflatable prick and shove it up yo skinny ass!
> We AIN'T gonna be
> AIN'T gonna be
> AIN'T gonna be
> Mules of the WORLD no mo![44]

According to Gilbert, "African American culture provides a model for feminine agency in the wise-girl rap of the 'Cannot' section," where

Chin demonstrates the "arbitrary composition of such racial stereo-types, [as] the Woman transforms from a Peking Opera performer to a Western man to a *Miss Saigon* sex-doll, before adopting the straight-talking sass of an urban black American."[45] The substitutive citations of various nativized female Asians point to racial stereotypes from the West that run from geisha, China doll, and Miss Saigon to the sexu-ally available Asian female in "Me So Horny," the 2-Live Crew rap song based on the encounter between U.S. servicemen and a Vietnamese hooker in the film *Full Metal Jacket*:

PRIVATE JOKER: I wanna slip my tube steak into your sister. What'll you take in trade?

PRIVATE COWBOY: What do you got?

DA NANG HOOKER: Hey, baby. You got girlfriend Vietnam?

PRIVATE JOKER: Not just this minute.

DA NANG HOOKER: Well, baby, me so horny. Me so HORNY. Me love you long time. You party?

PRIVATE JOKER: Yeah, we might party. How much?

DA NANG HOOKER: Fifteen dollar.

PRIVATE JOKER: Fifteen dollars for both of us?

DA NANG HOOKER: No. Each you fifteen dollar. Me love you long time. Me SO HORNY.

PRIVATE JOKER: Fifteen dollar too beaucoup. Five dollars each.

DA NANG HOOKER: Me sucky-sucky. Me love you too much.[46]

For a knowing audience of Chin's performance, such hypersexualized references of Asian women are partly about the sublimation of the Viet-nam War in American popular culture (musical, Hollywood film, rap) through the figure of the female Asian whore, a native whore who is sexually available but disposable, and always barely comprehensible in speech and/or action. The quick and varied citations of other tropes—geisha, China doll, Miss Saigon—also point to the way that Asian women in general are superficially nativized by U.S. imperial projects and disseminated to the rest of the world as consumable.

But exposing the "arbitrary composition" of Western racial stereo-types may be no more than a mere descriptor of colonial taxonomy, and such a sole focus can and often does obfuscate other racialized relationalities. The worldview or subjectivity of the heterosexual white male is not the only game plan in town. The China doll syndrome cited by Chin, for instance, may be a Western construction, but its cultural import in Singapore is more likely inflected through the trend of local Chinese men marrying mainland, working-class Chinese women rather than through a film star like Anna May Wong. Ironically, Chin's "Inscrutable Doll" invokes the mail-order doll bride from China who speaks Mandarin better than Chinese Singaporeans! But such resignifications are forestalled by an staunchly calibrated anti-(Western)-orientalist gaze. Besides, the blind spot of "deconstructive" embodiments for such a gaze is the inadvertent replication of nativized encounters or the instantiation of U.S. exotic tropes in the borderzones. For instance, the hyperbolic representation of helpless female orientals becomes essentialized in the moment of their redemption by the sassy female African American rapper who uses a decontextualized form of black rage to "save" her more docile and practically speechless Asian counterparts. The "agency" that is accrued to the "urban black American" by way of her forceful speech, expletives, and rap "mannerisms" is itself a racialized construction, but she is somehow presented as a more empowering stereotype than the orientalized Asian. Yet for audiences outside the United States, such as Singapore, the menacing female rapper is potentially instantiated as an exotic thug, since rap is mediated by U.S. music television and other sensationalistic images of tough neighborhoods in a black America they are unlikely to have encountered or studied. Hence, rather than speaking for her apparently more oppressed Asian counterparts, she ends up becoming nativized herself in an anti-orientalist critique about otherness. Such trappings of a deconstructive lens attuned only to a Western gaze can be productively addressed by applying visual sovereignty and minor epistemes as structuring modes of understanding.

In the case of Chin's performance, sorting out the audiences that she is addressing can help to recalibrate the gaze and political stakes of the minor-native in performance. But this is no easy task as there is no identifiable community, such as the Inuits, forming the core of her minor episteme. Rather, *Details Cannot Body Wants* addresses a very diverse female constituency with the amorphous, nativized Asian woman as its transnational centerpiece. As the show demonstrates, she could manifest in myriad forms that are shaped through Chin's body in a variety of languages, songs, and costumes. But her exoticism is never satisfactorily displayed, as the audience is "held hostage" by her inaccessibility and volatile transmogrifications. The minor-native episteme is in this case a performance technique and a reading practice anchored on the intersection of transcolonial feminisms and woman of color criticism. There are at least three audiences Chin's show is addressing: multiracial and transmigratory women in Singapore; female diasporic Asians and ethnic minorities in the United States and Australia; and an international audience who understands the gendered predicament of nativized female Asians in the global media of especially capitalist societies. These different audiences and the borderzones of their interaction "recognize the persistence of colonial power relations and the power of global capital, attend to the inherent complexities of minor expressive cultures on multiple registers, take a horizontal approach that brings postcolonial minor cultural formations across national boundaries into productive comparisons, and engage with multiple linguistic formations."[47]

Superb as it is, Chow's rhetorical riddle about the native who is falsely missed (as the titular question in her essay suggests) only to be rediscovered between the "defiled image and the indifferent gaze" necessitates a forceful reading against the binding cultural coordinates of the West. But the minor-native in the transcolonial borderzones invokes a different reading strategy and performance technique that considers the reinscriptive power of the colonial gaze as merely one of several power dimensions that must be configured for a critical understanding of transnational nativization. In other words, while we can neither ignore the native's persistent presence in our postcolonial modernity nor simply substitute it with a visual that is corrective of the "pornographic" gaze of the West, we have to move toward or stage an altogether different encounter while retaining the imaginary of the native as a form of tension for critique. Second, we need to situate our sense of space on less familiar or less trodden pathways using performance as a road map and a visual embodiment. For instance, while the inauguration of border studies around the U.S.-Mexican border has provided a model for considering the historic and contemporary effects of colonial annexation and exchange, it has also codified the relational coordinates in a bi-national metroplex. There are many other borders in the world with histories of violence, migration, and exchange that have not been adequately (if at all) studied. Meanwhile, much of the discourse continues to be generated through or against the dominant gaze of the straight white male and his mythic, nativized other. This classic dyad, a familiar colonial legacy of the West, continues to be a core problematic in border and postcolonial epistemologies. But could such a structuring optic be potentially transnationalized so that alternative borders are not exclusively narrated through its history and tropes? Can we see the native beyond his/her contradistinction to the white man as the standard bearer of difference? The transcolonial borderzones proposed here present a form of spatial relocation and interactional dynamic—who, what, and where we choose to perform and study—best served by the technics of performance and other transcolonial tactics such as visual sovereignty.

The politics of playing with nativized markers in transcolonial borderzones have to be understood in a critical field of cognate theories so that the minor-native can emerge as an analytic, particularly as it pertains to global literary and performance inquiries. In my particular approach, I have relied much on minor transnationalism as a navigational principle. Part of the critical riddle of the minor-native is figuring out whom its performance serves, and for what purpose; what its colonial and transnational conduits are; and how we come to know a minor-native performance is taking place. As pioneering proponents of minor transnationalism, Lionnet and Shih argue that it "points toward and makes visible the multiple relations between the national and the transnational" while emphasizing the minor's "inherent complexity and multiplicity."[48] This conception of minor transnationality is based not on a "major-resistant mode of cultural practice" but on a transversal movement of culture.[49] It produces "new forms of identification that negotiate national, ethnic, and cultural boundaries" whose coordinates are not pure to begin with, but "always already hybrid and relational as a result of sometimes unexpected and sometimes violent processes."[50] And unlike postnational, nomadic, or flexible models, its subjects are actually invested in their geopolitical space, and "often waiting to be recognized as 'citizens' to receive the attendant privileges of full citizenship."[51] These spells of difference demand an analytics tied to performance in the queer Asias and its attendant tropic spells.

The emergent minor-native in the transnational borderzone is not so much an identity or a demographic as it is a method for understanding minoritized or nativized acts, perceptions, and feelings in the transnational world. A witness and conspirator of this sea change, the brown boy springs from the wings of the stage, where he has been watching the native woman's show with a gleeful grin. And this is also where he takes his cue to leave with a bag of tricks made of and made for the tropic spells in the Asias, where each spellbinding performance attendant to his stories, alongside his critical companion, the native woman, now unfurls to a different gaze.

NOTES

Notes to the Introduction

1. Colin McPhee, *A House in Bali* (Singapore: Berkeley Books, 2000). For a study of his biography and musical accomplishments, see Carol Oja, *Colin McPhee: Composer in Two Worlds* (Washington: Smithsonian Institution Press, 1990).

2. Joshua Rosenblum, review of *A House in Bali*, by Evan Ziporyn, *Opera News*, October 14, 2010, http://shass.mit.edu/news/news-2011-opera-news-calls-ziporyns-new-opera-colossally-imaginative.

3. Quoted in ibid.

4. Certainly, one devastating legacy of these colonial encounters is the proliferation of child pornography and sex tourism in Southeast Asia. For instance, the disgrace of the former glam rock star turned pedophile Gary Glitter provided sensational but also short-lived media fodder around the exploitation of nameless boys and girls in this part of the world. See Thomas Fuller, "Gary Glitter Wears Out His Welcome in Southeast Asia," *New York Times*, August 21, 2008.

5. *To Catch a Predator* is a popular television series in which the show's host, Chris Hanson, and his team of producers plant online decoys who act as underaged

individuals to entrap adults who take the bait, and are then shamed and cited for their illicit sexual intent.

6. Thanks to Matthew Gutterl for suggesting this film as an example.

7. Joseph A. Boone, "Vacation Cruises; or, The Homoerotics of Orientalism," *PMLA* 101.1 (January 1995): 104. See also John C. Hawley, ed., *Post-Colonial, Queer: Theoretical Intersections* (Albany: State University of New York Press, 2001).

8. For a more recent study, see Joseph Massad, *Desiring Arabs* (Chicago: University of Chicago Press, 2007).

9. Philip Brett, "McPhee, Colin (1900–1964)," in *Encyclopedia of Gay Histories and Cultures*, ed. George Haggerty (New York: Garland, 2000), 579.

10. Oja, *Colin McPhee*, 116.

11. Ibid.

12. Ibid.

13. Quote from video "Colin McPhee: The Lure of Asian Music," uploaded by MichaelBlackwoodProd, September 7, 2011, last accessed October 31, 2012, http://www.youtube.com/watch?v=3ROcZdenux8&feature=related.

14. Oja, *Colin McPhee*, 88.

15. McPhee, *A House in Bali*, 116.

16. See, for instance, Malek Alloula, *The Colonial Harem* (Minneapolis: University of Minnesota Press, 1986), featuring black and whites from the 1930s.

17. Thomas Garvey, "Bali High," *Hub Review*, October 11, 2012, http://hubreview.blogspot.com/2010/10/bali-high.html.

18. Such a formulation owes its debt to early queer theory, particularly Eve Kosofsky Sedgwick, *Epistemology of the Closet* (Berkeley: University of California Press, 1990), which posits the endemic crisis of homosexual/heterosexual definitions as central to twentieth-century Western thought and knowledge; the groundbreaking interventions of Sue-Ellen Case, "Toward a Butch-Femme Aesthetic," in *Camp: Queer Aesthetics and the Performing Subject*, ed. Fabio Cleto (Ann Arbor: University of Michigan Press, 1999), 185–202, which posits a lesbian dyad as central to a field of inquiry (feminism); and more recent braidings of intersectional-assemblage studies from queer and woman of color critique collectives; see, for instance, Roderick Ferguson and Grace Hong, eds., *Strange Affinities: The Gender and Sexual Politics of Comparative Racialization* (Durham: Duke University Press, 2011).

19. See Anne McClintock, *Imperial Leather: Race, Gender, and Sexuality in the Colonial Contest* (New York: Routledge, 1995); and John Urry, *The Tourist Gaze* (London: Sage, 1992).

20. Michel Foucault, *Foucault Live (Interviews, 1961–1984)*, ed. Sylvère Lotringer (New York: Semiotext(e), 1996), 411.

21. For the originary colonial encounter, I have in mind what Michel de Certeau calls the "inaugural scene of conquest" in *The Writing of History* (New York: Columbia University Press, 1988), as well as what the American theater historian Patricia Ybarra calls "performing conquest" in her historiographic study on

Tlaxcalan performance cultures. Ybarra formulates "performing conquest" as a form of historiographic practice within a genealogy that includes "an organizing paradigm, policing tool, literary trope, form of political performance, foundational narrative of theatrical history, and epistemological object lesson." *Performing Conquest: Five Centuries of Theatre, History, and Identity in Tlaxcala, Mexico* (Ann Arbor: University of Michigan Press, 2009), 23.

22. To be clear, my zone of study in this book does not cover Asian Australian artists, but the influence of Australian AsiaPacifiQueer theorizing is acknowledged as a complement to U.S. and Euro queer theory.

23. Anna Lowenhaupt Tsing, *Friction: An Ethnography of Global Connection* (Princeton: Princeton University Press, 2005), 4.

24. Ibid., 6.

25. Ibid., xi.

26. Roderick A. Ferguson, *Aberrations in Black: Toward a Queer of Color Critique* (Minneapolis: University of Minnesota Press, 2003), 24. See also the work of scholars such as Gayatri Gopinath, Juana María Rodríguez, David Eng, Chandan Reddy, Martin Manalansan, Jasbir Puar, José Muñoz, Tavia Nyong'o, Jodi Melamed, and Grace Hong.

27. José Muñoz, *Cruising Utopia: The Then and There of Queer Futurity* (New York: New York University Press, 2009), 1.

28. *Oxford English Dictionary* (New York: Oxford University Press, 1992).

29. Dwight Conquergood, "Performance Studies: Interventions and Radical Research," *TDR: Theatre Drama Review* 46.2 (Summer 2002): 151.

30. Ibid., 146.

31. Edward Said, *Culture and Imperialism* (New York: Knopf, 1993), 51.

32. Laura Wexler, *Tender Violence: Domestic Visions in an Age of U.S. Imperialism* (Chapel Hill: University of North Carolina Press, 2000).

33. Mire Koikari, "Exporting Democracy?: American Women, 'Feminist Reforms,' and Politics of Imperialism in the U.S. Occupation of Japan, 1945–1952," *Frontiers: A Journal of Women Studies* 23.1 (2002): 24.

34. Naoko Shibusawa, *America's Geisha Ally: Reimagining the Japanese Enemy* (Cambridge: Harvard University Press, 2006), 56.

35. Ibid.

36. Allan Punzalan Isaac, *American Tropics: Articulating Filipino America* (Minneapolis: University of Minnesota Press, 2006), xviii.

37. Ibid.

38. Ibid., xvi.

39. Chay Yew, *Porcelain and A Language of Their Own: Two Plays* (New York: Grove, 1997).

40. Diana Taylor, *The Archive and the Repertoire: Performing Cultural Memory in the Americas* (Durham: Duke University Press, 2003), 13.

41. See, for instance, James Moy, *Marginal Sights: Staging Chinese in America* (Iowa City: University of Iowa Press, 1993).

42. Ibid., 9.

43. For critiques of the hetero-orientalist perspective, see Gina Marchetti, *Romance and the "Yellow Peril": Race, Sex, and Discursive Strategies in Hollywood Fiction* (Berkeley: University of California Press, 1994).

44. Dennis Altman, "Global Gaze/Global Gays," in *Sexual Identities, Queer Politics*, ed. Mark Blasius (Princeton: Princeton University Press, 2001), 102.

45. Olivia Khoo, "Sexing the City: Malaysia's New 'Cyberlaws' and Cyberjaya's Queer Success," in *Mobile Cultures: New Media in Queer Asia*, ed. Chris Berry, Fran Martin, and Audrey Yue (Durham: Duke University Press, 2003), 222.

46. U.S. Central Intelligence Agency, *The CIA World Factbook*, accessed November 1, 2012, https://www.cia.gov/library/publications/the-world-factbook/.

47. Connie Poh, e-mail message to author, March 31, 2003. See also National Arts Council brochure, *New Asia on Stage: Performing Arts Singapore* (Singapore: National Arts Council, 2000), which proclaims that "Singapore is New Asia, a thriving Asian city with a busy arts scene influenced by the traditional Asian heritage of its multicultural population and the contemporary beat of a young cosmopolitan city." For a discussion of the relation between Singapore's art, cultural industries, and New Asia, see Lee Weng Choy, "Authenticity, Reflexivity, and Spectacle; or, The Rise of New Asia Is Not the End of the World," *positions: east asia cultures critique* 12 (2004): 643–66.

48. Poh, e-mail.

49. Frank Chin, Jeffrey Paul Chan, Lawson Fusao Inada, and Shawn Wong, eds., *The Big Aiieeeee! An Anthology of Chinese American and Japanese American Literature* (New York: Doubleday, 1975).

50. See, for instance, Soek-Fang Sim, "Asian Values, Authoritarianism and Capitalism in Singapore," *Public* 8 (2001): 45–66.

51. See Beng-Huat Chua, *Communitarian Ideology and Democracy in Singapore* (London: Routledge, 1995), 159; and Michael Hill and Lian Kwen-Fee, *The Politics of Nation Building and Citizenship in Singapore* (London: Routledge, 1995), 202.

52. "Slavoj Zizek: Capitalism with Asian Values," last modified November 13, 2011, http://www.aljazeera.com/programmes/talktojazeera/2011/10/2011102813360731764.html.

53. For a comprehensive survey, see Sau-ling C. Wong and Jeffrey J. Santa Ana, "Gender and Sexuality in Asian American Literature," *Signs* 25.1 (Autumn 1999): 171–226.

54. See, for instance, Yen Le Espiritu, *Asian American Women and Men: Labor, Laws, and Love* (Lanham: Rowman and Littlefield, 2008), 117; a number of Asian American scholars such as Elaine Kim and King-Kok Cheung also have trenchant critiques on cultural nationalism's gender politics.

55. Chin et al., *The Big Aiieeeee!*, 34–35.

56. Lisa Lowe, "Heterogeneity, Hybridity, Multiplicity: Marking Asian American Differences," *Diaspora: A Journal of Transnational Studies* 1.1 (Spring 1991): 33–34.

57. Naoki Sakai, "'You Asians': On the Historical Role of the West and Asia Binary," *Japan after Japan: Social and Cultural Life from the Recessionary 1990s to the Present*, ed. Tomiko Yoda and Harry Harootunian (Durham: Duke University Press, 2006), 168.

58. Ibid., 170.

59. Ibid.

60. Vicente L. Rafael, "Translation, American English, and the National Securities of Empire," *Social Text* 30 (Fall 2009): 2.

61. Ibid., 3.

62. Michael L. Greenwald et al., eds., *Longman Anthology of Drama and Theatre: A Global Perspective* (New York: Pearson Longman, 2001).

63. The estimation is from James Brandon, *The Cambridge Guide to Asian Theatre* (Cambridge: Cambridge University Press, 1993), 252.

64. Greenwald et al., *Longman Anthology of Drama*, 252.

65. Antonin Artaud, *The Theater and Its Double* (New York: Grove, 1958), 50.

66. Ibid., 51.

67. Greenwald et al., *Longman Anthology of Drama*, 252.

68. Rey Chow, *Writing Diaspora: Tactics of Intervention in Contemporary Cultural Studies* (Bloomington: Indiana University Press, 1993), 3.

69. Michael Taussig, *Shamanism, Colonialism, and the Wild Man: A Study in Terror and Healing* (Chicago: University of Chicago Press, 1986).

70. Mattijs van de Port, "'It Takes a Serb to Know a Serb': Uncovering the Roots of Obstinate Otherness in Serbia," *Critique of Anthropology* 19.1 (March 1999): 21.

71. Ibid., 23.

72. Michael Taussig, "History as Sorcery," *Representations* 7 (Summer 1984): 87.

73. Alfred Métraux, *Voodoo in Haiti* (New York: Schocken, 1972), 15.

74. Taussig, *Shamanism*, 467.

75. Ibid., 444.

Notes to Chapter 1

1. The poem by Noel Coward is widely cited in travel guidebooks about Bali. Coward was said to have written this in the Hotel Bali guest book. See, for instance, Cameron Forbes, *Under the Volcano: The Story of Bali* (Melbourne: Black Inc. Press, 2007), 42.

2. Willard A. Hanna, *Bali Profile: People, Events, Circumstances, 1001–1976* (New York: American Universities Field Staff, 1976), 104.

3. Miguel Covarrubias, *Island of Bali* (New York: Knopf, 1937), 160.

4. James Boon, *The Anthropological Romance of Bali, 1597–1972: Dynamic Perspectives in Marriage and Caste, Politics and Religion* (Cambridge: Cambridge University Press, 1977), 6.

5. Hanna, *Bali Profile*, 102.

6. *Kecak* has been spelled differently over time (e.g., *kechak* and *ketjak*). Although *kecak* is sometimes referred to as *cak*, I make a formal distinction between *kecak*

and *cak*. *Cak* refers to the male chorus found in Sanghyang rituals from which *kecak* is derived. Sanghyang rituals consist of different exorcistic trance dances and are considered religious rituals. In contrast, *kecak* is popularly known as the "monkey dance" and is a secularized performing art form. I use *kecak* to refer to this performing art form in order to clarify the terminological confusion that may arise when *cak* and *kecak* are used interchangeably.

7. Adrian Vickers, *Bali: A Paradise Created* (Berkeley: Periplus, 1989), 92.
8. Hickman Powell, *The Last Paradise*, photographs by Andre Roosevelt (New York: Dodd, Mead, 1930).
9. Bali is relocated here as "Bali-Hai," the island of taboos to which American servicemen escape in *South Pacific*. Based on James A. Michener's Pulitzer Prize–winning book *Tales of the South Pacific* (1948), *South Pacific* was staged by Rodgers and Hammerstein as a musical play in 1949 and subsequently released as a musical film in 1958. As a musical theater production, *South Pacific* created stage history, had the "second-longest run of any musical in Broadway history (1,925 performances)," was seen by 3.5 million theatergoers who paid $9 million at the box office, and further gained "astronomic" profits from tours, sheet music, "dolls, cosmetics, dresses, lingerie, and so on." See David Ewen, *New Complete Book of American Musical Theater* (New York: Holt, Rinehart and Winston, 1970), 503. A recent and much less successful film adaptation starring Glenn Close was released in 2001.
10. Vickers, *Bali*; and Geoffrey Robinson, *The Dark Side of Paradise: Political Violence in Bali* (Ithaca: Cornell University Press, 1995).
11. I have found more than seventy newspaper articles in which "paradise lost" appeared as the headline or a description of Bali in the text itself. Here are only a few examples: Deborah Cassrels, "Paradise Lost as Once Beautiful Bali Buckles under Forklifts and Fallacies," *Weekend Australian*, September 29, 2012, 21; John McBeth, "Bali Struggles to Stay Idyllic," *Straits Times* (Singapore), June 8, 2011; Cindy Wockner, "Paradise Lost to Pollution and Poverty," *Courier Mail* (Australia), September 4, 2010, 65; "'It's Easy to Be Nervous on Streets After Dark': In Bali, Mike Smithson Revisits a Paradise Lost," *Sunday Mail* (South Australia), October 14, 2007, 78; Victor Dabby, "Paradise Found, Paradise Lost," *Gazette* (Montreal), October 13, 2007, J1; Neil Mercer, "Paradise Lost," *Sunday Telegraph* (Sydney, Australia), October 9, 2005, 84; Denny Lee, "Recovering Paradise Lost: A Bustling Bali on Upswing," *New York Times*, April 1, 2005, 9; Amalie Finlayson, "Paradise Lost," *Guardian*, October 14, 2002, 19; "Paradise Lost in Bali," editorial, *Augusta (GA) Chronicle*, October 17, 2002, A04.
12. Robinson, *Dark Side*, 4–9.
13. Transcribed from the film.
14. Susan Foster, *Choreographing History* (Bloomington: Indiana University Press, 1995), 10.
15. Ibid., 7.

16. Diana Taylor, *The Archive and the Repertoire: Performing Cultural Memory in the Americas* (Durham: Duke University Press, 2003), 20.

17. Joseph Roach, *Cities of the Dead: Circum-Atlantic Performance* (New York: Columbia University Press, 1996).

18. D. A. Miller, *Bringing Out Roland Barthes* (Berkeley: University of California Press, 1992).

19. Robinson, *Dark Side*, 5.

20. Ibid., 6.

21. Vickers, *Bali*, 2.

22. Covarrubias, *Island of Bali*, 160.

23. Quoted in Margaret J. Wiener, "Making Local History in New Order Bali: Public Culture and the Politics of the Past," in *Staying Local in the Global Village: Bali in the Twentieth Century*, ed. Raechelle Rubinstein and Linda H. Connor (Honolulu: University of Hawaii Press, 1999), 55, 56.

24. Ibid., 55.

25. "Colonial Era: Conquests and Dutch Colonial Rule," accessed October 15, 2012, http://bali_information.tripod.com/bali_guide/bali_conquest.htm.

26. Wiener, "Making Local History," 57–58.

27. Ibid., 57.

28. Originally published in German as *Love and Death in Bali*, Baum's novel was reprinted in 1989 with some revisions in the perception of *puputan* as suggested by its new subtitle, *The Powerful Account of Holocaust in Paradise*.

29. Clifford Geertz, *Negara: The Theatre State in Nineteenth-Century Bali* (Princeton: Princeton University Press, 1980).

30. Wiener, "Making Local History," 57. For other accounts of *puputan*, see Geertz, *Negara*; Beryl de Zoete and Walter Spies, *Dance and Drama in Bali* (Kuala Lumpur: Oxford University Press, 1973); and Covarrubias, *Island of Bali*.

31. Vickers, *Bali*, 91–92. "Ethical policy" also involved sending Indonesian elites to Dutch schools, where they were schooled in, among other things, Western political philosophies that ironically cultivated anticolonialism.

32. Wiener, "Making Local History," 84, note 12.

33. Ibid., 84.

34. Powell, *Last Paradise*, xiv–xvi.

35. Michael Hitchcock and Lucy Norris, *Bali, the Imaginary Museum: The Photographs of Walter Spies and Beryl de Zoete* (Oxford: Oxford University Press, 1995).

36. See Covarrubias, *Island of Bali*; and Michel Picard, "'Cultural Tourism' in Bali: Cultural Performances as Tourist Attraction," *Indonesia* 49 (1990).

37. Robinson, *Dark Side*, 6.

38. Covarrubias, *Island of Bali*, 160–66.

39. Robinson, *Dark Side*, 6.

40. Notably, the standardized appearance of the chorus developed only in the last thirty years.

41. *The Mysticism of Trance: Kecak Dance, Sanghyang Jaran Dance, Sanghyang Dedari Dance* (Jakarta: Maharani, 2007), DVD.

42. Ibid.

43. Marta Savigliano, *Tango and the Political Economy of Passion* (Boulder: Westview, 1995).

44. I am referring to a series of exchanges on the transnational listserv Balinese Arts and Culture Network (BACN), in which I participated from 2003 on. I will be discussing the exchange in more detail. The quotes hereafter are from the series of exchange from BACN.

45. BACN.

46. Ibid.

47. Ibid.

48. Ibid.

49. David Harnish, "[bacn] Walter Spies," online posting, BACN, November 28, 2003.

50. Founded in 1982, BACN was noted under the editorship of Raechelle Rubinstein as an "international interdisciplinary medium of communication for those seriously interested in the study of Bali." This description is found in BACN #37 (August 1997), edited by Raechelle Rubinstein, quoted in Michelle Chin, "[bacn] what is the BACN for?," online posting, BACN, June 11, 2003. Some of the world's most noted Balinese anthropologists, scholars, and writers, including Adrian Vickers, Michel Picard, Graeme MacRae, and H. I. R. Hinzler (president of the Walter Spies Foundation), are members of this electronic mail listserv.

51. Eng-Beng Lim, "Re: [bacn] Crossing cultures," online posting, BACN, January 8, 2003.

52. David Harnish, "[bacn] Walter Spies," online posting, BACN, November 30, 2003.

53. Andrew Charles, "Re: [bacn] walter spies and kecak," online posting, BACN, January 28, 2003.

54. Dieter Mack, "Re: [bacn] walter spies and kecak," online posting, BACN, February 3, 2003.

55. Ibid.

56. David Harnish, "Re: [bacn] walter spies and kecak," online posting, BACN, February 3, 2003.

57. Theodor William Dunkelgrün, "Re: Fwd: RE: [bacn] Crossing cultures," e-mail to author, January 9, 2003.

58. Ibid.

59. Dan Mcguire, "Re: Spies," online posting, BACN, January 11, 2003. The biography in question is by Hans Rhodius, *Schönheit und Reichtum des Lebens: Walter Spies, Maler und Musiker auf Bali, 1895–1942* (The Hague: Boucher, 1964).

60. Bruce Carpenter, "Re: [bacn] re: Walter Spies-Drake productions," online posting, BACN, November 20, 2003.

61. Graham MacRae, "RE: [bacn] Walter Spies," online posting, BACN, November 12, 2003.

62. Graeme MacRae, "Economy, Ritual and History in a Balinese Tourist Town" (PhD diss., University of Auckland, 1997), 21.

63. Dibia was at UCLA to stage *Body Tjak* in May 2002. During a panel entitled "Artist Alphabets: Conversations with Artists of *Body Tjak/Los Angeles*," organized by David Gere at UCLA's Department of World Arts and Culture, both Dibia and Keith Terry, directors/performers of *Body Tjak/Los Angeles*, denied that there were any traces of homoeroticism in *kecak* and wanted to give a "story" different from the one I had presented about Spies's involvement in *kecak*'s development.

64. In recent years, a growing corpus of work that reviewers call the anthropology of love has opened an ethnographic portal to transnational worlds where colonial affect, alternative intimacy, and other emotional binds are some of its organizing epistemes. These ways of understanding are crucial, as the authors often argue, for tracing new relational circuits, the formation of desire in political economies, and the cultural politics of neoliberalism. See, for instance, Elizabeth Povinelli, *The Empire of Love: Toward a Theory of Intimacy, Genealogy, and Carnality* (Durham: Duke University Press, 2006); Lisa Rofel, *Desiring China: Experiments in Neoliberalism, Sexuality, and Public Culture* (Durham: Duke University Press, 2007); and Nicole Constable, *Romance on a Global Stage: Pen Pals, Virtual Ethnography, and "Mail-Order" Marriages* (Berkeley: University of California Press, 2003).

65. Quoted in Vickers, *Bali*, 106.

66. Joseph A. Boone, "Vacation Cruises; or, The Homoerotics of Orientalism," *PMLA* 101.1 (January 1995): 104.

67. De Zoete and Spies, *Dance and Drama*, 72; and Covarrubias, *Island of Bali*.

68. I Wayan Dibia, *Kecak: The Vocal Chant of Bali* (Denpasar, Bali: Hartanto Art Books, 2000), 5.

69. Ibid., 7; Picard, "'Cultural Tourism' in Bali," 60.

70. Dibia, *Kecak*, 7.

71. De Zoete and Spies, *Dance and Drama*, 71.

72. Craig Latrell, "Circles of Meaning: A Cultural Approach to West Sumatran Theatre" (PhD diss., Yale University, 1998), 103.

73. I will be discussing the film more fully later.

74. De Zoete and Spies, *Dance and Drama*, 82.

75. Ibid.

76. Ibid., 85.

77. Ibid., 82, 85, 82.

78. Spies quoted in Ruud Spruit, *Artists on Bali* (Amsterdam: Pepin, 1997), 58.

79. See Covarrubias, *Island of Bali*; Dibia, *Kecak*; and Picard, "'Cultural Tourism' in Bali."

80. MacRae, "Economy, Ritual and History," 21.

81. Geoffrey Corbett Green, "Walter Spies, Tourist Art and Balinese Art in Inter-War Colonial Bali" (PhD diss., Sheffield Hallam University, 2002), 119.

82. Ibid.
83. Powell, *Last Paradise*, 228.
84. Ibid., 228–29.
85. Margaret Mead, *Letters from the Field, 1925–1975* (New York: Harper and Row, 1977), 160; Tessel Pollmann, "Margaret Mead's Balinese: The Fitting Symbols of the American Dream," *Indonesia* 49 (April 1990): 3.
86. Pollmann, "Margaret Mead's Balinese," 3.
87. Green, "Walter Spies," 110.
88. Ibid., 109.
89. These characterizations can be found in the popular press depicting their relationship. See, for example, "1927—Walter Spies," last accessed October 16, 2012, http://baliwww.com/bali/arts/spies.htm; and "Foreign Artists in Bali: 1904–1967," last accessed October 16, 2012, http://www.balix.com/multimedia/articles/artist/artist.html; as well as an excerpt at the Berlin Film Museum from the film *Bali—Insel der Dämonen*, last accessed October 16, 2012, http://www.artechock.de/arte/text/filminfo/b/ba/bainde.htm.
90. *Tabu* is notable for its Oscar-winning ethnographic cinematography of the "South Pacific" island on which it was filmed.
91. Green, "Walter Spies," 108.
92. Hitchcock and Norris, *Bali, the Imaginary Museum*, 75.
93. Tjokorda Gde Agung Sukawati, *Reminiscences of a Balinese Prince* (as dictated by Rosemary Hilbery) (Honolulu: University of Hawaii Press, Southeast Asian Paper No. 14, Southeast Asian Studies, 1979), 16.
94. Ibid., 18.
95. Ibid., 16.
96. Ibid.
97. Ibid.
98. Ibid.
99. Pollmann, "Margaret Mead's Balinese," 15.   100.   Ibid., 3.
101. Hitchcock and Norris, *Bali, the Imaginary Museum*, 30.
102. Ibid.
103. Ibid.
104. Pollmann, "Margaret Mead's Balinese," 2.
105. Ibid.
106. Ibid.
107. Pita Maha, meaning "great vitality," is an enclave of Balinese artists founded by Spies, the Dutch artist Rudolph Bonnet, and a local art patron and prince, Cokorda Gede Agung Sukawati. The organization had nearly a hundred members by the end of the 1930s. This cooperative of painters provided guidance to local painters, taught them skills that infused classical European as well as Balinese painting techniques, and developed a tourist market for their works.
108. Michel Picard, *Bali: Cultural Tourism and Touristic Culture* (Singapore: Archipelago, 1996), 32.

109. Pollmann, "Margaret Mead's Balinese," 2.

110. Powell, *Last Paradise*, xiv–xvi.

111. Boon, *Anthropological Romance*, 230.

112. Pollmann, "Margaret Mead's Balinese," 2.

113. Vickers, *Bali*, 109.

114. For a vivid description of the event, see Nicole Savarese, "Antonin Artaud Sees Balinese Theater at the Paris Colonial Exposition," *TDR* 45.3 (2001): 51–77.

115. Kathy Foley, "Trading Art(s): Artaud, Spies, and Current Indonesian/American Artistic Exchange and Collaboration," *Modern Drama* 35.1 (1992): 10–19.

116. Calonarang dance is a form of exorcistic trance dance depicting the ritualized conflict of a witch figure, Rangda, and a celestial lion-like figure, Barong, the guardian spirit of the village. In the most famous segment of the Calonarang, Rangda uses her magic to send Barong's army of male villagers into a trance, causing them to turn their krisses on themselves. However, Barong's protection keeps them from inflicting physical harm on themselves in spite of the krisses, and Rangda is finally pushed back to the graveyard.

117. For a discussion of Artaud's misconceptions as well as the legacy of Artaud's work, see Craig Latrell, "Neither Traveler nor Tourist: The Accidental Legacy of Antonin Artaud," in *Converging Interests: Traders, Travellers and Tourists in Southeast Asia*, ed. Jill Forshee with Christina Fink and Sandra Cate (Berkeley: Center for Southeast Asian Studies, 1999), 235–48.

118. Antonin Artaud, *The Theater and Its Double* (New York: Grove, 1958).

119. Ibid., 61.

120. Hitchcock and Norris, *Bali, the Imaginary Museum*, 30.

121. Hans Rhodius and John Darling, *Walter Spies and Balinese Art* (Amsterdam: Terra Zutphen, 1980), 39.

122. These are Walter Spies's film credits in *Island of Demons*.

123. See Hitchcock and Norris, *Bali, the Imaginary Museum*, 71; a similar phrase is repeated in Rhodius and Darling, *Walter Spies*, 37, and also in Claudia Orenstein, "Dancing on Shifting Ground: The Balinese Kecak in Cross-Cultural Perspective," *Theatre Symposium* 6 (1998): 117.

124. Latrell, "Circles of Meaning," 100.

125. See I Made Bandem, *Balinese Dance in Transition: Kaja and Kelod* (Kuala Lumpur: Oxford University Press, 1995), 28; Dibia, *Kecak*, 6–9; Orenstein, "Dancing"; Rhodius and Darling, *Walter Spies*, 37; Foley, "Trading Art(s)," 15–17; Hitchcock and Norris, *Bali, the Imaginary Museum*, 71; Latrell, "Circles of Meaning," 108; Picard, "'Cultural Tourism' in Bali," 60; and Philip F. McKean, "From Purity to Pollution? The Balinese *Ketjak* (Monkey Dance) as Symbolic Form in Transition," in *The Imagination of Reality: Essays in Southeast Asian Coherence Systems*, ed. A. L. Becker and Aram A. Yengoyan (Norwood, NJ: ABLEX, 1979), 299.

126. De Zoete and Spies, *Dance and Drama*, 83; Dibia, *Kecak*, 6–9.

127. See Dibia, *Kecak*, 8. A series of exchanges on the Balinese Arts and Culture News listserv has also alerted me to Mershon's contributions. There is an almost folkloric

general sense in which Mershon played a part in the choreography. The travel writer/ethnographer John Coast, for instance, briefly mentioned Mershon twice in his book, *Dancing out of Bali*, noting that "an American dancer, Katherine Mershon, had been responsible for selecting the trance chants and movements of the now famous Ketjak" (London: Faber and Faber, 1954, 86). Later in the book, Coast mentions California as the home of Mershon, "who had lived long in Bali before the war and had helped, with Walter Spies, to choreograph the original Monkey Dance" (211). Obviously, research on Mershon's as well as Rose Covarrubias's contribution to the form is needed in order to illuminate the gendered dimensions of the form.

128. Spruit, *Artists on Bali*, 62.
129. For those interested to find out more about Mershon and her possible contributions, see Katherine E. Mershon, *Seven Plus Seven: Mysterious Life-Rituals in Bali* (New York: Vantage, 1971); and Mershon's sections in *Traditional Balinese Culture: Essays*, ed. Jane Belo (New York: Columbia University Press, 1970).
130. Dibia, *Kecak*, 8.
131. Orenstein, "Dancing," 119.
132. De Zoete and Spies, *Dance and Drama*, 83.
133. Foley, "Trading Art(s)," 15.
134. Ibid.
135. Ibid., 16.
136. Dibia, *Kecak*, 9.
137. Ibid.
138. Bandem, *Balinese Dance*, 10.
139. Ibid., 12.
140. All phrases in quotation marks dealing with the plot of *Island of Demons* are translated from the German titles of the film. I thank Sue-Ellen Case for making the translations for me.
141. Bandem, *Balinese Dance*, 11.
142. Hanna, *Bali Profile*, 105.
143. For an account of just one participant of the "glittering orbit," see Deena Burton, *Sitting at the Feet of Gurus: The Life and Dance Ethnography of Claire Holt* (n.p.: Xlibris, 2009).
144. Boon, *Anthropological Romance*, 2.
145. Robinson, *Dark Side*, 1.
146. Ibid.
147. Ibid.
148. I am using the concept of performativity as Judith Butler formulates it in, among other places, "Critically Queer," *GLQ: A Journal of Lesbian and Gay Studies* 1.1 (November 1993): 17–32. For Butler, "performativity" refers to that which consists in a "reiteration of norms" that "precede, constrain, and exceed" the gender-performer in each bounded "act" (24). I relate the spelling of the Balinese exotic as a discourse to this conception whereby a normative exoticism is reiterated in multiple ways.

Notes to Chapter 2

1. A recent car crash involving a mainland Chinese immigrant driving a Ferrari and crashing into a cab, killing its local driver and Japanese passenger, has only fueled anti-Chinese sentiments. See http://bbs.chinadaily.com.cn/thread-749175-1-1.html.

2. C. J. W.-L. Wee, "Creating High Culture in the Globalized 'Cultural Desert' of Singapore," *TDR: The Drama Review* 47.4 (2003). Singapore became fully independent from the British Empire in 1965, following a brief union with Malaysia for two years (1963–1965). Through rapid economic development, it has accrued one of the highest per capita GDPs in the world, "higher than that of most developed countries" (US$60,900, 2012 estimate). See U.S. Central Intelligence Agency, *The World Fact Book*, accessed March 28, 2013, https://www.cia.gov/library/publications/the-world-factbook/geos/sn.html. Economists, however, point out that while Singapore has a "First World per capita income," its wage share is substantially lower than that of many OECD countries, and closer to Newly Industrializing Economies (NIEs) and Third World countries. Soon Teck Wong and Ong Lai Heng, "First World Per Capita Income, but Third World Income Structure? Wage Share and Productivity Improvement in Singapore," Singapore Department of Statistics, *Statistics/Singapore*, accessed June 14, 2005, http://www.singstat.gov.sg/ssn/feat/3Q2001/wage.pdf.

3. For a discussion of Singapore's pragmatic economic ideology and its relation to meritocracy, multiracialism, Asian values, and communitarianism, see Beng-Huat Chua, *Communitarian Ideology and Democracy in Singapore* (London: Routledge, 1995); and Diane K. Mauzy and R. S. Milne, *Singapore Politics under the People's Action Party* (London: Routledge, 2002), esp. chaps. 5 and 6.

4. Such a performative, materialistic rhetoric has engendered the image of the ugly and ungracious Singaporean. Prime Minister Goh Chok Tong proposed the creation of a Remaking Singapore Committee (RSC) to steer the aspirations and goals of the post-independence generation beyond the 5 Cs. As crucial as a matter of national security, the manifesto states that the RSC "will focus on the political, social and cultural aspects of our survival as a nation." Ironically, the RSC is structured as an offshoot of the earlier-established Economic Review Committee to help consolidate the larger and main goal of revitalizing the city-state's long-term economic fundamentals. For the full report, see "Remaking Singapore," accessed May 11, 2005, http://www.remakingsingapore.gov.sg.

5. The A. T. Kearney/Foreign Policy Magazine Globalization Index is reportedly "the first comprehensive empirical measure of globalization and its impact." Singapore has been consistently at the top of the list except for one year, 2003, when it was second. Largely European countries and the United States form the rest of the top ten. In 2004, the report notes that Singapore's rise to the top from its runner-up placing the year before was "solidified" in part by its bilateral free trade agreement with the United States in May 2003, "the first such agreement the United States had signed with an Asian nation" (54). It also notes rather

cryptically that as an "exception to the rule"—the rule being that "there is a strong positive relationship between globalization and political freedom"—Singapore has "tight government control over the media and limited individual liberties" even though it is the world's most globalized country with one of the freest, most open, and most modern economies in the world (59). For the full report and ranking, see "Measuring Globalization: A. T. Kearney/Foreign Policy Globalization Index, 2004, 2005, 2006, 2007," accessed November 29, 2009, http://www.atkearney.com/shared_res/pdf/2005G-index.pdf. For the 2004 report on cultural globalization, see Randolph Kluver and Wayne Fu, "The Cultural Globalization Index," *Foreign Policy*, February 10, 2004.

6. Audrey Yue, "Queer Singapore: A Critical Introduction," in *Queer Singapore: Illiberal Citizenship and Mediated Cultures*, ed. Audrey Yue and Jun Zubillaga-Pow (Hong Kong: Hong Kong University Press, 2012), 1–27.

7. See Lisa Duggan and Richard Kim, "A New Queer Agenda," *Scholar and Feminist Online* 10.1–10.2 (Fall 2011–Spring 2012), http://sfonline.barnard.edu/a-new-queer-agenda/preface/.

8. Dennis Altman, "On Global Queering," *Australian Humanities Review*, July 1996, http://www.lib.latrobe.edu.au/AHR/archive/Issue-July-1996/altman.html. Altman has also elaborated on this standpoint in "Rupture or Continuity? The Internationalisation of Gay Identities," *Social Text* 14.3 (1996): 77–94; "Global Gaze/Global Gays," *GLQ: A Journal of Gay and Lesbian Studies* 3.4 (1997): 417–36; and "The Emergence of Gay Identities in Southeast Asia," in *Different Rainbows*, ed. Peter Drucker (London: Gay Men's Press, 2000), 137–56.

9. Donald E. Morton, "Global (Sexual) Politics, Class Struggle, and the Queer Left," in *Post-Colonial, Queer: Theoretical Intersections*, ed. John C. Hawley (Albany: State University of New York Press, 2001), 208.

10. John D'Emilio made this argument in the context of America in his article "Capitalism and Gay Identity," in *Powers of Desire: The Politics of Sexuality*, ed. Ann Snitow, Christine Stansell, and Sharon Thompson (New York: Monthly Review Press, 1983). See also Henning Bech, *When Men Meet: Homosexuality and Modernity* (Chicago: University of Chicago Press, 1997); Kenneth Plummer, ed., *The Making of the Modern Homosexual* (London: Hutchison, 1981); and Steven Seidman, *Difference Troubles: Queering Social Theory and Sexual Politics* (Cambridge: Cambridge University Press, 1997).

11. Dennis Altman, *Global Sex* (Chicago: University of Chicago Press, 2001), 90.

12. In the U.S. academy, queer scholars of color are already intervening in this discourse with sensitivity to cultural difference as they formulate ways of making coalitional queer affiliations across the world. Arnaldo Cruz-Malavé and Martin Manalansan, for example, make a case for "queer globalizations" with an explicit call to deflect from the "colonizing gaze" of the "white scholar," and to unfix the legacy and grammar of "gay" as a structuring term for global interaction and coalition. Arnaldo Cruz-Malavé and Martin Manalansan, eds., *Queer Globalizations: Citizenship and the Afterlife of Colonialism* (New York: New York

University Press, 2002), 4. For an exemplary nuanced study, see also Martin Manalansan's wonderful book *Global Divas: Filipino Gay Men in the Diaspora* (Durham: Duke University Press, 2003).

13. J. K. Gibson-Graham, "Querying Globalization," in Hawley, *Post-Colonial, Queer*, 263.

14. See, for instance, Anne-Marie Fortier, "Queer Diaspora," in *Handbook of Lesbian and Gay Studies*, ed. D. Richardson and S. Seidman (London: Sage, 2002); Chris Berry, Fran Martin, and Audrey Yue, eds., *Mobile Cultures: New Media in Queer Asia* (Durham: Duke University Press, 2003); Gayatri Gopinath, *Impossible Desires: Queer Diasporas and South Asian Public Cultures* (Durham: Duke University Press, 2005); David Eng, *Racial Castration: Managing Masculinity in Asian America* (Durham: Duke University Press, 2001); Elisa Glick, Linda Holland, Sharon Holland, Daniel Balderston, and José Quiroga, "New Directions in Multiethnic, Racial and Global Queer Studies," *GLQ: A Journal of Lesbian and Gay Studies* 1.1 (2003): 123–35; Jasbir Puar, "Transnational Sexualities: South Asian (Trans)nation(alism)s and Queer Diasporas," in *Q&A: Queer in Asian America*, ed. David Eng and Alice Y. Hom (Philadelphia: Temple University Press, 1998), 405–24; Cruz-Malavé and Manalansan, *Queer Globalizations*; Hawley, *Post-Colonial, Queer*; and Cindy Patton and Benigno Sánchez-Eppler, eds., *Queer Diasporas* (Durham: Duke University Press, 2000).

15. As a neoliberal rhetoric, "New Asia" was a geopolitical imperative aimed at fostering regional links, technological growth, and the restructuring of (especially East and Southeast) Asian economies hit by the financial crises of the late 1990s. See, for instance, "East Asia Economic Summit Ends with Call for Building New Asia," *News Agency* (Singapore), October 16, 1999, http://www.xinhuanet.com/english/index.htm. Singapore in particular has actively embraced the cultural dimensions of this New Asian imaginary in the past decade as a way to instantiate the city-state's cosmopolitanism and touristic appeal. This form of cosmopolitan tourism is deftly integrated or suffused in recent performance projects and productions by the Singaporean director Ong Keng Sen, notably his pan-Asian Shakespearean productions and the Flying Circus Project. For just two of the many interesting debates about Ong's work, see Yong Li Lan, "Ong Keng Sen's Desdemona, Ugliness, and the Intercultural Performative," *Theatre Journal* 56.2 (2004): 251-73; and Helena Grehan, "Questioning the Relationship between Consumption and Exchange: TheatreWorks' Flying Circus Project, December 2000," *positions: east asian cultures critique* 12.2 (2004): 565-86.

16. C. J. W.-L. Wee, "Staging the Asian Modern: Cultural Fragments, the Singaporean Eunuch, and the Asian Lear," *Critical Inquiry* 30 (Summer 2004): 771–99. For a postcolonial history of Singapore's development from the perspective of a theater historian and critic, see Jacqueline Lo, *Staging Nation: English Language Theatre in Malaysia and Singapore* (Hong Kong: Hong Kong University Press, 2004), esp. chaps. 1 and 2. See also Eng-Beng Lim, "Glocalqueering in New Asia: The Politics of Performing Gay in Singapore," *Theatre Journal* 57.3 (2005):

383–405; and William Peterson, *Theater and the Politics of Culture in Contemporary Singapore* (Middletown: Wesleyan University Press, 2001).

17. Showcase, press release, November 25–December 2, 2002.

18. August Strindberg, *Five Plays*, trans. Harry Carlson (Berkeley: University of California Press, 1983), 205.

19. The term "glocal" (global + local) is said to be popularized by the sociologist Roland Robertson, who notes that the term "glocalization" was coined by Japanese economists who published in the *Harvard Business Review* in the late 1980s. Rendered in Japanese as *dochakuka*, it refers to "the simultaneity—and co-presence—of both universalizing and particularizing tendencies." Roland Robertson, "Comments on the 'Global Triad' and 'Glocalization,'" in *Globalization and Indigenous Culture*, ed. Inoue Nobutaka (Tokyo: Institute for Japanese Culture and Classics, Kokugakuin University, 1997). See also Roland Robertson, "Glocalization: Time-Space and Homogeneity-Heterogeneity," in *Global Modernities*, ed. Mike Featherstone, Scott Lash, and Roland Robertson (London: Sage, 1995); William Thornton, "Mapping the 'Glocal' Village: The Political Limits of 'Glocalization,'" *Continuum* 14.1 (April 2000): 79–89; and Frederic Jameson and Masao Miyoshi, eds., *The Culture of Glocalization* (Durham: Duke University Press, 1998). The term is now widely circulated in the field of cultural studies, particularly around "global/local linkage, disjuncture and fracture at the neo-capitalist border: the counterlogic of *both/and*." Rob Wilson and Wimal Dissanayake, eds., *Global/Local: Cultural Production and the Transnational Imaginary* (Durham: Duke University Press, 1996), 5.

20. "Filth for the Eyes, Food for the Soul," *Asian Boys Vol. 1*, program notes, 2.

21. TNS produces a varied program that promotes an ongoing social commitment, not only through its main season, but also by sponsoring annual community theater festivals for young people aged thirteen to twenty-five, educational theater programs in schools, and various community forums and platforms.

22. Community clubs are found in every constituency or residential precinct and serve as neighborhood centers for social and cultural activities. Singapore's prime minister, Goh Chok Tong, representing the dominant People's Action Party, happens to be one of Marine Parade's democratically elected officials.

23. Both Tan and Sharma are Singaporean citizens, have professional theater degrees in their corresponding fields from the University of Birmingham in England, and are more proficient in English than in their mother tongues. Tan was also mentored by Richard Schechner at New York University in 1997 for three months on a Fulbright scholarship.

24. The Necessary Stage, http://www.necessary.org/About/about.htm. TNC productions have toured Cairo, Glasgow, Berlin, London, Melbourne, Taipei, New Delhi, Macau, and Pusan.

25. Singapore Media Development Authority, *Report of Censorship Review Committee (CRC)* (Singapore: Ministry of Information, Communication and the Arts, 2003), 51.

26. Ibid., 15.
27. Ibid., 21.
28. Ibid.
29. Ibid., 51.
30. Ibid.
31. Ibid.
32. The committees and ministries include the following: Censorship Review Committee (CRC); Media Development Authority (MDA); Economic Review Committee (ERC); Remaking Singapore Committee (RSC); Ministry of Information and the Arts (MITA); National Arts Council (NAC); and the Public Entertainment Licensing Unit (PELU).
33. Singapore Media Development Authority, *Report of CRC*, 51.
34. Alvin Tan, quoted in Sonia Kolesnikov-Jessop, "Singapore Loosens Censorship," United Press International (UPI), September 4, 2003.
35. David Clive Price, "Singapore: It's In to Be Out," *Time*, August 10, 2003.
36. See Goh Chok Tong, "Speech by Prime Minister Goh Chok Tong at Remaking Singapore Report Presentation and Appreciation Lunch on Saturday, 12 July 2003," http://app.mfa.gov.sg/pr/read_content.asp?View,3283.
37. See Baden Offord, "Singapore," in *Encyclopedia of Gay Histories and Cultures*, ed. George Haggerty (New York: Garland, 2000), 821.
38. Chen, a film graduate from Boston University, also received his MA in English from the National University of Singapore and attended a seminar on feminism with Sue-Ellen Case, who was in residence as a Visiting Fulbright Professor while Chen was pursuing his degree in 1999.
39. The R(A) or Restricted (Artistic) ordinance is a state-imposed regulation that ensures that theatrical and filmic productions with contentious, presumably adult themes in sexuality (in other words, homosexuality), violence, nudity, and other such suggestive scenes are available only to audiences over eighteen for theater and twenty-one for film. See "New Play Set to Ruffle Feathers," *ProjectEyeball*, October 11, 2000, 2.
40. A critic from *Salon.com* calls Pierre et Gilles's photo-art "an unabashed mix of commercial and high art, glamour, poetry and homoeroticism." Glen Helfand, "Pierre et Gilles," *Salon.com*, March 1, 2001, http://dir.salon.com/sex/feature/2001/03/01/pierre_gilles/index.html. For more images, see Bernard Marcadé, *Pierre et Gilles: The Complete Works, 1976–1996* (New York: Taschen, 1997). Evidently, the publicity photo shot of *Asian Boys* had incorporated this aesthetic by fusing elements of sadomasochistic and toy images with a sensibility of glossy high fashion.
41. *Asian Boys Vol. 1*, Program notes, 2.
42. All quotes from *Asian Boys* are from a version of the playtext supplied by the playwright. I also rely on transcriptions from my notes at the performance and a videorecording of the production.
43. *Asian Boys Vol. 1*, playtext. Ibid.

44. Ibid.

45. Ibid.

46. Ge Lan from China, Meena Kumari from India, and Anita Sarawak from Malaysia are Asian stars affectionately recuperated alongside their Hollywood counterparts as international queer icons for their comparable cinematic excess, tragedy queen personas, and outlandish styles.

47. Written between 500 BCE and 300 CE by Bharata, the *Natyasastra* is an ancient Indian treatise on dramaturgy and histrionics that covers all aspects of theater and many other art forms. See Bharata Muni, *Natyasastra of Bharatamuni* (Baroda: Oriental Institute, 1980).

48. Ibid.

49. For a comprehensive account of this tale, see James R. Brandon's Indian theater chapter in *The Cambridge Guide to Asian Theatre* (Cambridge: Cambridge University Press, 1993), 65–66.

50. Indians are a minority in Singapore. As a result, Indian and other South Asian myths and cultures are often less considered and less privileged in mainstream media. For an interesting discussion of India's omission from New Asia, and Singapore's location in "New Asian intercultural structures," see Rustom Bharucha, "Foreign Asia / Foreign Shakespeare: Dissenting Notes on New Asian Interculturality, Postcoloniality, and Recolonization," *Theatre Journal* 56.1 (2004): 1-28.

51. *Asian Boys Vol. 1,* transcribed playtext.

52. National Day Parade is a spectacular event in Singapore featuring thousands of participants from schools, civil ministries, military units, corporations, and grassroots organizations. The parade is broadcast live on virtually all available television channels. For television viewers in particular, it has become a yearly ritual during the start of the parade to see parliamentary and elected officials take their seats by rank at the podium. As the camera focuses on the podium, viewers watch endless streams of People's Action Party (PAP) officials in their signature white uniforms walking in order to their seats. The plethora of white-uniformed officials serves as a timely reminder of the party's dominance in local politics. Having led the country from rags to riches since its independence from the British in 1965, PAP officials are highly respected by their constituents for building the nation into a global city-state. In the 2001 election, the Singapore government, controlled by the PAP, was returned to office, losing only two out of eighty-four seats to opposition parties. PAP's margin of victory (75.3 percent) was also its largest since 1980.

53. "State, Artists Work Together to Develop Arts," *Straits Times*, December 9, 1999, Forum, 42.

54. Lyrics of the song "A Whole New World" as used in the production. Alan Menken (music), Howard Ashman (arrangement), and Tim Rice (lyrics), "A Whole New World," *Walt Disney Pictures Presents Aladdin Original Motion Picture Soundtrack* (Burbank: Walt Disney Records, 1992).

55. *Asian Boys Vol. 1*, transcribed playtext.

56. Ibid.

57. Notably, the visibility of these artistic and commercial signifiers of gay sexuality is based on the fantasy, embodiment, and eroticization of certain types within the gay community, from "Asian" to "Latino" to "Jews," or from "Military," "Suit & Tie," "Muscle," "Hairy Chest," "Cowboy," and "College" to "Bears." Gay white male, however, is the unmarked standard.

58. *Asian Boys Vol. 1*, playtext.

59. Ibid.

60. Peterson, *Theater and the Politics of Culture*, 153.

61. Ng's performance was part of an arts festival co-organized by the Artists' Village and 5th Passage. His performance in 1994, titled *Brother Cane*, was condemned by the National Arts Council after it became a focal point of controversy following the sensationalized coverage by the *New Paper*. Ng was charged with obscenity and banned from performing in Singapore indefinitely. For discussion of this event, see Sanjay Krishnan, Lee Weng Choy, Sharaad Kuttan, Leon Perera, and Jimmy Yap, eds., *Looking at Culture* (Singapore: Artres Design and Communications, 1996). In 2012, the performance artist Zihan Loo created a reenactment performance of this incident at the Substation titled *Archiving Cane*.

62. As I have argued, global queering theorists often choose to look at evidence that gay cultures are alike in many different ways. Others speak about international homoerotic traditions or signs in Western terms or frames of understanding: coming out, gay, Pride Parade, and so forth. Even in their nuanced critique of "global queerness," Chris Berry and Fran Martin contend that "the moment of cultural globalization is characterized precisely by challenges to the authority of the West from forces of cultural difference unleashed by decolonizations and the ensuing complex global economic and cultural shifts." Without denying the historic, colonial legacies of the West, such a formulation continues to perpetuate the premise in which "the West" (which West, whose West?) is always already dominant and the sole colonizing or influential force in the gay world. Such an approach tends to neglect other complex forces at play within geopolitical regions and also the nation-state. See Berry and Martin, "Syncretism and Synchronicity: Queer 'n' Asian Cyberspace in 1990s Taiwan and Korea," in Berry et al., *Mobile Cultures*, 88.

63. See the report on Vincent Lounge's website: http://www.vincentzs.com/VLoungeP3.html.

64. Conversation with a gay male immigrant from Hong Kong who works at the club, May 26, 2012.

65. Conversation with a young Singaporean Chinese male at Backstage, August 22, 2003.

66. Gail Wan, "Singapore Emerging as Asia's New Gay Entertainment Capital," Agence France Presse, September 14, 2003.

67. Price, "Singapore: It's In to Be Out."

68. "Singapore Tries to Loosen Up," Associated Press, September 15, 2002.

69. Price, "Singapore: It's In to Be Out."

70. Simon Elegant, "The Lion in Winter," *Time* (Asian edition), July 7, 2003.

71. Ibid.

72. The event was said to generate around $4 million for Singapore tourism, a small but significant amount in this niche market.

73. Although the party was considered "Asia's Mardi Gras," there was and still is an official sanction against "gay marches" in Singapore. Hence, the "welcome party," mass dancing extravaganza (featuring music mixed by famous deejays from the United Kingdom and the United States), and "poolside recovery" were all conducted at designated venues.

74. Sonia Kolesnikov-Jessop, "In the Pink," *South China Morning Post* (Hong Kong), December 2, 2003.

75. "Singapore Developer Pitches Chic Apartment at Asia's Gay Community," Agence France Presse, November 13, 2003.

76. "Out and About," *Nation* (Thailand), December 19, 2003.

77. See Kolesnikov-Jessop, "In the Pink"; and idem, "Shake Your Booty on the Bar for a Better Singapore," *South China Morning Post*, August 6, 2003.

78. Wan, "Singapore Emerging."

79. See "Out and About."

80. Elegant, "Lion in Winter."

81. Singapore is about 274 square miles. For a list of gay saunas and queer bars, see http://dragoncastle.net/singapore.shtml.

82. Prior to this gay awakening, when Singapore was considered the fearsome father-state, it was already seen as "probably the cruisiest" city in Asia. See Peterson, *Theater and the Politics of Culture*.

83. Lee Kuan Yew, "From Third World to First World," in *From Third World to First: The Singapore Story, 1965–2000* (New York: HarperCollins, 2000), 762.

84. Ibid.

85. Acronym for Severe Acute Respiratory Syndrome, an epidemic that affected many Asian countries after the disease was spread by a Chinese national in Hong Kong to several other tourists staying at the same hotel.

86. See Chua Mui Hoong, "It's Not about Gay Rights—It's Survival," *Straits Times*, July 9, 2003.

87. The labels on the republic have been scattered around debates on "Asian values" that Singapore's leaders are charged for using in their governance. See Neil Englehart, "Rights and Culture in the Asian Values Argument: The Rise and Fall of Confucian Ethics in Singapore," *Human Rights Quarterly* 22.2 (2000): 548–68; Francis Fukuyama, "Confucianism and Democracy," *Journal of Democracy* 6.2 (1995): 20–33; Chua Beng-Huat, "'Asian Values' Discourse and the Resurrection of the Social," *positions: east asia cultures critique* 7.2 (1999): 573–92; Bilahari Kausikan, "Governance That Works: Hong Kong, Singapore, and 'Asian Values,'"

Journal for Democracy 8.2 (1997): 24–34; and Mark Thompson, "Whatever Happened to 'Asian Values'?" *Journal for Democracy* 12.4 (2001): 154–65.

88. The early litigious and prosecutorial fervor of Singapore's rulers is chillingly captured by a prominent dissident, Francis Seow, in his autobiographical account, *To Catch a Tartar: A Dissident in Lee Kuan Yew's Prison* (New Haven: Yale University Southeast Asia Studies, 1994). Other famous cases include the academic Christopher Lingle, who fled the country and was tried in absentia for writing a column titled "Smoke over Parts of Asia Obscures Some Profound Concerns" for the *International Herald Tribune (IHT)* on October 7, 1994. Lingle, who was a visiting professor at the National University of Singapore, had insinuated that repressive means were used in certain unnamed East Asian states in conjunction with the use of a "compliant judiciary to bankrupt opposition politicians." Singapore's leaders, Senior Minister Lee Kuan Yew, his son, Deputy Prime Minister Lee Hsien Loong, and Prime Minister Goh Chok Tong sued the *IHT* and were awarded a total of US$665,000 despite a published apology from the paper. For accounts of this famous episode and others, see Gordon P. Means, "Soft Authoritarianism in Malaysia and Singapore," *Journal of Democracy* 7.4 (1996): 103–11; and Christopher Lingle, *Singapore's Authoritarian Capitalism* (Fairfax: Locke Institute, 1996).

89. Much of Singapore's bad press is concentrated in the Western discourse. Its reputation in Asia appears more positive. For instance, the efficiencies of Singapore's economy and legendary urban planning are so admired by China that a mini Singapore was to be built there in the form of a massive China-Singapore Suzhou Industrial Park (SIP). The project was initiated in 1994 at a cost of US$30 billion and its objective was to build a "modern, industrial city over 20 years covering 70 kilometres, a veritable second Singapore." For many reasons, the project failed eventually and called into question the infallibility of Singapore's reputed economic successes. See K. K. Lim, "A Second Singapore: Why We Succeed and Fail," *Singapore for Democracy*, May 2001, http://www.sfdonline.org/Op%20Pages/OPMay01.html.

90. Notably, foreign-born nationals form a quarter of its population of four million, and as Singaporeans become more mobile, many are choosing to live overseas.

91. Geert De Clercq, "Singapore Considers Legalizing Homosexuality: Lee," *Reuters*, April 24, 2007, http://www.reuters.com/article/2007/04/24/us-singapore-lee-idUSSP5349120070424.

92. Pierre Bourdieu, *Language and Symbolic Power* (Cambridge: Polity, 1991).

93. Quoted in Elegant, "Lion in Winter."

94. See Wayne Arnold, "Singapore Lets Its Hair Down," *International Herald Tribune*, July 14, 2003.

95. Richard Florida, *The Rise of the Creative Class: And How It's Transforming Work, Leisure, Community and Everyday Life* (New York: Basic, 2002).

96. Chua, "It's Not about Gay Rights—It's Survival." The *Straits Times* has a daily circulation of 400,000 and a readership of 1.23 million in Singapore. It "strives to

be an authoritative provider of news and views, with special focus on Singapore and the Asian region." UCLA Asia Institute, Asia Media, accessed December 31, 2003, http://www.asiamedia.ucla.edu/fmwebpages/st.asp.

97. Quoted in Chua, "It's Not about Gay Rights—It's Survival."

98. References to Singapore as a nanny-state are too numerous to list here. Prime Minister Goh Chok Tong himself has acknowledged this label and responded to it: "The irony is, western journalists decry Singapore as a nanny state. But many Singaporeans want it that way. They are worried that we're shifting the burden of responsibility and decision-making back to them." Quoted from *Channel NewsAsia*, August 17, 2003.

99. Dereka Rushbrook, "Cities, Queer Space, and the Cosmopolitan Tourist," *GLQ: A Journal of Lesbian and Gay Studies* 8.1–2 (2002): 183–206.

100. Karl Ho, "'London of Asia' Here? First Scrap Rules on Nightspots," *Straits Times*, March 25, 2003.

101. Singapore Ministry of Information and the Arts (MITA), *Renaissance City Report*, February 9, 2000, http://www.mita.gov.sg/renaissance/ES.htm.

102. "Singapore Has Long Been 'Switzerland of the East,'" *Business Times*, September 18, 1999, 3.

103. In the executive summary of the *Renaissance City Report*, Singapore wants to become a "global arts city" as part of a "nation-building" imperative. This artistic aspiration has been covered by the international press. See, for instance, wired reports by Salil Tripathi, "Artistic Ambitions Don't Play Well in Uptight Singapore," *Australian Financial Review*, December 14, 2002; and Zeida Cawthorne, "Lion City Stalking Global Arts Title," *South China Sunday Morning Post*, June 14, 1998.

104. Even Lee Kuan Yew had acknowledged that Singapore's rapid economic ascendancy and focus had compromised local cultural and artistic developments. To rectify the situation, the ambitious Singapore government put down US$353 million to build a performing arts center, Esplanade: Theaters on the Bay, to position the country as a world and regional cultural nerve center. The recently opened mammoth arts complex aims to showcase "world-class" productions, high-profile musicals, and brand-name philharmonic orchestras. Singapore's leaders hope, as the *New York Times* reports, that the Esplanade will "become instantly imprinted on the world's architectural and artistic consciousness." It is also hoped that as "Singaporeans develop their taste for the arts, . . . the rest of the world will acquire a taste for Singapore." Wayne Arnold, "Singapore Offers an Architectural Symbol for the Arts," *New York Times*, December 3, 2002. Singapore's explicit desire was and always has been to be a cutting-edge city-state.

105. Singapore Ministry of Information and the Arts, *Renaissance City Report*.

106. Rushbrook, "Cities, Queer Space," 188.

107. This phrase is often used by the government to justify the implementation of various policies.

108. Singapore Ministry of Information, Communication and the Arts, 2000 Census, accessed December 10, 2003, http://www.sg/flavour/people_7.asp. For the full statistical figures, see www.singstat.gov.sg/keystats/c2000/religion.pdf.

109. William Peterson, "Singapore," in *Encyclopedia of Religious Practices* (Farmington Hills: Gale Group Press, 2005).

110. The National Council of Churches of Singapore (NCCS) "Statement on Homosexuality" can be accessed on various religious websites: http://www.anglican. org.sg/nccs_homosexuality.html, accessed November 10, 2003; http://www. methodist.org.sg/others/nccs.htm, accessed November 11, 2003.

111. Ibid.

112. Deputy Prime Minister Lee Hsien Loong, interview with Christopher Gunness, "Out in Asia," BBC, aired November 13, 2000.

113. The penal code sections in question are Section 377, "Whosoever voluntarily has carnal intercourse against the order of nature with any man, woman or animal, shall be punished with imprisonment for life, or with imprisonment for a term which may extend to 10 years, and shall also be liable to a fine"; and Section 377A, "Any male person who, in public or private, commits or abets the commission of or procures the commission by any male person of, any act of gross indecency with another male person, shall be punished with imprisonment for a term which may extend to 2 years." There are no provisions under this law against lesbian sex.

114. Senior Minister Lee was interviewed by Riz Khan on CNN in 1998 and by Terry Gross on National Public Radio, United States, in 2000, while Deputy Prime Minister Lee appeared on BBC's program "Out in Asia," hosted by Christopher Gunness, in 2000.

115. In 1998, responding to a self-identified Singaporean "gay man" who called in to CNN and asked about the "future" of gay people in Singapore, Senior Minister Lee remarked, "I don't think an aggressive gay rights movement would help. But what we are doing as a government is to leave people to live their own lives so long as they don't impinge on other people. I mean, we don't harass anybody." In 2000, Deputy Prime Minister Lee told Gunness on BBC, "As you say, homosexual people are not harassed or intimidated or squeezed in Singapore. But neither do we encourage homosexual lifestyles to be publicly flaunted or legitimised or presented as being part of a mainstream way of life." In 2003, Prime Minister Goh reiterated these positions—"I do not encourage or endorse a gay lifestyle"—but with an appeal for their social "acceptance" at the National Day Rally Speech.

116. E-mail correspondence with the owner of a gay sauna in Singapore. "Saunas" in Singapore feature a wide variety of facilities, from sun-bathing decks, mini-gyms, Jacuzzi pools, movie screening rooms, "private rooms," shower stalls, and dining areas to actual steam saunas.

117. At the World Human Rights Conference in Vienna in 1993, the Singaporean foreign minister, Wong Kan Seng, claimed, "Homosexual rights are a Western

issue, and are not relevant at this conference." Quoted in Chris Berry, *A Bit on the Side: East-West Topographies of Desire* (Sydney: Empress, 1994), 73.

118. Senior Minister Lee has stated that there is a "fundamental difference between Western concepts of society and government and East Asian concepts." See Amartya Sen, "Human Rights and Asian Values," *New Republic*, July 14 & 21, 1997, 34; see also Eric Jones, "Asia's Fate: A Response to Singapore School," *National Interest* 35 (1994): 2. According to Lee the core of this difference is that Singaporeans have "little doubt that a society with communitarian values, where the interests of society take precedence over that of the individual, suits them better [than democracy]." See Daniel Bell, "A Communitarian Critique of Authoritarianism: The Case of Singapore," *Political Theory* 25.1 (1997): 16. Critics have pointed out that Lee had sought to integrate his "Asian values ideology" with a particular interpretation of Eastern philosophies such as Confucianism to justify his authoritarian style of governance. For more on this debate, see Uri Gordon, "Machiavelli's Tiger: Lee Kuan Yew and Singapore's Authoritarian Regime," *Singapore Window*, March 2000, http://www.singapore-window.org/swoo/000614ug.htm.

119. Bell, "Communitarian Critique," 2.

120. Michel Foucault, *History of Sexuality* vol.1, *An Introduction*, trans. Robert Hurley (New York: Vintage, 1990).

121. "Thio Li-Ann's Parliamentary Speech on 377A," accessed March 29, 2013, http://www.yawningbread.org/apdx_2007/imp-359.htm.

Notes to Chapter 3

1. To explore "cruising" as a queer theoretical move in performance studies, see José Muñoz, *Cruising Utopia: The Then and There of Queer Futurity* (New York: New York University Press, 2009); and Sue-Ellen Case, Susan Foster, and Philip Brett, eds., *Cruising the Performative: Interventions into the Representation of Ethnicity, Nationality, and Sexuality* (Bloomington: Indiana University Press, 1995). Theoretical cruising, like gay male cruising, expands conditions of possibility for alternative relationalities and connections without a destination in mind. The associative acts of cruising—to entice, solicit, please, or seek, or to advance with ease, semblance of ease, or minimal effort, as in sailing or driving on "cruise control"—are exemplified by different modalities of walking or sashaying around town waiting for some "business" to happen or someone nice to appear randomly. As Nguyen Tan Hoang notes, one of the critical possibilities of gay male cruising is the way it "swerves from or evades capitalist/national time viewed as re-productive, in the sense that such a logic deems public cruising to be 'wasteful' loitering or strategically opportunistic." But as he cautions, such a "celebration of gay male cruising as a subversion of heteronormative time frames" may be limited as it "privileges urban space and freedom of movement/reservoirs of time that remain inaccessible to a lot of queers." Carolyn Dinshaw, Lee Edelman, Roderick A. Ferguson, Carla Freccero, Elizabeth Freeman, Judith

Halberstam, Annamarie Jagose, Christopher Nealon, and Nguyen Tan Hoang, "Theorizing Queer Temporalities: A Roundtable Discussion," *GLQ: A Journal of Lesbian and Gay Studies* 13.2–3 (2007): 192.

2. Esther Kim Lee, *A History of Asian American Theatre* (Cambridge: Cambridge University Press, 2006), 1.

3. The reporter Joyce Wadler, who collaborated with Boursicot for her book *Liaison,* writes that the Frenchman believed Shi was a woman despite knowing him socially as a man. Shi's preposterous stories of gender masquerade, including how he was a woman in the cover of a man to prevent his father from taking a second wife who could bear him a son, convinced Boursicot to believe otherwise. See Joyce Wadler, "The True Story of M. Butterfly: The Spy Who Fell in Love with a Shadow," *New York Times,* August 15, 1993.

4. Katrin Sieg, *Ethnic Drag: Performing Race, Nation, Sexuality in West Germany* (Ann Arbor: University of Michigan Press, 2002), 25. Native drag is in a way comparable to Katrin Sieg's formulation of "ethnic drag," which she used to discuss specific ethnic masquerades that are staged by West Germans in the post-Nazi period that are illuminated by the strategies of drag performance. For instance, a fraught site is ethnographic documentaries that attempt to use drag to work through "racial domination, submission, and objectification that structure colonial and East-West relations."

5. E. San Juan Jr., "Symbolic Violence and the Fetishism of the Sublime: A Metacommentary of David Hwang's *M. Butterfly,*" *Journal of Intercultural Studies* 23.1 (2003): 2.

6. Renato Rosaldo, "Imperialist Nostalgia," *Representations* 26 (1989): 107-22.

7. Dean MacCannell, *Empty Meeting Grounds: The Tourist Papers* (New York: Routledge, 1992), 33.

8. Ibid., 30.

9. Ibid., 32.

10. Neferti Tadiar, *Fantasy Production* (Hong Kong: Hong Kong University Press, 2004), 9.

11. David Eng, *Racial Castration: Managing Masculinity in Asian America* (Durham: Duke University Press, 2001), 159.

12. Ibid.

13. Ibid., 142.

14. Elizabeth Freeman, "Time Binds, or, Erotohistoriography," *Social Text* 84–85, vol. 23, nos. 3–4 (Fall–Winter 2005): 57.

15. Gayatri Gopinath, *Impossible Desires: Queer Diasporas and South Asian Public Cultures* (Durham: Duke University Press, 2005), 12.

16. See, for example, Roderick A. Ferguson, *Aberrations in Black: Toward a Queer of Color Critique* (Minneapolis: University of Minnesota Press, 2003); Gopinath, *Impossible Desires;* Allan P. Isaac, *American Tropics: Articulating Filipino America* (Minneapolis: University of Minnesota Press, 2006); Martin F. Manalansan, *Global Divas: Filipino Gay Men in the Diaspora* (Durham: Duke University Press,

2003); Eng-Beng Lim, "Glocalqueering in New Asia: The Politics of Performing Gay in Singapore," *Theatre Journal* 57.3 (2005): 383–405; and Eng, *Racial
Castration.*

17. Robert Lomax is the white male protagonist in *The World of Suzie Wong.*

18. Karen Shimakawa, "'I Should Be—American!': Abjection and the Asian (Ameri-
    can) Body," in *National Abjection: The Asian American Body Onstage* (Durham:
    Duke University Press, 2002), 25.

19. Guy Haydon, "My Life with Suzie Wong," *South China Morning Post* (Hong
    Kong), December 17, 1994, 4.

20. Ibid.

21. Ibid.

22. Ibid.

23. Mason quoted in Haydon, "My Life with Suzie Wong."

24. Ibid.

25. Jasbir Puar, *Terrorist Assemblages: Homonationalism in Queer Times* (Durham:
    Duke University Press, 2007).

26. For a discussion of this citation in the context of the U.S.-Vietnamese war, see
    Sylvia Chong, *The Oriental Obscene: Violence and Racial Fantasies in the Vietnam
    Era* (Durham: Duke University Press, 2011).

27. "We Meet Again," *South China Morning Post*, April 6, 2008, 7.

28. "What's the Big News?" *Life Magazine*, October 6, 1958, 2.

29. William Shatner, *Up till Now: The Autobiography* (New York: St. Martin's, 2009),
    62.

30. For Ferdinand as "America's Boy," see James Hamilton-Paterson, *America's Boy:
    A Century of United States Colonialism in the Philippines* (New York: Henry Holt,
    1999). For Japan as "a boy of 12," see Sam Jameson, "A Sunday in December:
    The American Shogun," *Los Angeles Times*, December 3, 1991; Naoko Shibusawa,
    America's Geisha Ally: Reimagining the Japanese Enemy (Cambridge: Harvard
    University Press, 2006), 55; U.S. Senate Committee on Armed Services and
    Committee on Foreign Relations, Military Situation in the Far East, *Hearings to
    Conduct an Inquiry into the Military Situation in the Far East and the Facts Sur-
    rounding the Relief of General of the Army Douglas MacArthur from His Assign-
    ment in the Area*, 82nd Cong., 1st sess., pt. 1, May 3, 1951, 312–13. For Vietnam
    as "not worth the life of a single American boy," see Robert D. Johnson, "The
    Progressive Dissent: Ernest Gruening and Vietnam," in *Vietnam and the
    American Political Tradition: The Politics of Dissent*, ed. Randall Bennett Woods
    (Cambridge: Cambridge University Press, 2003), 58.

31. Shibusawa, *America's Geisha Ally*, 57.

32. Viet Le, photographer, *Untitled (Philip)*, chromagnetic print, 12" x 12" framed
    edition of four. From *pictures of you* series, 2003–2010.

33. For example, Tisa Chang of Pan Asian Repertory Theater noted that "Asian-
    American actors were generally limited to roles like geisha girls and exotic
    houseboys" before the "transformative 1970s." Steven McElroy, "Theatre: The

Geisha-and-Houseboy-Liberation Theater," *New York Times*, May 20, 2007. Also see various essays in David Eng and Alice Hom, eds., *Q&A: Queer in Asian America* (Philadelphia: Temple University Press, 1998), esp. chap. 7, Richard Fung, "Looking for My Penis: The Eroticized Asian in Gay Video Porn," 115–34; and Gina Maséquesmay and Sean Metzger, eds., *Embodying Asian/American Sexualities* (Plymouth: Lexington Books, 2009).

34. Shu-mei Shih and Francoise Lionnet's introductory remarks in their seminal anthology, *Minor Transnationalism* (Durham: Duke University Press, 2005), 1–27.

35. Judith Halberstam, *In a Queer Time and Place: Transgender Bodies, Subcultural Lives* (New York: New York University Press, 2005).

Notes to the Conclusion

1. Rey Chow, "Where Have All the Natives Gone?," in *Writing Diaspora: Tactics of Intervention in Contemporary Cultural Studies* (Bloomington: Indiana University Press, 1993), 50.

2. Chin Woon Ping, *Details Cannot Body Wants*, in *Postcolonial Plays: An Anthology*, ed. Helen Gilbert (London: Routledge, 2001), 276–85.

3. This could be a reactive Asiacentrism, a counter-Eurocentric position, or the disciplinary practice or legacy of area studies. See, for instance, Mark Johnson, Peter Jackson, and Gilbert Herdt, "Critical Regionalities and the Study of Gender and Sexual Diversity in South East and East Asia," *Culture, Health and Sexuality: An International Journal for Research, Intervention and Care* 2.4 (2000): 361–75.

4. Leslie Rabine, *Global Circulation of African Fashion* (Oxford: Berg, 2002), 12.

5. I am thinking of Guillermo Gómez-Peña and Coco Fusco's influential performance installation, *Couple in the Cage*, which modeled a deft critique of the imperial, anthropological gaze by playing precisely with such a question as Latin American performance artists who can signify otherwise (as natives). See Coco Fusco and Guillermo Gómez-Peña, *Couple in the Cage: A Guatinaui Odyssey*, directed by Coco Fusco and Paula Heredia (New York: Third World Newsreel, 1993), DVD.

6. Consider the facetious commentary in Teresa Hsiao, "A White Man's Guide to Dating Asian Girls," *Huffington Post*, May 31, 2012, where dating an "Asian girlfriend" as the quintessential oriental princess has become a rite of passage for all white men. In fact, "to 'Date an Asian chick' has become akin to 'Go sky-diving' or 'Live in New York' in the veritable white guy bucket list." This entry of Asian exotica was prompted by the recent marriage of the Facebook founder and CEO, Mark Zuckerberg, and Priscilla Chan.

7. Chow, "Where Have All the Natives Gone?," 38.

8. Ibid., 29.

9. Ibid.

10. Gayatri Chakravorty Spivak, "Can the Subaltern Speak?," in *Colonial Discourse and Post-Colonial Theory: A Reader*, ed. Patrick Williams and Laura Chrisman (New York: Columbia University Press, 1994), 66–111.

11. Chow, "Where Have All the Natives Gone?," 38.

12. Victor Bascara, *Model-Minority Imperialism* (Minneapolis: University of Minnesota Press, 2006), xvii.

13. Ibid., xvi.

14. Francoise Lionnet and Shu-mei Shih, *Minor Transnationalism* (Durham: Duke University Press, 2005).

15. Walter Mignolo, *Local Histories/Global Designs: Coloniality, Subaltern Knowledges, and Border Thinking* (Princeton: Princeton University Press, 2000).

16. Hemispheric Institute, http://hemisphericinstitute.org/hemi/; Jill Lane, *Blackface Cuba, 1840–1895* (Philadelphia: University of Pennsylvania Press, 2005); Diana Taylor, *Archive and the Repertoire: Performing Cultural Memory in the Americas* (Durham: Duke University Press, 2003).

17. Francoise Lionnet, "Creole Vernacular Theatre: Transcolonial Translations in Mauritius," *MLN* 118.4 (September 2003): 913.

18. Ibid.

19. Edward Bruner, *Culture on Tour: Ethnographies of Travel* (Chicago: University of Chicago Press, 2004).

20. Ibid., 18.

21. Lionnet, "Creole Vernacular Theatre," 913.

22. Leo Ching, *Becoming Japanese: Colonial Taiwan and the Politics of Identity Formation* (Berkeley: University of California Press, 2001), 11.

23. Helen Gilbert, "Introduction to *Details Cannot Body Wants*," in Gilbert, *Postcolonial Plays*, 274.

24. Ibid.

25. Chin, *Details Cannot Body Wants*, 277.

26. Ibid.

27. Ibid.

28. Ibid.

29. Ibid., 278.

30. Gilbert, "Introduction," 274.

31. Ibid., 273.

32. Michelle Raheja, "Reading Nanook's Smile: Visual Sovereignty, Indigenous Revisions of Ethnography, and *Atanarjuat (The Fast Runner)*," *American Quarterly* 59.4 (December 2007): 1160.

33. Ibid., 1161.

34. Ibid., 1179.

35. Ibid., 1174.

36. Ibid., 1161.

37. Ibid., 1175.

38. Ibid., 1159.

39. Ibid., 1175.

40. Ibid., 1178.

41. Ibid.

42. Lionnet and Shih, *Minor Transnationalism*, 9.
43. Gilbert, "Introduction," 274.
44. Chin, *Details Cannot Body Wants*, 280.
45. Gilbert, "Introduction," 274.
46. *Full Metal Jacket*, directed by Stanley Kubrick (Burbank, CA: Warner Home Video, 1987), VHS.
47. Lionnet and Shih, *Minor Transnationalism*, 11.
48. Ibid.
49. Ibid., 7.
50. Ibid., 8, 9.
51. Ibid., 8.

INDEX

Affects, 51; nativized, 141
Afong Moy, 24
African American woman, 186
Agnes (character from *Asian Boys, Vol. 1*),
102–3, 106–7, 113–14; construction of, 117;
Singapore represented in, 109–10; U.S.
traditions and, 109–10
"Aiiieeeee," 30
Altman, Dennis, 118
America Is in the Heart (Bulosan), 150
American exceptionalism, 4
American Idol, 25
"Americanization," xiii–xiv
*American Tropics: Articulating Filipino
America* (2006) (Isaac), 21
Anal sex, 133–34
Angels in America (Kushner), x

Anonymity, 74, 159
Anthropological gaze, 18, 43, 217n5
Anthropology: of love, 199n64; visual, 44–45
A/P/A. *See* Asian/Pacific/American
Archives, 51
Archiving Cane (2012), 209n61
Artaud, Antonin, 36–37, 82
ASEAN. *See* Association of Southeast
Asian Nations
Asia, 34–35; global, 12; imagery, 24, 118; as
native boy, 4. *See also* Diaspora; Inter-
Asia; *specific places*
"Asian," 135, 136
Asian America, xiv, 26–27, 138–39, 143;
"Aiiieeeee," 30; cultural nationalism, 30, 32;
masculinity in, 142; performance art, 11,
162, 164–65; U.S. imperial histories in, 14

ABOUT THE AUTHOR

Eng-Beng Lim is Assistant Professor of Theatre Arts and Performance Studies at Brown University, where he is on the Gender and Sexuality Studies Board at the Pembroke Center for Teaching and Research on Women, and a faculty affiliate of the Center for the Study of Race and Ethnicity in America, the Department of East Asian Studies, and the Department of American Studies.